Hand assessment:
A clinical guide
for therapists
Second edition

Catherine Stuart Simpson

APS Publishing
The Old School, Tollard Royal, Salisbury, Wiltshire, SP5 5PW
www.apspublishing.co.uk

British Library Cataloguing in Publication Data
A catalogue record for this book is available from the British Library

© APS Publishing 2005
ISBN 1 9038772 9 6

Printed in the UK by Cromwell Press Ltd., Trowbridge, Wiltshire

Contents

Acknowledgements

Thanks are due to so many people who have helped me with this book, some may even be unaware of how helpful they were.

First to Roswyn Hakesley-Brown for her encouragement and practical support to start the project and, more importantly, continue it.

I am particularly indebted to Annette Leveridge and Karen Murray for their willing agreement to read the final version in its raw state, and their extremely helpful comments. Annette also kindly agreed to write the foreword.

Similarly, thanks are due to Claire Taylor, Ann Chadwick, Hilary Simpson, Mark Willetts, Edith Davies, Elizabeth Mason, Jane Smith, Wendy Mudge, Helen Theobolds, Adrienne Foster, Mr I Bhoora, Mr R D Loynes, Nora Price and Professor M Topping for reading chapters, all of whom immediately agreed to give their precious time. The constructive advice offered was very much appreciated.

My husband and family have been extremely patient. I am very grateful for this, as well as their assistance in wrestling with the computer, graphs and formulae, tracking solder wire, the continual use of practice hands and assistance with proof reading.

I have been very fortunate to have the support of library staff, particularly Linda Brain, librarian of the PGMC, Staffordshire General Hospital and her staff for their cheerful and resourceful help. All the staff of the British Library were also extremely helpful.

I am grateful to those who have helped me track down information and equipment. Amongst my colleagues this includes Norma Bate, Val Phillips, Shirley Francis, Irene Nation, Denise Hanlon, Rhona Hardwick, Kevin Evans, Helen Phillips, Shiona Walker, Janette Turner, Sally Hurley and Carol David. Also Dr Ing Helmut Heck and Fräulein Maria Fathmann for assistance detailing recording range of movement measurements. Helen Snoad and May Woods of the British Lymphology Society also provided valuable information on measuring lymphoedema. Mary Wilding and Linda Miller of Biometrics Ltd gave information on the E-LINK.

I have been lucky enough to visit other departments and see how they use different apparatus to assess hands. I am particularly grateful to Sarah Woodbridge, Derby Royal Infirmary for demonstrating the BTE and monfilaments. Also to Nicky Burr, Anna Pratt and Debbie Carter at Mount Vernon Hospital for the demonstration of the BTE, MULE and DEXTER systems.

I am indebted to Nick Davies, of Birmingham University, who enabled me to meet Professor Alan Wing of Birmingham University and Ben Bishop of Muse Virtual Presence and other key people involved in the future of hand assessment.

Plates 1.1 and 1.2 are the commissioned work of Helen Taylor and form part of the portfolio for her BA[Hons] in Professional Media at Cheltenham and Gloucester College of Higher Education. Richard Cooper of BTE. kindly allowed me to reproduce the the photograph of the work simulator [Plate 15.1] and Rehab Robotics Ltd provided the photograph of the HATS System [Plate 15.2] and gave permission to reproduce it.

The drawings are the work of Jane Fallows and all other photographs of Alistair Rose, both medical illustrators. I have been most grateful for their professionalism, patience and experience. Robert

Timmerman, Irene Wharton and my mother, Agnes Farrow, kindly agreed to model for some of the plates. These photographs were produced by kind permission of Mid Staffordshire General Hospitals NHS Trust. However, this work reflects my personal view and opinions, not necessarily the policy of the Trust. Similarly, any problems referred to in the text are gained from long experience in the National Health Service and from discussion with other therapists from around the country. It cannot be inferred that these exist in the hospital where I am currently working.

Others who have helped with illustrations are Val Angeles of Promedics, UK suppliers for North Coast Medicalwho loaned the equipment for plates 5.1, 11.2. and 13.1.

Figure 1.1 represents work jointly undertaken with Karen Murray and Hayley Bagnall.

Valery Marston of APS Publishing has been extremely supportive throughout the production coping with my cold feet and silly questions.

Finally, thanks must go to Irene Wharton and Eleanor Grant for their support, which has kept me going throughout the period of production.

I am very grateful to all of the above; however, any deficiencies within the book are mine and not theirs.

Catherine Stuart Simpson

Preface

This book grew out of the initial reading done for the HATS project. I was lucky enough to be able to participate in the design phase and clinical evaluation of the project, which was funded by the European Telematics Commission for the Elderly and the Disabled DGX111. Led by Professor Mike Topping, from Staffordshire University, the team was made up of engineers, surgeons and therapists from Sweden, Germany and the United Kingdom and was a thoroughly enjoyable time, while being a period of intense personal development. The aim and outcome of the HATS project was a computerised hand assessment system.

The main aim of the book is to detail methods of assessing the hand for the benefit of physiotherapists and occupational therapists working in general hospitals or health centres, where they may see a huge variety of conditions and problems. Often in this situation, there may be little or no support from clinical specialists from their own profession. Also, there are immense pressures relating to staffing and time available for the large number of patients attending. Following a long period of budgetary control, many centres have limited specialised measuring equipment available. When money does become available for equipment, it can be difficult to decide what to purchase. I hope this book will be of some assistance for those coping with these problems and lay the basis for departmental protocols.

While writing the book, I have developed an interest in the history of assessment and, whenever possible, I have gone back to the original papers and spent quite some time in the British Library. Although I remain frustrated by my lack of skill in foreign languages, it has been fascinating to discover how tests developed, why they were so named and how this interweaves with social history. I believe that, by understanding these processes, it will help us to move to new processes. It is a matter of interest to note that R Fortescue Fox, who is the first person recorded in Britain to use a finger goniometer dorsally, developed his work at 126 Great Portland Street; not a dynamographic pear's throw (see *Chapter 8*) away from the first registered address of the British Association of Hand Therapists. The 1917 London telephone directory lists him as living at 36 Devonshire Place West. I could imagine him walking round the corner each morning. I have tried to share this interest and hope that others find it of some appeal.

The historical perspective shows that we need to improve our measuring technique, as well as our tools and there is a huge need for therapists to carry out simple research on the reliability of the methods currently in use.

The future of the National Health Service and hand therapy holds many exciting possibilities and challenges for which we must prepare. As Sir William Osler (1849–1919) said, "The best way to prepare for tomorrow is to do today's work superbly well". Only by taking the greatest care in the selection and execution of methods used to assess the patient, subjectively and objectively, will we obtain the information needed to meet the rehabilitation needs of our patients, now and in the future.

Catherine Simpson
June 2001

Foreword

Catherine Simpson, a hand therapist with many years of experience, has produced a manual on hand assessment that will benefit occupational therapists and physiotherapists, be they experienced or new to the field of treatment of conditions affecting the hand.

Natalie Barr, who pioneered hand therapy with other therapists after the Second World War and, in the ensuing years, in rehabilitation centres, such as Farnham Park, Chessington, and Grimsby, was herself a source of inspiration to many young therapists new to the treatment of the hand who are leaders in the field today. Natalie led the way to development of skills, including methods of assessment of the hand, which are today able to be supported by evidence of validity and reliability and which can be standardised.

Catherine describes the hand assessment tests in the manual with clarity and enthusiasm, offering the reader many options and good referencing to follow up the advice given. It is good to have a manual that will not only be an aide-memoire to experienced hand therapists but, as Catherine herself writes, will benefit students and those occupational therapists and physiotherapists who do not work in specialised hand units, and who may not have the resources and knowledge to develop appropriate skills in assessment.

Catherine has not focussed purely on assessment tests devised and evolved in the United Kingdom, but has cast her net across the world, creating a wide spectrum for her readers.

The British Association of Hand Therapists has set Standards for Hand Therapy, which should be achieved by all Chartered Physiotherapists and/or State Registered Occupational Therapists involved in the management of trauma or dysfunction of the hand and upper limb.

Standard II states the 'Assessment is a continuous process by which the acquisition of relevant quantified and other data will result in the formation of treatment plans related to goals which have been actively set with the patient and which are targeted towards a positive outcome'.

Catherine Simpson has given her readers the means to achieve this standard, looking not only at the present, but to the future as well.

Thank you Catherine for giving us some insight into this many faceted topic.

Annette Leveridge

Chapter 1
Introduction to assessment

It is difficult to underrate the value of the hand. It is the means by which we interact with our environment and other creatures; therefore, small impairments can have far reaching consequences. Hand therapy intervention, in the form of physiotherapy and occupational therapy, is crucial to address the effects of impairment and, in order to do this effectively, the first task must be to carry out an assessment. Assessment must be selective to meet the needs of the patient and accurate, repeatable and valid; this presents challenges to the therapist. This chapter explores these themes further.

The importance of the hand

There is scarcely a task of daily living in which the hand is not involved in some way, using it for support or holding, manipulating and locating objects at will. The hand is able to carry out a huge variety of tasks. It can support the entire body weight, can grasp and wield a hammer, or use a needle, hold onto a rope tightly enough to preserve life, or use the rapid, fine and controlled movements needed to play an instrument. The brain enables the hand to carry out these tasks, coordinating muscle activity in the hand and throughout the body to ensure successful completion. The hand is, therefore, an extension of the brain and yet the brain is also an extension of the hand. The hand is a useless tool without the brain; however, the hand also transmits much vital data to the brain, enabling it to function, by seeking out information on the form, structure and texture of objects. A good example of this is holding an ice cream cone; information from the eye and previous knowledge subconsciously alert the holder to the problem that, if held too loosely, the cone will drop, but, if held too tightly, it will disintegrate. The hand transmits information on the texture, shape, and strength of the cone, allowing the brain to control the strength of grip. Therapists are only too aware of this, as touch is a tool of their profession. A joint may be seen to be swollen, but only by palpation can the temperature, area, quality, and fluidity of swelling be determined and assimilated by the brain. It has been demonstrated that impaired sensation results in deterioration of function (Moberg, 1958; 1991).

Furthermore, the hand is significant in communication. Across all cultures, hand gestures form an important part of non-verbal communication; it is just the meaning of individual gestures that vary. Appreciation is shown by applause; from babyhood, clapping is a sign of pleasure. Through touch, our intimate relationships are formed and confirmed. In working relationships, touch is conventionally used for the same purposes; in the handshake on meeting, and confirming an agreement.

The hand is also used to demonstrate status and belonging to a group. The ancient tradition of saluting is a mark of respect and the differing salutes of the Royal Navy, Royal Air Force, Army, and a variety of scouting and guiding organisations, are a symbol of belonging to the group. The mason's handshake identifies others in the group and also their rank within the group (Knight, 1987). The ring is used as a mark of commitment to a relationship, including friendship, engagement and marriage, or to signify status, such as the Monarch's ring and Bishop's ring. Literature and speech patterns recognise this symbolic quality of the hand, including cleansing following a regretted act, notably Lady Macbeth and Pontius Pilate, and the recognition of power, for example 'It is out of my hands'.

The significance of the hand in activity, communication and symbolism is demonstrated by the fact that, across many cultures, it is painted and adorned. This includes the exotic henna hand paintings and uncut fingernails of the Far East, and the tattoos, elaborate manicures and nail paintings of the West. These not only please the individual, they can identify and confirm belonging to a particular group (see *Plates 1.1* and *1.2*).

The importance of the hand, therefore, is both physical and spiritual (Brand, 1988). It is hardly surprising that hand injury or disease have profound effects on the individual, making the effective treatment of such conditions of vital importance. The World Health Organisation (WHO, 1980) defines impairment as 'any loss or abnormality of psychological or anatomic structure'. We are all aware, from personal experience, that a small cut on the hand, or a fingernail broken below the quick can impact on function. How much more significant then are the effects of more serious impairment. The impairment results in either disability or handicap. Disability is 'any restriction or lack… of ability to perform an activity in the manner, or within the range considered normal for a human being' (WHO, 1980). The definition of handicap is 'a disadvantage for a given individual, resulting from an impairment or disability that limits or prevents the fulfilment of a role that is normal (depending on age, sex, and social and cultural factors) for that individual' (WHO, 1980).

The crucial importance of the hand means that any significant injury or disease requires

Plate 1.1 Nail art – a current western fashion

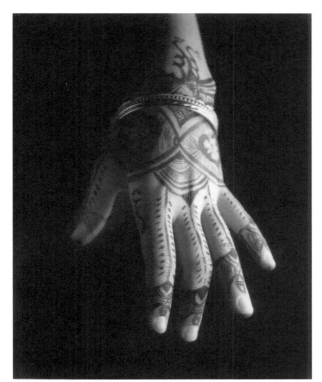

Plate 1.2 Hand decorated with an oriental henna pattern

intervention to prevent disability or handicap occurring. Intervention may be medical, psychological, surgical or therapeutic, provided by an occupational therapist or physiotherapist. Occasionally, only one practitioner may be involved, but it is possible that all may be involved. The first step in any therapeutic approach must be assessment (British Association of Hand Therapists, 1998; Chartered Society of Physiotherapy, 2000).

The challenge of assessment

Hand assessment has been accurately described as the cornerstone of hand therapy (Nicholson, 1992) and has been usefully defined as the 'process of examination by which the quality of a patient's hand function is quantified and judged' (Bear-Lehman and Abreu, 1989). It is, therefore, more than pure examination; it is about taking into account subjective and objective factors, and combining the data to get a full picture of that individual patient. The subjective assessment is formed by those elements, which cannot be measured, including the history, description of symptoms, and past medical history. The objective assessment is any part of the assessment that can be measured or quantified. The therapist will need to use many sources to obtain the full picture; this can include reference to medical notes, X-rays, other colleagues' findings, the patient and, finally, with the patient's agreement, the patient's relatives and close friends.

Assessment serves many purposes that benefit patients, individually and collectively, and the professional. From the perspective of the individual patient, these include identifying the cause, prioritising problems, monitoring progress, and selection for surgery. Collectively, assessment enables comparisons to be made within departments, nationally, and internationally to evaluate the effects of treatment, which furthers professional knowledge and status.

The therapist must use the assessment process to identify the range of problems related to the impairment, disability, and handicap. The cause of the problem[s] must be established; for example, patients are frequently referred from general practitioners with the request, 'Hand pain—please treat'. Assessment enables the therapist to isolate the probable cause of the pain. Depending on the patient's history and tests administered, it will be possible to differentiate between pain referred from a neck problem, a local tenosynovitis in the hand, wrist instability, or inflamed joints, and many other causes. Only once the cause of a problem is isolated does it become possible to decide on an appropriate intervention or treatment modality; in the absence of a universal panacea for hand problems, this is essential. Time is the most precious resource that health care professionals have; therefore, time must be used to maximize health gains within available budgets (Appleby, 1998). A haphazard application of treatment, for example the application of paraffin wax baths to all patients on the grounds that it will do no harm, is time wasting and of dubious value. It may be that therapy is not the best way forward for the patient, and it may be necessary to recommend referral to a medical, surgical, or psychology colleague.

When problems are identified and the cause ascertained, assessment enables them to be prioritised. It then becomes possible to formulate goals, a treatment plan, and predict outcome on an estimated timescale. The treatment plan may include a whole variety of therapeutic interventions; electrotherapy, thermal, manual, exercise, splinting, education, and adaptation. Assessment can also be a useful tool to explain to the patient why they may be experiencing functional problems, and illustrate what can be done about them (Roberts, 1989). It is important that, in formulating the treatment plan, the patient's lifestyle, needs, and aspirations are taken into account, and that the plan is acceptable to them. The planning process must be open and honest, and explained fully to the patient, so that he/she can make an informed decision to consent to or reject treatment.

Assessment may be undertaken to select patients for surgery (Tooby, 1993). Information yielded by the assessment can assist in ascertaining a patient's suitability for surgery; this cannot necessarily be ascertained accurately in a busy surgical outpatients clinic. In rheumatoid arthritis, this information can include the involvement of other joints, function, cognition, compliance, and motivation of the patient, all of which could affect the outcome of surgery and the potential gain for patients.

For the individual patient, the final reason for assessing is to chart progress. The initial assessment forms a baseline measure for the patient, and subsequent measurements allow progress to be monitored, and this can be of interest and encouragement to patients, giving positive feedback on their efforts. As long ago as 1920, Albee and Gilliland found the use of repeated measurements during treatment aroused and maintained the interest of patients in their progress. They named this Metrotherapy and actively incorporated it into treatment (Salter, 1955). The frequency of this measuring should reflect the rate of progress; if joint range is increasing rapidly, several measurements in one session will encourage the patient to greater efforts. Conversely, if progress is slow, and improvement occurs slowly over a period of weeks, frequent measures showing no change will have a negative effect.

On a collective level, the initial and final assessment allows for the interventions to be evaluated; these can be surgical or therapeutic. This facilitates discussion and reflective practice, and has the potential to be the most effective means of progressing skills at the level of the individual therapist, which will, in turn, benefit patients. At departmental level, national, and even international level, it provides information for audit and the establishment of evidence-based practice. This is of particular importance to therapists. In 1916, Lovett and Martin wrote 'Impressions that electricity of one kind or another, or test, or exercise were beneficial have filled the literature; unsupported assertions, marvellous cures and fantastic treatments have too often been advanced on the slenderest of grounds'. Yet there continues to be relatively little hard data on the effects of therapy intervention (Tallis, 1989). Despite advances in the last ten years, there is still much to be done (Watkins, 2001). As evidence-based practice becomes the norm in the National Health Service, such information on treatment effectiveness becomes invaluable. This will advance the knowledge of the profession and improve their status and value within the team. Consequently, it is important to use comparable measures; therefore, measures selected should be as reliable as possible, valid, sensitive, and acceptable to the patient (Fess, 1986;1995;1998; Chartered Society of Physiotherapy, 2000). Fess (1995) gives clear instructions for the evaluation of assessment instruments. The instrument must be an accurate measurement unit, meeting national standards, which can be tested in the clinical area. Intra-rater, then inter-rater reliability, must be established. Reliability is a pre-requisite to the establishment of validity, meaning that the test measures the phenomenon for which it was designed (this is expressed as a correlation co-efficient). The test must be administered in a standard manner, with no alteration of the tool, and normative data should be available. Finally, the test must be responsive over time or sensitive to change, as this enables clinically important changes to be recorded over time (Rosen and Jerosch-Herold, 2000). Fess cites only four tools currently in use that meet her strict criteria; these are the volumeter, the goniometer, Jamar dynamometer, and the Semmes-Weinstein monofilaments.

It is now well-documented that the use of standardised tests is surprisingly sparse (Hammond, 1996; Jeffreson and Hammond, 1997; Winward *et al*, 1999; Murray *et al*, 2000). Some therapists working in non-specialised units do not have access to all of these tools, and their requests for equipment have to be prioritised against other departmental needs (Murray *et al*, 2000). It is important to continue to state the case for necessary equipment and to evaluate the methods currently used.

In order to obtain useful information on the outcome of intervention, irrespective of the tool used, it is important that certain safeguards are built into the assessment process:

- as far as practically possible, the same therapist should assess the patient on each occasion; rotational schemes and leave commitments do not always make this possible. On most measurements, intra-rater reliability is greater than inter-rater reliability

- as far as practically possible the assessment should be carried out at the same time of day and at the same point in the session. The patient may be affected by early morning stiffness and, therefore, if measurements are taken at different times of the day, a false impression of improvement or deterioration is created. Similarly, measurements of mobility and stiffness may be affected by the interventions applied and, therefore, measurements should be made consistently, either at the start or close of treatment

- it is important that every one in the same department measures the same thing in the same way. Therefore, it is useful to use training time to standardise measurement-taking and to follow up with regular checks that this is still the case. It is surprising how easily techniques become adapted to individuals and this will affect the reliability of certain measures

- all measuring equipment should be calibrated regularly, in the setting in which it is used, to ensure accuracy, and should also be handled and stored carefully to prevent damage. Even the humble tape measure alters in length (Heck *et al*, 1999).

In her challenging book, Yekutiel (2000) advocates ceasing the habit of separating assessment and treatment. This is an interesting concept. Does this established habit have a negative effect by demonstrating loss? This will depend on the patient and condition. Patients with progressive disease, such as motor neuron disease, will not welcome confirmation of their deterioration, of which they are all too aware. In discussion with colleagues, as part of reflective practice, it became clear that an adolescent with challenging behaviour made better progress and behaved in an acceptable manner when not assessed on arrival. Instead, she was given tasks to carry out and the assessment took place in an informal manner. It would appear that the assessment process was viewed negatively, as a test. Sometimes, it can be hard to separate assessment and treatment. For example, when using manual muscle testing (see *Chapter 10*), the tests may often resemble treatment, using the muscle without resisting, and then applying an increasing resistance as the muscle strengthens. Yet the therapist continues to evaluate strength and movement, even when not assessing formally. Similarly, it can be difficult to separate assessment and treatment in hypersensitivity (see *Chapter 11*). Therefore, although there will be some situations where the assessment process will be informal and incorporated into the treatment, it must still be present. Findings should also be presented in a positive manner.

If patients find the assessment process challenging, so do many therapists. Time is a hard taskmaster, particularly in the National Health Service where the number of patients requiring treatment is infinite. A full hand assessment can take 90 minutes (Roberts, 1989); however, in the clinical situation, this is not always possible due to high referral levels. The majority of hand therapists (Murray *et al*, 2000) set aside 30 minutes; therefore, it is essential that only relevant measurements be taken. A plethora of useless measurements is of no help to the therapist, surgeon, or physician, while lack of hard data gives no basis for assessing progress. Brand and Hollister (1999) state:

> *'Measure what is relevant to the patient's condition and measure it with precision. Record what is relevant and record it in a way that makes it easy to see and review at a glance. There must be flexibility in the setting and later modification of the goals. There must not be flexibility in the disciplines of accurate measurement. It is better not to measure than to record figures that are meaningless. Measurements and tests must always be servants to the educated, alert and sensitive mind'.*

The guideline (see *Page 8*) has been developed, based on experiential learning and known contra-indications. However, findings must always be reviewed in the light of what is known about the individual patient. A useful guiding principle is to ask what will be known when each component of the assessment is complete. Findings eliminating a problem or the cause of the problem can be as useful as confirmatory findings.

Although function has been included in the later stages of the assessment, this does not have to be the case. It may fit more comfortably in the start of the assessment; such decisions can only be made when the history is taken. At the end of the assessment, the therapist should be able to identify any impairment, disability and/or handicap.

The quality and depth of the assessment can be improved when both the physiotherapist and occupational therapist are involved. The pooling of information and use of each professional's particular skills are to the patient's benefit; however, communication is vital to prevent duplication, which only serves to confuse the patient. Departmental culture is significant in achieving an optimum level of communication; however, individuals must also expend effort on their working relationships to achieve and maintain it.

Time can be used more efficiently if the assessment is carried out in a specific area where all the assessment tools and papers are kept together. This area should be well lit so that measurements can be read and recorded accurately. If possible it should be quiet to enable both the patient and therapist to concentrate on the assessment, without distraction, and to ensure confidentiality. Sometimes it may be necessary to assess the patient at the bedside, in their home or even the workplace. It is also important to set aside a small amount of time to clean the tools used, either by washing or wiping with a solution of all purpose detergent and water, followed by drying or by using a disinfectant wipe. This will help prevent infections being passed from patient to patient.

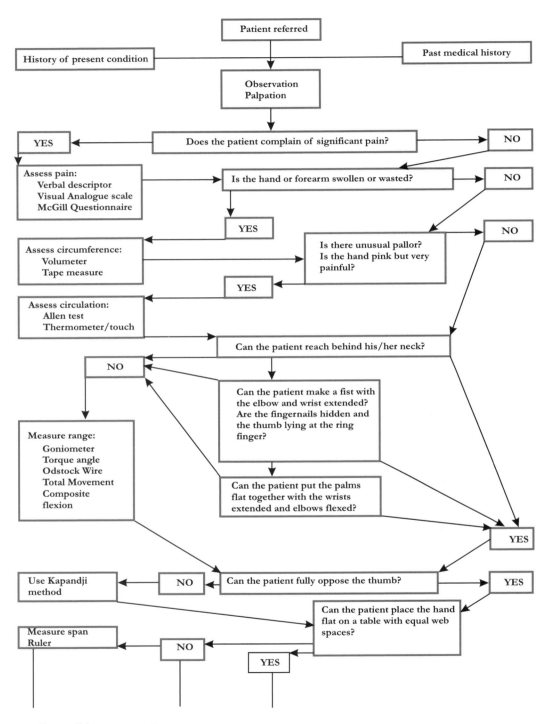

Figure1.1: A possible sequence in assessment

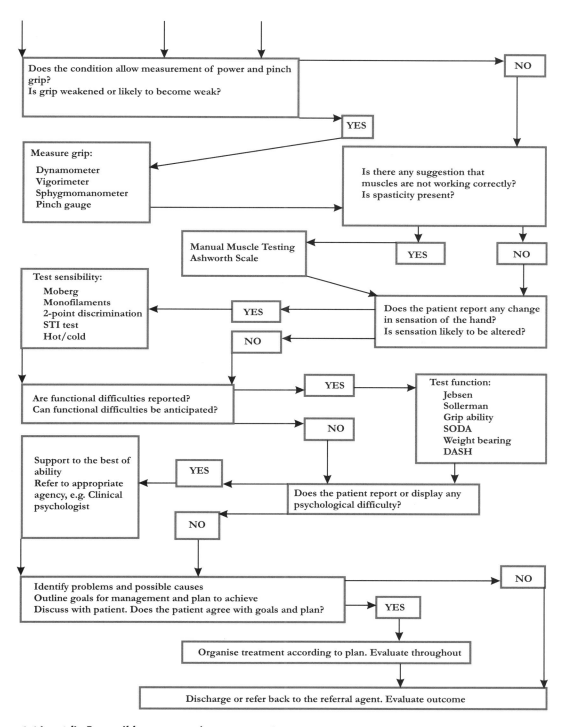

Figure 1.1(contd): A possible sequence in assessment

The recording process may be speeded up by the use of prepared charts; however, no chart will cover all possibilities and it can be very difficult to locate the correct box on a crowded chart. A selection of different A4 sheets for different tests may be a solution. Discussions relating to treatment options should also be recorded, as should any reasons for non-intervention, and discussion of side effects or potential dangers. The importance of meticulous record-keeping cannot be overemphasised. Records may be requested as part of an insurance claim, litigation regarding an injury or clinical negligence, or in the event of the sudden death of a patient. In addition, patients have the right to read their clinical records; therefore, records must follow a logical sequence, be accurate, contemporaneous, legible (Chartered Society of Physiotherapy, 2000), and subjective value judgments should be avoided.

Records should be made in permanent ink; black is the preferred colour (CNST, 2000). Corrections should not be made with correction fluid; an error is crossed out with a straight line and initialled. Every entry must be dated, signed, with the full name of the therapist written underneath the signature. If a student has carried out the assessment or treatment, the supervisor should countersign the record. The record must be secured and stored to minimize losses (CNST, 2000). To aid this, each side of the record sheet should be numbered for clarity and the patient's name and identification number placed at the top of each page as, over a period of time, the pages may become separated. If there is an omission in the notes, this cannot be added against a previous date; the date the omission was identified should be recorded. Abbreviations should be avoided unless locally agreed (Chartered Society of Physiotherapy, 2000). Digits should always be identified by name, not number, to ensure clarity.

Successful clinical decision-making and rehabilitation of the hand is dependent on a thorough, relevant and accurate assessment and recording of these findings. This book will describe how and when to collect the subjective and objective information on impairment, disability and handicap needed for a thorough hand assessment.

To summarise

- The hand has physical, sensory and spiritual significance
- Even minor impairment can result in severe disability and handicap
- Successful rehabilitation is dependent on assessment to identify the causes of problems and prioritise and plan treatment
- Initial and final assessments can form the basis of evidence-based practice therefore, measures must be accurate, reliable, valid and relevant
- Careful recording is essential.

References

Appleby J (1998) Measuring Efficiency in the NHS. *Man Rev* **3**:2

Bear-Lehman J, Abreu BC (1989) Evaluating the hand: Issues in reliability and validity. *Physical Ther* **69**(12): 1025–33

Brand P (1988) The mind and spirit in hand therapy. *J Hand Ther* **July-September**:145–7

Brand PW, Hollister A (1999) *Clinical Mechanics of the Hand*, 3rd edn. CV Mosby, St. Louis: 322

British Association of Hand Therapists (1998) *BAHT Standards for Hand Therapy*. British Association of Hand Therapists, Woodlands, 25 Mountview. Billericay. Essex

Chartered Society of Physiotherapy (2000) *Core Standards*. Chartered Society of Physiotherapy, 14 Bedford Row, London

CNST (2000) *Clinical Risk Management Standards*. Version 01.N.H.S. Litigation Authority. June 2000. Standard 6: Health Records :65–82

Fess EE. (1986) The need for reliability and validity in hand assessment instruments. *J Hand Surg* **11A**(5): 621–3

Fess EE (1995) Guidelines for evaluating assessment instruments. *J Hand Ther* **8**: 144–8

Fess EE ed (1998) Making a difference: The importance of good assessment tools (guest editorial). *Br J Hand Ther* **3**(2): 11

Hammond A (1996) Functional and health assessments used in rheumatology occupational therapy: A review and United Kingdom survey. *Br J Occ Ther* **59**(6): 254–9

Heck H, Simpson CS, Murray K, Smith J, Alcock S, Fathmann M (1999) *HATS Evaluation; Study Work Package 13*. Staffordshire University

Jeffreson P, Hammond A (1997) Upper limb/hand function assessments in current use with rheumatology patients. *J Nat Ass Rheumat Occ Therapists* **11**(1): 33–37

Knight S (1987) *The Brotherhood*. Grafton Books. London

Chapter 2
History

History taking is probably the most important part of the assessment, as it generally forms the first contact between the therapist, the patient, and possibly the patient's relative. It can elicit important information that will assist in the choice of further tests, diagnosis, and planning. It is essential that the therapist establish a rapport and empathy with the patient quickly. Rapport can be defined as a sense of mutuality, understanding, harmony, accord, confidence, and respect underlying a relationship between two persons (Glanze, 1986) and forms the basis of successful communication, while empathy is understanding without over-involvement (Foster, 1997). This chapter looks at ways of facilitating this process and the type of information that must be elicited by the interview. It should be remembered that this is not easy or the vast proportion of complaints in the NHS, which are related to staff attitude (Woodyard and Darby, 1996) would not occur.

General principles

The old maxim 'You never get a second chance to make a first impression' is very apt here. This interaction can set the tone for the relationship, which can help or hinder the subsequent treatment plan and patient's progress. The consultation will almost certainly be of greater importance to the patient than the therapist. The patient may have an injury or condition that may threaten their livelihood or independence; furthermore, they may be in pain and find themselves in an alien environment. The therapist must display confidence, even if it is not felt, and interest in the patient. Some stumbling blocks to this are:

- cases may become routine to the therapist, but are never routine to the patient. Even if the case is not routine, some of the aspects, such as the opening remarks and questions, will be. Make these sound fresh and interesting, verbally by intonation and non-verbally by appearing alert, interested, and making eye contact

- at all times, it is important to make a supreme effort to expunge any extraneous matters from the mind and concentrate on the current patient

- patients kept waiting beyond their appointment time should be given a genuine apology and explanation, in order to ensure that the consultation gets off to the best possible start.

Many patients appear to have rehearsed a speech about their condition and it is usually best to let them make it. Often, this will include their biggest worry, for example, will they be able to work or will their problem get better? Sometimes, they would like an instant answer to such a question. At this point, it is usually best to explain that more information is needed before you can answer. If, after the assessment is completed, the question still cannot be answered then they should be told that you do not know the answer, but that you will do your best to ensure that, if at all possible, they will attain their goal. The therapist should not feel threatened by patients bringing a list of written questions. The answers can be given at the appropriate stage in the consultation. While it is important to structure the interview, it should not be done so rigidly as to make the therapist sound disinterested or prevent the patient giving vital information.

Patient's personalities and language skills are extremely diverse. Some patients may volunteer little more than monosyllabic answers; others may be extremely verbose and tell long-winded and apparently pointless tales. It is important that the therapist has the social skills to draw out the silent, encourage the vague to be specific, and cut off the long-winded, politely, where necessary.

Verbal and physical abuse by patients should not be tolerated; however, often a patient may appear ungracious, truculent, or abrupt. Effort expended in building up a relationship with these patients usually pays dividends; they may reveal personal problems that are the cause of this behaviour, or may turn out to have an enchanting personality, hidden below an outer reserve.

Often, by listening carefully to the history, the therapist will gain insight into the patient's condition, which can help diagnosis. Additionally, this will illuminate the patient's perception of their condition, which may be realistic, wildly pessimistic, or over optimistic. Open questions will elicit more information, to either confirm or refute the impressions formed (Foster, 1997). In addition to listening skills, the therapist should use observational skills to monitor the patient's non-verbal behaviour, which may support or contradict information given, as well as give an insight into any fear, shame, or anger that the patient may be experiencing, and which could affect their recovery (Brand, 1988). The therapist should use words and phrases that are simple, clear, and understandable to the patient and relatives (Martin and Gupta, 1992). The appropriate use of humour can facilitate rapport and create a relaxed atmosphere (Sullivan, 2001). Inappropriate use could jeopardise the therapeutic relationship; consequently, humour should be used with caution.

A question that often arises is, should a relative or the patient's partner be present for the assessment? Relatives may be able to give useful information about the patient's abilities pre-injury or how function is affected. The patient may have a hearing or speech problem and need assistance. Support for the treatment programme may be needed, for example, to reinforce the home exercise programme. If a partner is not involved in the process, they may be overprotective, which may slow rehabilitation; conversely, some patients perform better when their relative is not present. When the patient is under 16 years of age, he/she should, usually, be accompanied by a responsible adult, in order to obtain consent to treatment and, where language skills are undeveloped, give the history (Department of Health, 2001). Ultimately, in other cases, the person who decides on this is the patient, who should be asked this question discreetly so that he/she can refuse without offending his/her relative. If it is decided to leave the supporter in the waiting area, a brief word afterwards summing up the session, with the patient's consent, maintains good communication diplomatically. Consent and the summary of the discussion should be recorded.

Sometimes, the involvement of the relative causes barriers to rapport and history-taking. If the relative tries to dominate the interaction, the therapist's social skills will again be needed to maintain respect for the relative's view, but not excluding the patient. Useful phrases in this context can be, 'Is that how it feels, Mr. Bloggs?' Relatives may also describe vividly how put upon they feel by the patient's dependence; in this instance, a useful phrase is, 'It's a difficult situation for you both, neither of you wanted it'. Sometimes, patients bring small children or babies with them and this can prove disruptive to the department and a distraction for the parent; if this is the case, they should be gently and tactfully discouraged from bringing them. Depending on the age of the child, a firm word from the therapist may curtail bad behaviour. Prevention is better than cure and, depending on the child's age, a toy or drawing may prove a distraction. If the child has behaved well, praise will be appreciated by parent and child.

Woodyard and Darby (1986) provide a useful rule of thumb for patient interactions. 'Perhaps the single, simplest piece of advice one can give to staff is that they should treat patients, as they would wish their families and themselves to be treated. But this is easier said than done.' Reflective practice and peer review helps develop this concept.

Setting the scene

Ideally, the area for history-taking should be private, so that personal details are not overheard. In practice, in many departments, this has to take place in a quiet corner or behind curtains or it may be necessary to carry out the assessment by the bedside, in the home or workplace.

The patient should feel secure and be comfortable, both in temperature and position, to encourage them to relax. In winter, outpatients should have the opportunity to hang up outdoor clothing, but should not be asked to remove indoor clothing until the history is taken. The therapist should ensure that patients can maintain their personal space and should position him/herself at the same level as patients; this aids equality and establishes rapport. If the therapist perches on a plinth and patients are seated on a lower chair, they may feel that the therapist is dominating the interview. Conversely, if the therapist hides behind a barrier or lurks at a distance, the patient will perceive this as disinterest or may, in turn, attempt to dominate the interview. The therapist should sit either at right angles to, or facing the patient, to facilitate eye contact; both the therapist and the patient should be able to initiate or withdraw eye contact during the interview (see *Plate 2.1*).

Note taking is a vital legal requirement for professionals and it is important that such records are contemporaneous, legible, dated, signed, factual and accurate. Some therapists advocate that notes are made as soon after the consultation as possible (Trombly, 1995), although this method relies on the memory of the therapist. Inexperienced therapists sometimes prefer to make rough notes and write these up later; however, this can cause undue stress by increasing his or her workload. Patients usually expect notes to be made and a brief explanation will reassure those who do not. Record taking should not dominate the interview.

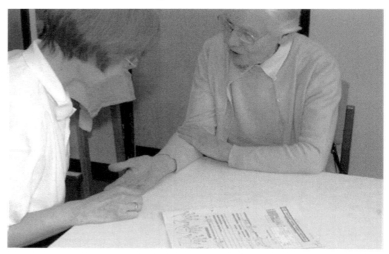

Plate 2.1 Position the patient and therapist to facilitate rapport

It is useful to listen to the patient's history and reflect a summary back to the patient; in the summary, use the adjectives that the patient has used, i.e., 'Let me see if I have got this correct, you have had a stinging pain in your wrist since Christmas, which never goes away, but is worse at night.' This process serves the purpose of checking that the facts are correct, while letting the patient know that the therapist has, indeed, understood the problem. It should then be written down on the record. This approach permits eye contact to be maintained and the patient, not the record card, is the centre of attention. Writing time allows the patient to reflect on any questions they may have or further information to supply.

The structure of the interview

- start with an introduction. Always introduce yourself and ensure that the status and name of any patient supporter is known. Introductions should include the therapist's role and why he/she is seeing the patient If the patient has consented to the presence of a student, he/she should also be introduced

- outpatients should be given an appointment time that is acceptable to them

- ensure that you are talking to the correct patient by checking name, address and date of birth

- ensure that the following information is recorded:
  - the patient's name
  - date of birth
  - address

- general practitioner
- consultant
- unit number, or NHS number
- telephone number (home, work and mobile numbers are useful in case an outpatient appointment is to be altered)

- determine the patient's dominant hand. For simplicity this is generally taken to be the hand that the patient uses to write with, and a variety of methods exist to obtain more accurate detail (Oldfield, 1971; Moynihan and Breathnach, 1995; Gabbard *et al*, 1997; Lui and Fess, 2000; Cary and Adams, 2003). There is considerable variance between reported preference and actual preference and this can have implications for research, normative values, and the extent of the disability experienced by individual patients (Moynihan and Breathnach, 1995; Lui and Fess, 2000)

- ascertain the patient's occupation. If the patient gives his/her occupation as unemployed, it is useful to establish clearly the type of work he/she may be seeking. Often, it is necessary to know exactly what type of work is undertaken; for example, engineers may do heavy manual labour, work requiring the utmost dexterity, or use a computer all day. When a person has retired it useful to know what his/her employment was; this gives insight into the patient's life and an idea of his/her anticipated strength, dexterity, and sensitivity

- enquire about the management of activities of daily living, so that these can be explored further at a later date, if necessary

- establish hobbies or leisure pursuits of importance to the patient. If the patient is involved in sport or music, it is useful to know at what level he/she practices, as this will affect his/her needs and attitude to recovery. An explanation of the purpose behind these questions is needed, to avoid seeming impertinent

- define the event or problem that has resulted in the consultation. Sir Lancelot Spratt, the fictional surgeon in the books written by Richard Gordon, advised his students not to ask, 'What brought you here?' Inevitably, the answer would be, 'the Number 9 bus'. Personal experience has confirmed that this question needs to be rephrased to elicit the information required

- note any slurring of speech as the patient answers, as this is sometimes of clinical significance in cases of upper motor neuron problems.

Trauma patients

If trauma is the cause of the problem, find out when the injury occurred and calculate how much time has elapsed since it happened. Establish what treatment or surgery has been given to date. Ascertain where the patient was when the injury occurred and did it happen at home, at work, or during leisure pursuits, as this can have some bearing on the patient's injury and recovery. For example, a fall from a moving horse will generate greater forces than a slip on the kitchen floor, and cause greater bony and soft tissue damage. It is also important to ascertain if the location was clean or dirty, as infection can delay healing and the return to normal function. It is useful to know the mechanism of injury, including the position of the hand and direction of force, as this will highlight structures that may have been damaged (American Society for Surgery of the Hand, 1990; Nicholson, 1992).

Depending on the event it may be very difficult for the patient to talk about the accident and therefore questions should be phrased as sensitively as possible. There may be pending legal claims and it can be helpful to be aware of these. The therapist should always remain nonjudgmental; some accidents may have occurred in embarrassing circumstances or as part of the commission of an alleged criminal act.

- *Problems relating to trauma—find out:*
  - When?
  - Where?
  - How?
  - What happened next?

Box 2.1 Summary of enquiry for trauma patients

Surgery

Following surgery, obtain the date, why it was performed, the type of surgery and any complications, such as damaged tissues, which cannot be repaired. Information on this may have to be obtained from the patient's medical notes.

Musculo-skeletal problems

For problems unrelated to trauma or surgery, find out when the problem first appeared, if it occurred suddenly or insidiously, and is it localised or generalised. Enquire on the progression, if any, of symptoms and any other associated occurrences. The effects on work, leisure and home life must be established. Ask the patient to describe what makes the problem better and what makes it worse. If the patient is unable to supply any, make informed suggestions, such as cold, warmth, or a particular time of day to facilitate further responses (American Society for Surgery to the Hand, 1990). When the patient reports clunks and clicks, note the terminology used (it may be significant), and ask the patient to show where these are felt and when.

Note the effects of previous medical and therapeutic treatment on the condition (Nicholson, 1992). If an intervention has been unhelpful in the past, it is likely to be so again, or the patient may have very positive or negative feelings to a particular treatment modality based on past experience.

All patients

The patient's general state of health at the time of consultation should also be ascertained. A special enquiry should be made into any known allergies to ensure the allergen is excluded from treatment. If, for example, the patient has a latex allergy, non latex gloves and hand equipment should be used. All current medication should be recorded.

Smoking is relevant to the general health of the patient; therefore, the patient should be asked if he/she is a smoker. Smoking may affect healing through its effects on the peripheral circulation. Explain these effects to the patient to enable him/her to make an informed choice on stopping or continuing the habit. The Smoking Cessation Service may be helpful here.

Take the previous medical history with dates. Always obtain further information from medical notes, colleagues and X-rays as necessary. Of particular note are:

- any previous hand injury or condition
- any condition that may result in the patient becoming unconscious or ill while in the department; e.g. diabetes, epilepsy, hypertension, narcolepsy, or cardiac problems. Establish trigger factors when relevant; these may be significant when choosing treatment options
- any condition or treatment that may have a lasting systemic effect, such as tuberculosis, or radiotherapy following cancer. Certain treatment modalities will be contraindicated
- any psychological, emotional or social problems that may be longstanding or recent (See below).

The patient may have splints that are worn or have been abandoned. The type and purpose of such splints should be established and arrangements made to inspect them. It is important to discover the reason why splints have been abandoned.

Find out what the patient's goal is and what is important to the patient. This could be to hold his/her baby at the christening, to write a letter that is legible, or return to work. This will help with goal setting and determining a successful outcome.

Finally check the patient's understanding of what he/she has been told, that he/she has no further questions and gives consent for the assessment to proceed.

Psychological or emotional problems

Psychological or emotional problems that may hinder progress are extremely relevant (Nicholson, 1992; Bexon and Salter, 2000). This is of particular importance when patients have been involved in a workplace accident and may develop a phobia about a particular tool (Bexon and Salter, 2000). Even if they do not develop a phobia, they usually find it hard to go back to where the injury occurred and look at the machinery involved. This seems to be easier if it takes place in a social manner, going back to thank colleagues for their good wishes for example. One patient revealed that it was not the sight of the circular saw that upset him, but his blood, which was still on the walls of the building that he had been constructing. Because of the importance of the hand to status and spirituality (see *Chapter 1*), it is not surprising that a small physical impairment can have a huge emotional effect (Rumsey *et al*, 2003). A broken fingernail, so trivial and common, is generally regarded with annoyance and irritation.

Although psychological problems are rarely divulged immediately, once the therapeutic relationship is established, the patient is more likely to open up. This can be facilitated if the therapist sits beside the patient who is undertaking a task (Cheshire, 2000). The patient's current drug regime may indicate any recent or longstanding psychological problems that are being treated. Sometimes a question, such as 'Do you dream about the accident?' will elicit information, as it shows that the therapist has some understanding of the problems. Patients who are unable to work or have chronic hand pain may become depressed. Depending on the information obtained from patients about their emotions, the therapist may decide to administer the Hospital Anxiety and Depression Scale Questionnaire (Zigmond and Snaith, 1983; Snaith and Zigmond, 1994) or seek help from a psychologist or community psychiatric nurse.

It may also become apparent that the patient has social problems, which may be financial problems or related to care of a child, elderly relative or pet (Salter, 1987). In these cases a referral to a social worker should be advised. The social worker will be aware of statutory and voluntary support available locally.

Hospital Anxiety and Depression Scale is a reliable and valid scale for detecting anxiety and depression in medical patients. It is well accepted with response rates reported of 95–100%. It is stable enough to withstand situational influences, but becomes less stable over long periods of time. It is sensitive to changes in the course of diseases and to psychotherapeutic and psycho-pharmacological intervention. Well researched throughout the world, it can be used for international comparisons (Herrmann, 1997).

To obtain the questionnaire and manual, it is necessary to register on-line prior to purchasing the manual forms (Snaith and Zigmond, 1994).

Box 2.2 Hospital Anxiety and Depression Scale

Questionnaire

As time for assessment in a busy department is always pressing, the patient can be given a questionnaire to complete before the consultation, either through the post or when he/she is in the waiting area. This gives him/her the opportunity to focus on his/her problem and collect relevant data, such as a medication list. The completed questionnaire can then act as a springboard for further discussion. Some therapists use the Health Assessment Questionnaire (HAQ), Modified Health Assessment Questionnaire (MHAQ), Arthritis Impact Measurement Scale 2 (AIMS2) or DASH Questionnaire to facilitate this and develop a measurable outcome (see *Chapter 12*).

The next step

While taking the history, the process of observation, described in the next chapter, is begun. When the history is completed, the therapist should have knowledge of the patient as a whole, not just the hand problem, an idea of possible causes of the hand problem and the range of objective tests and measurements that will be needed. These can be started when the observation phase is completed.

To summarise

- establish rapport and empathy with the patient and relatives by genuine interest and concentration. This will help gain the required information
- matching, or mirroring, the patient's posture and communication style can help create rapport
- use verbal, listening, observational and social skills
- answer questions as honestly and as fully as possible
- get further information when necessary.

References

American Society for Surgery to The Hand (1990) *The Hand Examination and Diagnosis*, 3rd edn. Churchill Livingstone, Edinburgh: 5–8

Bexon C, Salter M (2000) Assessment. In: Salter M, Cheshire L, eds. *Hand Therapy Principles and Practice*. Butterworth-Heinemann, Oxford: 51–57

Brand P (1988) The mind and spirit in hand therapy. *J Hand Ther* Jul –Sept: 145–47

Cary I, Adams J (2003) A comparison of dominant and non-dominant hand function in both right- and left-handed individuals using the Southampton Hand Assessment Procedure (SHAP). *Br J Hand Therapy* **8**(1): 4–10

Cheshire L (2000) Psychosocial aspects of hand therapy. In: Salter M, Cheshire L, eds. *Hand Therapy Principles and Practice*. Butterworth Heinemann, Oxford: 58–69

Department of Health (2001) *Reference Guide to Consent for Examination or Treatment*. Department of Health, London

Foster M (1997) Assessment. In: Turner A, Foster M, Johnson S, eds. *Occupational Therapy and Physical Dysfunction: Principles Skills and Practice*, 4th edn. Churchill Livingstone, Edinburgh: 164–67

Gabbard C, Iteya M, Rabb C (1997) A lateralized comparison of handedness and object proximity. *Can J Exp Psychol* **51**(2): 176–80

Glanze WD, ed (1986) *Mosby's Dictionary of Medicine and Nursing*. CV Mosby, St Louis

Herrmann C (1997) International experiences with the Hospital Anxiety and Depression Scale—A review of validation data and clinical results. *J Psychosom Res* **42**(1): 17–41

Lui P, Fess E (2000) Establishing hand dominance: Self-report versus the Waterloo Handedness Questionnaire. *J Hand Ther* **13**(1): 71–2

Martin LJ, Gupta A (1992) Hand sssessment. *Plastic Surgic Nurs* **12**(3): 89–94

Moynihan JB, Breathnach CS (1995) A survey of manual preference, skill and strength in undergraduates. *Irish J Psycholog Med* **12**(4): 127–31

Nicholson B (1992) Clinical evaluation. In: Stanley BG, Tribuzi SM, eds. *Concepts in Hand Rehabilitation*. FA Davis, Philadelphia: 59–91

Oldfield RC (1971) The assessment and analysis of handedness: The Edinburgh Inventory. *Neuropsychologia* **9**: 99–113

Rumsey N, Clarke A, White P, Hooper E (2003) Investigating the appearnace-related concerns of people with hand injuries. *Br J Hand Therapy* **8**(2): 57–61

Salter MI (1987) *Hand Injuries: A Therapeutic Approach*. Churchill Livingstone, Edinburgh: 18

Snaith RP, Zigmond AS (1994) *HADS: Hospital Anxiety and Depression Scale*. Windsor NFER, Nelson

Sullivan JL (2001) Hand therapy: The healing touch with a touch of humor. *J Hand Ther* **14**(1): 3–9

Trombly C (1995) *Occupational Therapy for Physical Dysfunction*, 4th edn. Williams and Wilkins, Baltimore: 32

Woodyard J, Darby M-A (1996) Vicious circles. *Health Serv J* **26 September**: 30–31

Zigmond AS, Snaith RP (1983) The Hospital Anxiety and Depression Scale. *Acta Psychiatr Scand* **67**: 361–70

Chapter 3
Observation

History taking is exacting. Despite this, it is during this phase that the observation of the hand begins. It is hardly surprising that palmists claim to tell a person's future and past by studying the hand, as life leaves its mark on the hand (see *Plate 3.1* and *3.2*). Similarly, looking at the hand can reveal much about the patient's condition and his/her level of function. Furthermore, in cases where the problem is unilateral, there is a natural control for comparisons. Touch is a core skill of therapists and during the observation phase palpation will be essential to confirm or clarify the information obtained by the eyes, without causing unnecessary pain. Colditz (2000) recommends touching the unaffected hand first to establish trust.

Euclid, the Egyptian mathematician who lived circa 300 BC, is reputed to have said, 'What can be seen, cannot be seen at once in its entirety'. This statement illustrates the need for a structured, observational approach. It is, therefore, suggested that this starts with the whole person and then focusses on specific features. The areas requiring observation are considered as follows: posture, structure, colour, temperature, skin, wounds and scars, and the method for recording them is described.

Life leaves its mark upon the hand—the hands of an older person

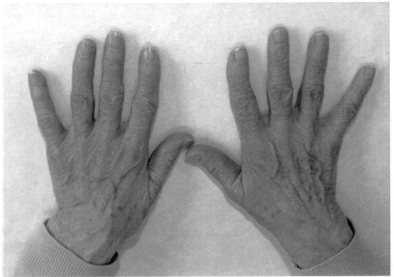

Plate 3.1: Dorsal view

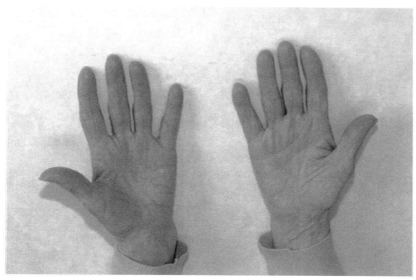

Plate 3.2: Palmar view

Preparation

During the course of the assessment, it will be necessary to see the whole upper limb (ASSH, 1990; Nicholson, 1992) and the patient will need to remove indoor clothing; this presupposes privacy. In order to maintain patient comfort and equality, do not ask the patient to remove indoor clothing until the history is taken and the limb needs to be observed. Always explain why this is necessary (Chartered Society of Physiotherapy, 2000):

- to establish if the problem is localised
- to observe the interaction of muscular effort of the shoulder and elbow joints
- to ascertain any proximal lack of movement or wasting acquired as a result of disease or injury
- to establish the presence of any misalignment in the shoulder or elbow as function will inevitably be affected

For future visits suggest the patient wears a sleeveless T-Shirt. Alternatively, such instructions can be included in the appointment letter.

Observational considerations

Posture

When first meeting the patient, note the general posture of the patient when sitting and walking. General posture can give an indication of the patient's general well-being—if hunched it may mean he/she is depressed or has a kyphosis. Often, just by looking at patients in the waiting area, in the few seconds before they are called in, it is possible to tell by their posture and facial expression whether they are better or worse. Note the speed and quality of movements for any abnormality and the facial expression.

Posture may also be significant in a work-related disorder or referred pain (Boyling, 2000). Observe how the patient is holding the hand; it may be in an abnormal position, for example, the patient may be protecting or cradling it. The patient may make no effort to use the hand, for example, when taking off clothes or handling the appointment card. These can be important visual clues to the way the patient feels about the hand and how the hand feels to the patient.

Observe the position of the hand at rest; the normal hand adopts a flexed posture with the fingers cascading down from the index finger. If this does not occur, consideration should be given to the presenting posture and possible reasons why it has occurred, for example, an extended finger can indicate a ruptured flexor tendon or it can indicate a lack of passive movement due to rigidity. Wrist flexion in the relaxed hand causes the fingers to gently flex; this is known as the tenodesis effect, and if this does not occur it is a sign of a significant hand problem. The presence and type of any splinting or fixation should also be noted and relevant enquiries made about it (see *Chapter 2*).

Tremor may be present and there may be clues from the history as to the cause of the tremor (e.g. history of Parkinson's disease or alcohol abuse). It can be assessed by the use of drawing an Archimedes spiral. The patient is shown a spiral and asked to copy it. The greater the tremor, the more jagged and shaky the spiral will appear; this can be used to demonstrate the effect of treatment (Cooper *et al*, 2000) or progression of disease over time.

Structure

The presence, type and location of any deformities present in the hand should be noted. Deformity is defined as a condition of being distorted, disfigured, flawed, malformed or misshapen (Glanze, 1986). There are many types of deformity that can occur in the hand; some of these are acquired (see *Box 3.1*) through disease, such as rheumatoid arthritis, or trauma, such as claw hand, which occurs in combined ulnar and median nerve injury.

Mallet Finger—the DIP joint is held in flexion

Boutonnière—the PIP joint is flexed and the DIP joint hyper-extended

Swan-Neck—the PIP joint is hyper-extended; the DIP joint flexed

Ulnar Drift—the fingers and/or wrist lie in ulnar deviation

Claw Hand—all the arches of the hand are flattened; the MCP joints are hyper-extended, the PIP and DIP joints are flexed

Dupuytren's Contracture—the MCP may be flexed; the PIP and DIP joints are flexed. This usually, but not always, occurs in the little and ring fingers

Intrinsic Plus—the MCP joints are flexed and the PIP and DIP joints are extended

Box 3.1: Common acquired deformities of the hand

There are also many congenital deformities. The American Society for Surgery to the Hand (ASSH, 1990) classifies these as follows:

- failure of formation of parts
- failure of differentiation or separation of parts
- duplication
- overgrowth
- undergrowth
- congenital constriction band syndrome
- generalised skeletal abnormalities.

These deformities should be carefully recorded, and photography is useful. Sometimes adults with congenital deformities, who have been unable to use one hand from childhood, or have limited use, acquire some small injury to their useful hand. These patients suffer a disproportionate disability; measurements, such as grip strength, will appear within normal range, but will be abnormally low for them.

Observe any absence of digits or parts of digits. Childhood amputations can be difficult to spot in the adult, as colour, hand posture and use will appear normal. In these cases, the extent, cause and date of amputation should be ascertained. There may be clubbing of the terminal phalanx, a sign of general ill health (Stuttaford, 2000); this observation will assist the therapist in taking the past medical history.

The presence of any lumps and bumps on the hand may be significant. Nodules or osteophytes can occur at the margin of DIP joints (Heberden's nodes) or at the PIP joints (Bouchard's nodes) and these may indicate the presence of osteoarthritis. Small, firm swellings at the wrist or palmar digital crease may well be ganglia. Sometimes a ganglion or a mucous cyst arises from the DIP joint; these tend to have thin walls and there may be grooving of the fingernail distal to the cyst. Malignant tumours occur rarely in the hand, although basal and squamous cell skin cancers may occur dorsally in the elderly (ASSH, 1990). Should the therapist be the first to spot a suspect lesion, this should be drawn immediately to the attention of the referring doctor without causing the patient anxiety.

Hand size

Large hands can be a feature of acromegaly, a chronic metabolic disease marked by the gradual enlargement of the bones of the extremities, jaw and face. It is, however, more likely that hand size will be affected by oedema or wasting.

Following surgery or trauma, it is almost inevitable that the hand will be swollen. This can be judged by the absence or decreased prominence of palmar or dorsal creases, particularly over the PIP joints. The swelling may be confined to a joint/joints or digits, therefore the location of swelling should be noted. The swollen hand, digits or joints should be measured as appropriate (see *Chapter 5*). Gentle palpation should be used to assess the feel of joint swelling to ascertain if it is organised or fluid. Synovitis is suggested if the joint feels 'boggy' on palpation. Palpation will indicate the presence of pitting oedema or identify tissues with a rigid or woody feel, indicating that elasticity may be affected.

Conversely, comparison with the other hand may indicate muscle wasting. Wasting may be visible particularly at:

- the forearm
- the first palmar interosseous space when the thumb is adducted
- the other interosseous spaces (dorsally and volarly)
- over the thenar eminence
- the fifth metacarpal may be visible at the ulnar border, if the hypothenar eminence is wasted (Salter, 1987; Bexon and Salter, 2000).

The location of muscle wasting should be noted and measured as appropriate (see *Chapter 5*) and the contraction of wasted muscles tested to ascertain if wasting is due to nerve or tendon damage (see *Chapter 10*).

Colour

Compare the colour of the affected and non-affected hands or, in bilateral conditions, the colour of the tester. The affected hand may be blanched, cyanosed or darkened. Differentiation is easy in Caucasian patients, however, colour change can be difficult to identify in deeply pigmented skin, even for the experienced observer. Unilateral change of colour may be usual for that patient, for example, following an earlier hemiplegia, and this should be established. It may be that colour change is generalised throughout the hand or limb, or localised to one or more digits. The presence and location of any demarcation line should be noted. These findings can give an indication of the circulation to the hand and fingers and the ulnar and radial pulses can be palpated to confirm that they are present; this is essential if any form of thermal treatment or elevation is to be contemplated. If pulses are present, arterial patency can be tested using the Allen test (see *Chapter 14*) (Allen, 1929; ASSH; 1990).

The temperature of the skin may be colder or warmer than expected from the surroundings and can be judged by touch. Touching the hand gently and comparing with the opposite hand will help reveal the cause of discolouration; if hot, rubor may be the result of inflammation or infection or, if cold, pallor may be due to poor circulation. It is possible for unpractised hands to detect 2° C changes in temperature while a practised hand can detect 1.25° changes (Brand and Hollister, 1999). Alternatively, skin temperature can be tested using disposable thermometer strips; these should not be applied immediately after holding the hand (Brand and Hollister, 1999). Temperature indicators or strip thermometers are available from hand therapy equipment specialists.

Note the colour and distribution of any bruising. During the history taking, it is important to ensure that the cause of the bruising is ascertained; patients often knock or trap their hand during the recovery phase and it may be that further injury has occurred. Alternatively, forearm or upper limb bruising may be the result of rough handling. If abuse is suspected, then advice must be taken immediately from the head of department. Action taken will depend on the nature of the suspected abuse.

Skin

Dorsally the skin should be thin and mobile, while the palmar surface should have thick and tethered skin; any deviation from this should be noted, as should any lesions or irregularities (ASSH, 1990). Often the palmar skin may be calloused, reflecting the work and hobbies of the patient and, if there has been a period of disuse, these will change in texture and appearance, becoming softer and paler. The presence and condition of such callosities should be noted. Early signs of Dupuytren's contracture may be noticed as a small disruption in the palm of the hand.

The skin may be dirty reflecting the condition of the hand at the time of injury or demonstrate recent use. It is generally a sign of recovery for a patient to apologise for attending with dirty hands. When a hand is protected from use by a splint, for example following a tendon repair, the presence of dirt may indicate overuse and presents the opportunity to discuss this.

Touching the skin on the hand may give an indication of any lack of sensation. Sometimes this can be suspected from the history and patient's report; however, in some cases, such as where the origin of hand pain lies in the cervical spine, the presence or absence of sensation is significant. Any suspected loss must be fully tested (see *Chapter 11*), but at this stage it is possible to get an indication of the existence, scale and severity of any problem.

Sweating abnormalities, excess or absence, are often a sign of nerve damage. If the hand is sweating profusely, it may indicate an autonomic nervous system disorder (Tubiana *et al*, 1996), complex regional pain syndrome or anxiety. The location and amount of sweating should be noted (Tubiana *et al*, 1996) (see *Chapter 11*). The amount of sweating can be assessed by:

- visual estimation
- touching the hand with the dorsum of the therapist's fingers (Salter, 1987; Bexon and Salter, 2000)
- the use of a skin resistance meter (Bexon and Salter, 2000), although these do not appear to be commercially available
- ninhydrin sweat test (see *Chapter 11*)
- trace the blunt end of a pen across the skin. It will stick if sweating is present. If it does not stick, sweating is not present and this normally indicates peripheral nerve damage.

The texture of the skin may appear scaly and dry, as after the removal of a cast, or it may be shiny and thin.

Hairs should be equally present on both hands (Malick and Kasch, 1984) (unless, of course, the hand and forearm were shaved prior to surgery). Dark, dense, coarse hairs, appearing to grow in an ulnar direction are a feature of complex regional pain syndrome (Downs-Wheeler, 2000). Similarly, an increase or absence of hairs can demonstrate a peripheral nerve disorder (Waylett-Rendall, 1988).

Fingernails

The presence, length, condition and colour of the fingernails are important diagnostic tools for therapist and doctor. The soft palmar tissue of the fingertips will lack support if nails are absent. Nails bitten below the quick have an affect on function, best demonstrated by attempting to pick up a pin (Zook, 2000). Enquiries about nail biting can clarify if the condition of the nails is self-inflicted or pathological, for example nail growth may be slowed following nerve injury (Waylett-Rendall, 1988). Conversely, nails extending more than 0.5 cm beyond the end of the fingers interfere with grip and fine function and the patient should be encouraged to cut them to gain maximum benefit from treatment (Stegink Jansen, 2000).

Thickened or ridged nails indicate systemic disease or disuse. Transverse ridges may be the result of an episode of general ill health, affecting the nail growth (Stuttaford, 2000). Longitudinal ridges and splitting can be the result of trauma, as is a hooked nail deformity (Zook, 2000). Pitting of the nails may be the result of psoriasis (Stuttaford, 2000). In nerve injury, nails may become harder and ridged and over time become smaller and curving towards the palm (Waylett-Rendall, 1988). In cases of nerve damage or reflex sympathetic dystrophy (or type 1 complex regional pain syndrome), the finger pads become atrophied giving a pencil pointing appearance (Waylett-Rendall, 1988).

The natural nail colour is of particular significance in the diagnosis of general health. In liver disease the nails may be slate grey, blue in cardio-pulmonary problems, and tiny haemorrhages that appear like small wood splinters under the nails are a diagnostic feature in heart valve infections (Stuttaford, 2000). In some deeply pigmented Africans it may be necessary to look at the mucous membranes in the mouth or eye to identify changes, such as cyanosis. Where there is rubor around the nailbed, this can indicate infection or paronychia (Zook, 2000). Discoloured nails (yellow, green or brown), which are flaking or lifted, can result from fungal infection (Stuttaford, 2000); this may occur if the patient has not kept the finger tips clean while casted.

Subungual malignant melanoma may be characterised by a pigmented area, or melanonychia, with disruption and enlargement of the nail. If a pigmented area appears on the nail, a scratch should be made proximally and distally to the area and a watch maintained on nail growth. If the scratch and pigment grow at the same rate a subungual haematoma is likely; if only the scratch grows, then it may be a nevus (collection of blood vessels) or melanoma and a biopsy will be necessary (Zook, 2000). It is usual to carry out a biopsy if the area is greater than 6mm. If there is any persistently unhealed area around the nails, it may indicate a squamous cell carcinoma. The therapist should seek medical advice immediately when suspecting either of the above conditions, without making the patient unduly anxious.

Wounds

An agreement should be reached with referring doctors regarding the removal of wound dressings. Any dressing will impede the movement of the hand and this is in direct proportion to the size and security of the dressing. Consequently, it is usually necessary to remove dressings to assess the wound and allow movement, provided removal or movement is not contraindicated and aseptic technique is used. The site of the wound should be noted, as should the type of wound, which may be:

- tidy
- untidy
- open
- closed.

Any surgical or medical treatment to the wound should be recorded; this should include the type and method used for closure or fixation. The state and stage of healing should be observed.

The colour of an open wound is often significant; it may be red, yellow or black. The colour of surrounding tissues and quality of such tissues also warrants attention. Any suspected infection should be reported to the referring doctor without delay; this can be identified by:

- warmth

- rubor
- pulsating pain
- presence of pus
- smell

The size of the wound should be recorded. If the wound is regularly shaped, this can be measured using a disposable measuring tape or sterile ruler. For irregularly shaped wounds, a clear acetate sheet can be held above the wound and an outline made in felt tip pen (Baldwin *et al*, 1992). This can then be traced onto the patient's record sheet. Alternatively, a Polaroid photograph can be taken at a given distance and recorded on a grid, giving a visual record of healing and wound state.

Dressings should be renewed when the treatment session is completed, or when that part of the assessment is finished. Irrespective of age or sex, the patient may be unable to look at his/her hand; if this is the case, he/she should not be forced to do so. If this reluctance persists, the patient may require support from a psychologist. Reassure an anxious patient that, when healed, the hand will look much better. Before and after photographs or reassurance from other patients can be helpful.

Scars

The location, mobility, vascularity and condition of scars should be noted, as these may affect movements in the hand if the skin is tethered or adhered to underlying tissues. It is necessary to touch the scars to ascertain this and to gain an impression of any hypersensitivity. If hypersensitivity is present, it can be assessed using a visual analogue scale (VAS) (see *Chapter 4*) or the Three Phase Sensitivity Test (see *Chapter 11*). Scar pliability can be measured using specialist tools. These devices have poor inter-rater reliability; therefore, the same therapist should use them consistently (Baldwin *et al*, 1992; MacDermid *et al*, 2000). Palpation around the scar may indicate if there is induration (or hardening) and, by gently moving the skin, adherence can be noted.

Burn scars require specialised testing using a formalised scale (Baldwin *et al*, 1992). This is an extremely specialised area, usually undertaken in regional centres and, therefore, is not covered here.

Posture—of the body, of the hand

Splinting/cast/fixation

Tremor present

Deformity present—acquired/congenital

Amputation present

Size—wasting/swelling

Skin—colour, temperature, bruises, condition, callosities

Sweating—excessive/absent/normal

Hair presence/pattern

Nail lengths, colour, condition

Wound size, state

Scars—mobility, vascularity, condition, hypersensitivity

Box 3.2: Checklist for observing the hand

Recording

The significant factors observed can be noted on simple sketches of the hand. Four simple line drawings of the hand can be pre-printed onto the record sheet or applied to the sheet at the point of choice, using an inexpensive, rubber-stamping system, showing the palmar and dorsal aspects of the left and right hands. These should show the major wrist, palm and digital creases. Sketches facilitate the accurate drawing of wounds and scars. To facilitate this process the drawings should represent the patient's hands as they appear across the table.

In the case of congenital abnormalities, or severe injury, photographs of the hand taken with the patient's consent and maintained as part of the medical record can be a quick and easy way of recording severe problems. Video recording offers a chance of assessing movement, over a period of time, and again these can be stored as part of the record. It can be tempting with photography to use artistic licence, such as angles, which enhance or minimise deficits; however, as with all medical assessments, the angle of shot and pose should be standardised (Brand and Hollister, 1999). When the services of a medical photographer are available better results will be obtained.

The importance of history taking, listening and observing cannot be over-emphasised. As therapists spend proportionally more time with individual patients than their colleagues, it is possible for their history and observations to provide vital diagnostic clues, which may relate to general health or upper motor neuron lesions.

The next step

When this part of the assessment and the history are completed, the therapist will be ready to select and to begin some objective measures, which will give an expanded picture of the patient's condition.

To summarise

- view the whole upper limb. Consider posture, structure, colour, skin and wounds
- observe, palpate as necessary and record any deviations from the normal on all tissues
- record on simple sketch drawings of the hand

References

Allen EV (1929) Thromboangiitis obliterans: Methods of diagnosis of chronic occlusive arterial lesions distal to the wrist with illustrative cases. *Am J Med Sci* **178**: 237–44

American Society for Surgery to The Hand (1990) *The Hand Examination and Diagnosis*, 3rd edn. Churchill Livingstone, Edinburgh: 9; 13; 45–6

Baldwin JE, Weber LJ, Simon CLS (1992) Wound scar management. In: *Clinical Assessment Recommendations*, 2nd edn. American Society of Hand Therapists, Chicago: 21–28

Bexon C, Salter M (2000) Assessment. In: Salter M, Cheshire L, eds. *Hand Therapy Principles and Practice*. Butterworth-Heinemann, Oxford: 51–7

Boyling J (2000) The Prevention and Management of Occupational Hand Disorders. In Salter M, Cheshire L, eds. *Hand Therapy Principles and Practice*. Butterworth-Heinemann, Oxford: 221–22

Brand PW, Hollister A (1999) *Clinical Mechanics of the Hand*, 3rd edn. CV Mosby, St Louis: Ch12

Chartered Society of Physiotherapy (2000) *Core Standards*. Chartered Society of Physiotherapy, London

Colditz JC (2000) Passion of practice: The intuition of treatment. *J Hand Ther* **13**(1): 12–18

Cooper C, Evidente VG, Hentz JG, Adler CH, Caviness JH, Gwinn-Hardy K (2000) The effect of temperature on hand function in patients with tremor. *J Hand Ther* **13**(4): 276–88

Downs-Wheeler MJ (2000) *Complex Regional Pain Syndrome*. Basic Workshop for BAHT Conference, Edinburgh, Frenchay Hand Centre, Bristol

Glanze WD, ed (1986) *Mosby's Dictionary of Medicine and Nursing*. CV Mosby, St Louis

MacDermid JC, McOwan C, Kramer JF, Wilton J, Roth JH (2000) Pliability measures of scar: Reliability of two devices. *J Hand Ther* **13**(1): 72

Malick MH, Kasch M, eds (1984) *Manual on Management of Specific Hand Problems*, Series I. Aren Publications, Pittsburgh

Nicholson B (1992) Clinical Evaluation. In: Stanley BG, Tribuzi SM, eds. *Concepts in Hand Rehabilitation*. FA Davis, Philadelphia: 59

Salter MI (1987) *Hand Injuries: A Therapeutic Approach*. Churchill Livingstone, Edinburgh: 18–21

Stegink Jansen CW, Patterson R, Viegas SF (2000) Effects of fingernail length on finger and hand performance. *J Hand Ther* **13**(3): 211–17

Stuttaford T (2000) Digital Diagnosis. *The Times* 30/11/2000

Tubiana R, Thomine J-M, Mackin E (1996) *Examination of the Hand and Wrist*. Martin Dunitz, London

Waylett-Rendall J (1988) Sensibility, evaluation and rehabilitation. *Orthopaed Clin N Am* **19**(1): 43–56

Zook EG (2000) Understanding the perionychium. *J Hand Ther* **13**(4): 269–76

Chapter 4
Pain

This chapter considers the phenomenon of pain and why the assessment of this is of such significance to therapists. The subjective methods of assessing pain are described, the background to quantification of pain is explained and four methods to quantify pain objectively are described; these are the visual analogue scale, the numerical rating scale, the verbal descriptor scale and the McGill Questionnaire.

What is pain?

Pain is not a simple sensation, but a complex phenomenon encompassing body and soul (Haker, 2000). It has been defined as an unpleasant sensation and emotional experience associated with actual or potential tissue damage, or described in terms of such damage (Merskey and Bogduk, 1994). Pain can be likened to being in love. It is an intensely personal, complex event, often affected by culture, previous experience and knowledge, which cannot be felt by another person and is difficult to describe. As the person who is in love (or pain) struggles to identify the significant, relevant features of his/her state and express his/her feelings, the listener can only interpret what he/she is told in the light of his/her own knowledge, culture and experience. This is further complicated when the experience happened some time ago. In essence, this is the problem confronting the therapist who is assessing pain.

Pain can occur either as a result of obvious trauma or inflammation, or may occur seemingly in isolation. The extreme sensibility of the hand, coupled with its functional activities, make hand pain particularly distressing for the patient. Furthermore, many factors other than clinical considerations affect the reaction to pain: these include personal factors, such as culture and social class, and emotional factors, such as anxiety, depression, and fear (Schofield, 1995). Pain cannot be seen or felt by the examiner and assessing it is essentially subjective, and liable to interpretation by the clinician through his or her own levels of expectation, experience, and bias.

The use of an informal comment (e.g. slight pain, very painful) is not sufficient to assess pain (Browne, 1996). The therapist needs to assess pain carefully to identify the cause. This enables efforts to be made to attempt to rectify the problem, and where appropriate, manage the pain and provide a baseline for management, so that the therapist and patient can ascertain if pain is improving. The therapist must ensure that pain does not inhibit active movement, so that additional problems, such as stiffness of the shoulder, occur.

In some cases, the cause of pain may be glaringly obvious; a laceration or haematoma will inevitably be painful, as are localised inflamed joints. At times, however, the therapist must become a detective and look for clues in the patient's history and description of pain. This is especially true when there is no history of trauma and there are no other factors, such as loss of movement, swelling, or weakness. The 'detective therapist' requires a detailed knowledge of anatomy and an awareness of conditions, their signs and symptoms. The site and nature of the pain need to be established (Schofield, 1995). If not already known, the onset and duration of pain should be ascertained and the effects of pain on function must be noted. Using the clues presented, the 'detective therapist' can select a suitable physical test, which may confirm the cause or eliminate it from the search. If the therapist cannot find an underlying cause for the pain, then it does not mean that pain does not exist (Schofield, 1995).

Qualitative aspects of pain

Observation

Huskisson (1974) reported the findings of Lim and Guzman, who researched the visible manifestations of induced pain in a prison population, and concluded that this was an unreliable method of measuring pain. Despite this, the therapist should observe the patient throughout the assessment. Facial movements, such as grimaces, widening of the eyes, biting lips, restlessness or cradling of the hand, may all indicate that pain is present and affecting the patient. Such signs of discomfort can corroborate or contradict the patient's verbal account and pain measurements. More importantly, however, the therapist should be aware that actions increasing the patient's pain will hinder the assessment or could provoke a violent reaction from the patient.

Site

The first question must be, 'Where does it hurt?' The patient may point with a finger indicating a sharp pain, or the whole hand indicating a wider or diffuse pain. The therapist must be aware of which anatomical structures may be directly involved at this site and also the nerve distribution to the area, in order to identify referred pain, when present. Gentle palpation will help localise pain and identify tender areas. Clinical reasoning, or the thinking process, requires that relevant tests be applied to assess patients. The site of the pain should be recorded on a body/hand chart.

Type of pain

Pain may be constant or intermittent. If intermittent, precipitating or exacerbating factors must be identified whenever possible, for when the pain occurs can be relevant. Numbness, tingling, and pain occurring in the thumb, index, middle and ring fingers at night, relieved by putting the hands out of bed, could be carpal tunnel syndrome. This can be confirmed by Gilliatt's and Phalen's tests (see *Chapter 14*). Pain localised to the tendons of Abductor Pollicis Longus and Extensor Pollicis Brevis, which is worse on wringing out a dishcloth, suggests de Quervain's tenosynovitis, confirmed by Finkelstein's test (see *Chapter 14*). Wrist pain occurring only on weight bearing may be due to a disruption of the triangular fibrocartilage complex (see *Chapter 13*), while pain confined to the anatomical snuffbox and which is worse on palpation may well be a fractured scaphoid that has gone undetected (ASSH, 1990).

The words used to describe the pain can also be helpful: 'stabbing', 'burning', 'like insects creeping' or 'throbbing'. Further factors will be needed to confirm or eliminate suspicions, for example, 'throbbing' pain could indicate infection and this could be confirmed by rubor, raised temperature, swelling or malaise.

How the patient copes with the pain is also relevant (Schofield, 1995). For example, the patient may find heat helpful, conversely ice may be beneficial, and these findings can be useful when deciding on treatment strategies.

Allodynia is defined by Merskey and Bogduk (1994) as, 'Pain due to a stimulus which does not normally provoke pain'. Pain can be identified as allodynia by using the Semmes Weinstein monofilaments (see *Chapter 11*). The patient is touched in the area where allodynia is reported and in a normal area. If the monofilaments cause pain, allodynia is confirmed.

Function

Function is almost certainly affected to some degree by pain; therefore, the therapist should enquire whether pain affects the patient's life and activities (Schofield, 1995). This may appear slight, for example, the patient may not be able to use a particular tool in the garden, or so severe the patient may be unable to self-care. The significance to the patient will depend on the individual's circumstances and preferences, and it is helpful at this stage to ascertain these if not already established. Identifying a particular goal, such as being able to feed the cat independently, can be used as an outcome measure and gives a patient-orientated goal to work towards.

Quantifying pain

Background

Where pain is the main problem experienced by the patient, it is important to quantify it to ascertain if treatment is of benefit. Efforts have been made to quantify pain; these are the visual analogue scale, numerical rating scale, the verbal descriptor scale and the McGill Pain Questionnaire. The visual analogue scale and the verbal descriptor scale both stem from the work of Freyd (1923), who based a linear scale with four verbal prompts to form the graphic rating scale to measure psychological phenomena; he attributes this to the Scott Co Laboratory. Huskisson (1974), Joyce *et al* (1975) developed the visual analogue scale from this and Keele (1948) developed the verbal rating scale. These scales all have a place, but the clinician must select the ones that meet the requirements of the particular clinical situation, as no single tool is suitable for all occasions. It is often suggested that confirmation of results can be obtained by using two methods in conjunction (Carlsson, 1983; Wewers and Lowe, 1990). Pain measurement can be affected by a variety of patient-related factors; these can include:

- education level
- the nature of the physical illness
- the presence of affective disorders
- visual ability
- the ethnic background of the patient (Flaherty, 1996).

It has been shown that minor changes in numerical and analogue scales can affect patient behaviour (Scott and Huskisson, 1976). All methods, except the McGill Pain Questionnaire, are one-dimensional, measuring pain intensity, and it has been argued that one-dimensional measures are not the best measure of such a multifaceted problem (Flaherty, 1996).

Visual analogue scale (VAS)

The patient is asked to place a mark on a line to indicate the amount of pain he/she is experiencing. This tool has proved useful to quantify pain and measure its intensity (Huskisson, 1974; Joyce, 1975). It has been well-researched on a variety of pain types, including acute, chronic, progressive, cancer and postoperative pain (Flaherty, 1996; Chok, 1998). The absolute form (there are no prompting words along the line (Carlsson, 1983)) is generally regarded as the method of choice for quantifying pain in a clinical setting. Furthermore, it has also been shown to be significantly accurate for remembered pain (Revill *et al*, 1976). Freyd himself felt it was a universal measure and it is believed that it can be used across cultural boundaries (Wewers and Lowe, 1990); however, this assertion should be viewed with caution (Edwards, 1991). It has been suggested (Fagan *et al*, 1990) that the VAS was unsuitable for the elderly; however, this has been shown to be incorrect (Tiplady *et al*, 1998).

The VAS is suitable for many clinical situations and has the advantage of being quick to administer, taking less than five minutes to test and two minutes to score (Flaherty, 1996). Furthermore, while demanding minimum effort from the patient, it is interesting to complete (Freyd, 1923). There are, however, exceptions to its use.

Do not use VAS:

- if the patient is unable to grasp the abstract concept of a line representing pain, or poor language skills renders him/her unable to understand the explanation of the concept. It has been claimed that written instructions on the top of the sheet may help overcome this (Gift, 1989; Mottola, 1993; Flaherty, 1996); however, this may not always be the case and it lengthens the assessment considerably
- if the patient has a visual impairment and is unable to see the line clearly
- if the patient is unable to sit at a table, as it has been shown that the starting position and the way the line is viewed can affect the scoring (Wewers and Lowe, 1990)
- if the patient cannot hold a pen due to arthritis, dressings or intravenous infusion or has a hand tremor, modify the procedure. To do this, the therapist places the pen point at the extreme left hand of the scale and moves the pen to the right along the line. When the patient indicates that this is the point that he/she wishes to register, the therapist makes a mark on the line (Gift, 1989). Alternatively, the patient points to the spot on the line and the therapist may record the mark (Mottola, 1993). It should be noted that it is not known how these modifications affect reliability.

Preparing the scale.

Prior to testing, prepare the scale by drawing a horizontal line on a piece of paper. In practice, and to facilitate scoring (Mottola, 1993), this is usually ten centimetres long, but could be of any length, although a five centimetres line has been shown to be least accurate (Revill, 1976). There should be vertical stops at 90° to the horizontal and ½ inch (about 1.25 cm) high (Cline *et al*, 1992; Mottola, 1993). At the extreme left hand edge, the words 'No pain' appear and at the extreme right hand end the words 'Worst pain possible' appear (Revill, 1976). No other words or prompts should be shown. The verbal instructions needed are given below.

Figure 4.1: The visual analogue scale

There has been some debate concerning the choice of a horizontal or vertical line (Scott and Huskisson, 1979a). It is probably best used horizontally (Mottola, 1993).

The scale should not be photocopied to avoid distortion to the length (Gift, 1989; Mottola, 1993). Either use a computer printout (Cline, 1992) or preprint on the record sheet. It is possible to purchase pads that have a card cover printed with the words above and a cut out showing the line. When the line has been marked the cover can be raised and the measurements are visible. The disadvantages of this system are: the shortness of the line, the cover will inevitably become marked, which may influence the patient's selection, and the completed result could be difficult to incorporate into the record.

How to test using VAS

- collect the tools needed: scale, pen and a ruler that measures in millimetres
- ensure that the patient is sitting at a table with the scale immediately in front of him/her (Mottola, 1993)
- if the patient normally wears glasses for reading, he/she should put these on
- explain to the patient that the line represents his/her pain. Indicate that the left end represents no pain at all and the right end represents the worst pain that he/she can possibly imagine (Revill *et al*, 1976). Ask him/her to take the pen and mark on the line the point at which his/her pain is currently. If pain is intermittent, ask him/her to mark the line at the point that would represent his/her pain when last experienced. Note what the instruction was
- when the scale is marked, place the ruler along the line with zero at the intersection of the vertical stop and the horizontal line. The score is taken from the intersection of the pen mark against the horizontal line and recorded in millimetres in the notes (Mottola, 1993)
- the test is repeated in the same way using an identical blank scale, either after a pain relieving treatment has been given or at the next attendance. There is debate as to whether the patient should see his/her earlier test(s) (Scott and Huskisson, 1979b; Gift, 1989). This is a matter of preference, but the record should show if earlier tests have been seen or not.

Recording of VAS

Always keep charts as part of the record and ensure that they are dated, signed and numbered. Where two tests are carried out on one day, record the date and time or note pre-treatment and post-treatment.

To facilitate the therapist's overview of treatment over a period of time, a table can be inserted into the patient records showing all pain scores together. An

Table 4.1 A means of recording the overview of pain measurement

Date	Time	VAS Score	Tester	Tester Signature
1/3/01	9.0.a.m	96	I A-S	
1/3/01	9.30.a.m	78*	I A-S	
2/3/01	10.0.a.m.	82	I A-S	
2/3/01	10.30.a.m.	65*	I A-S	

*Patient did not have previous test result.

additional column can be added to give a verbal comment made by the patient.

Reliability of VAS

Little and McPhail (1973) compared the VAS with the Beck depression inventory and found significant reliability (p<0.001). Revill *et al* (1976) demonstrated significant test/retest reliability; Joyce *et al* (1975) found the scale more sensitive than a graphical rating scale. Gift (1989) shows that there is high inter-rater reliability.

The VAS has been validated against the McGill Pain Questionnaire (Gift, 1989). This shows that it has concurrent validity, defined as, 'The degree to which scores on an instrument are correlated with some external criterion measured at the same time' (Flaherty, 1996). Construct validity has been defined as, 'The degree to which an instrument measures the construct (e.g. pain) under investigation' (Flaherty, 1996), and this has been shown to be good for the VAS (Maurer and Jezek, 1992). Discriminate validity, described as an approach to construct validity that involves assessing the degree to which a single method of measuring two constructs yields different results, was demonstrated by Joyce *et al* (1975).

Numerical Rating Scale (NRS)

The numerical rating scale can be used to measure the intensity of acute, chronic or progressive pain, and the effectiveness of relief. This involves either a vertical scale with 0 at the bottom, or a horizontal scale with 0 at the left hand end. A variety of scales, for example, of 0–5, 0–10, 0—20, and 0–100, may be used and marked on the line. Downie *et al* (1978), using a vertical 11-point numerical scale, found it more reliable than the visual analogue scale. This has not been consistently repeated when other ranges are used (Scott and Huskisson, 1976; Ekblom and Hansson, 1988). An 11-point scale is, therefore, both simple and reliable, although clearly a wider scale gives greater scope for sensitivity. However, as always, the same tool must be used consistently. It is particularly suitable where time is limited and the patient can appreciate the concept of 'marking pain' by numbers, but has difficulty accepting the abstract concept of a line representing pain.

NRS is simple and quick to administer, taking less than five minutes, easy to score and can be used in any setting without disruption to the ward or patient. Additionally, it can be used as a verbal scale if patients are unable to use a pen, read, or have limited English and it could be used on the telephone if a patient with a chronic problem sought advice. Furthermore, it can be used easily as part of a computerised assessment and record, which is significant with the development of the electronic patient record and electronic health record (see *Chapter 15*). However, there are certain situations where it must be used with caution. NRS is not suitable for patients who may have cognitive problems or young children who cannot differentiate numbers (Flaherty, 1996). Scott and Huskisson (1976) found that certain numbers were preferred on the numerical scale.

Preparing the scale

Prepare a vertical scale with 0–10 marked at equal incidents. Below the zero, it should read 'No pain at all' and, above the ten, 'Worst pain possible'. This will confirm verbal instructions given to the patient. If this method is used consistently in the department, it is helpful if it is printed on the patient record sheet. Alternatively, it can be photocopied or printed out by computer as required.

How to test NRS

- collect the tools needed—scale and pen
- if the patient can use a pen, ask him/her to sit at a table with the scale in front of him/her
- if the patient normally wears glasses for reading, he/she should put them on
- show the patient the scale and explain that these numbers represent the severity of his/her hand pain—0 is no pain at all and 10 the worst pain possible. Ensure that he/she grasps the concept of the worst pain possible (Scudds, 2001)
- ask the patient to circle the number most representing his/her hand pain at that moment
- if the patient cannot use a pen or see the chart, even when wearing glasses, ask him/her to tell you which number most represents his/her pain at that moment
- repeat the test using a blank identical chart, either after giving a pain relief treatment or at the next attendance.

Worst pain possible
10
9
8
7
6
5
4
3
2
1
0
No pain at all

Figure 4. 2: A numerical rating scale

Recording

Recording as for VAS.

Verbal Descriptor Scale (VRS)

This system, first described to test response to analgesics by Keele (1948), involves three to five numerically ranked words and the patient is asked to say which word best describes his/her pain. Such a scale is given below; different words can be used, and those used here follow the definitions given by Keele.

The verbal descriptor scale is simple, easy to perform and to score and can be used to measure acute, chronic and progressive pain. It can be used easily in any setting, even where the patient cannot see or cope with the numerical rating scale or the visual analogue scale (Flaherty, 1996). There are, however, limitations to this system; it creates artificial categories where delays may be caused if the patient has difficulty selecting a word which they may not have used themselves (Schofield, 1995) or the word selected may not reflect the pain felt (Flaherty, 1996). There may be some words that patients may rank relatively highly or prefer, but it is not known what these may be (Scott and Huskisson, 1976). It is not suitable for those who have poor language skills, nor does it cross cultural barriers (Schofield, 1995). It is less sensitive than the NRS or VAS (Scott and Huskisson, 1976). Consequently, the principle use of the system can be as a confirmation to the NRS or VAS.

0 =	**No** pain	
1 =	**Slight** pain (an awareness of pain without distress)	
2 =	**Moderate** pain (pain distracts attention from a routine occupation, such as reading or housework)	
3 =	**Severe** pain (pain fills the field of consciousness to the exclusion of other events)	
4 =	**Agonising** pain (there will be motor symptoms, such as restlessness or shock syndrome)	

Figure 4. 2: A verbal descriptor scale, as used by Keele (1948)

Preparing the scale

Select the words with definitions and print these on a sheet. It is possible to use those of Keele (1948), or to develop one's own to reflect current language with which the patient will be familiar.

How to test the Verbal Descriptor Scale

- collect the tools needed, scale and pen
- if the patient can use a pen he/she should sit at a table with the scale in

front of him/her

- if the patient normally wears glasses for reading, he/she should put these on
- ask the patient to read the scale and circle the word he/she feels best fits his/her pain
- if the patient is unable to read or use a pencil, read out the words and definitions and ask him/her to say which is the most apt
- score using the number beside the word
- repeat using the same protocol either after a pain relieving treatment or at the next attendance.

Recording

Record as for VAS.

The McGill Pain Questionnaire

Several questionnaires exist to assess pain; the McGill is probably the best known. Developed by Melzack and Torgerson in 1971, it measures many dimensions of pain and recognises that every pain has unique qualities. It measures location, pattern over time, sensory, affective and pain intensity, i.e. qualitative and quantitative. Melzack and Torgerson identified the range and scope of words used to describe pain and the words were given a rating. These words, grouped as sensory, affective and evaluative, alone are insufficient and, therefore, the questionnaire also includes a body chart and a variation of Keele's simple scale. The McGill Questionnaire has been shown to be reliable over a variety of patient types (Byrne *et al*, 1982; Chok, 1998) and studies have demonstrated construct (Kremer and Atkinson, 1981), concurrent and predictive validity. It is, therefore, most useful where it is necessary to address the multidimensional nature of pain, such as for legal work. Melzack (1975) demonstrated, using data obtained from 297 patients, that the Questionnaire provides information suitable for statistical purposes and is sensitive enough to detect different methods of relieving pain. These qualities make it particularly suitable for research purposes. The Questionnaire should be carried out by the interview method, as asking the patient to complete it can give lower scores (Klepac *et al*, 1981). This is useful where hand pain may well prevent extensive writing. The chief disadvantage of this method in the clinical setting, where the practitioner may have limited time or the patient feels unwell, is that the long version can take 30 minutes—although the short version can take only 10 minutes. Furthermore, it can be difficult for those with poor language skills or cultural groups and subgroups to whom some of the descriptors may be unclear (Byrne *et al*, 1982; Flaherty, 1996).

The next step

When this part of the assessment is complete, the therapist should have a thorough knowledge of the site, occurrence and severity of pain. Further tests may well be needed to ascertain the cause of pain and its impact on other functions. The therapist must consider ways of relieving pain, possibly by using the physical modalities available. Alternatively, it may be necessary to discuss pain control with the referring doctor.

To summarise

- find out as much as you can about the site, type, causes and relief factors of pain
- no one method of quantifying pain is suitable in all situations
- measure the intensity of pain using either the visual analogue scale or the numerical rating scale; confirm with the verbal rating scale if necessary
- the McGill Pain Questionnaire will provide a fuller picture and is suitable for research, legal work and complex pain cases.

References

American Society for Surgery to The Hand (1990) *The Hand Examination and Diagnosis*. 3rd edn. Churchill Livingstone, Edinburgh: 86–90; 103–6

Browne R (1996) Accepting the challenges of pain management. *Br J Nurs* **5**(9): 552–5

Byrne M, Troy A, Bradley LA *et al* (1982) Cross-validation of the factor structure of the McGill Pain Questionnaire. *Pain* **13**:193–201

Carlsson AM (1983) Assessment of chronic pain1; Aspects of the reliability and validity of the visual analogue scale. *Pain* **16**: 87–101

Chok B (1998) An overview of the visual analogue scale and McGill Pain Questionnaire. *Physiother Sing* **1**(3): 88–93

Cline M, Herman J, Shaw ER, Morton DM (1992) Standardisation of the visual analogue scale. *Nurs Res* **41**(6) 378–80

Downie WW, Leatham PA, Rhind VM, Wright V, Branco JA, Anderson JA (1978) Studies with pain rating scales. *Ann Rheum Dis* **37**: 378–81

Ekblom A, Hansson P (1988) Pain intensity measurements in patients with acute pain receiving afferent stimulation. *J Neurol Neurosurg Psychiatry* **51**: 481–86

Edwards N (1991) Letter. *Res Nurs Health* **14**: 81

Fagan D, Lamont M, Jostell K-G, Tiplady B, Scott DB (1990) A study of the psychometric effects of chlormethiazole in healthy young and elderly subjects. *Age Ageing* **19**: 29–31

Flaherty S (1996) Pain measurement tools for clinical practice and research. *J Am Ass Nurse Anaesthet* **64**(2): 135–40

Freyd M (1923) The graphic rating scale. *J Educat Psychol* **14**: 83–102

Gift A (1989) Visual analogue scales: Measurement of a subjective phenomena. *Nurs Res* **38**(5): 286–88

Haker E (2000) A touch of pain. *Physiother* **86**(12): 618

Huskisson EC (1974) Measurement of pain. *Lancet* **Nov 9th**: 1127–31

Joyce CRB, Zutshi DW, Hrubes V, Mason RM (1975) Comparison of fixed interval and visual analogue scales. *Eur J Clin Pharmacol* **8**: 415–20

Keele KD (1948) The pain chart. *Lancet* **July 3rd**: 6–8

Klepac RK, Dowling J, Rokke P, Dodge L, Schafer L (1981) Interview vs paper-and-pencil administration of the McGill Pain Questionnaire. *Pain* **11**: 241–46

Kremer E, Atkinson JH (1981) Pain measurement: construct validity of the affective dimension of the McGill Pain Questionnaire with chronic benign pain patients. *Pain* **11**: 93–100

Little JC, McPhail N (1973) Measures of depressive mood at monthly intervals, *Br J Psychiatry* **122**: 447–52

Maurer GL, Jezek SM (1992) *Pain Assessment in Clinical Assessment Recommendations* 2nd edn. American Society of Hand Therapists: Chicago: 95–108

Melzack R (1975) The McGill Pain Questionnaire: Major properties and scoring methods. *Pain* **1**: 277–99

Melzack R, Torgerson WS (1971) On the language of pain. *Anesthesiol* **34**(1): 50–59

Merskey H, Bogduk N (1994) *Classification of Chronic Pain*. International Association for the Study of Pain, Seattle: 210

Mottola CA (1993) Measurement strategies: The visual analogue scale. *Decubitus* **6**(5): 56–58

Revill SI, Robinson JO, Rosen M, Hogg MIJ (1976) The reliability of a linear analogue for evaluating pain. *Anaesthsia* **31**: 1191–98

Schofield P (1995) Using assessment tools to help patients in pain. *Prof Nurse* **10**(11): 203–6

Scott J, Huskisson EC (1976) Graphic representation of pain. *Pain* **2**: 175–84

Scott J, Huskisson EC (1979a) Vertical or horizontal visual analogue scales. *Ann Rheum Dis* **38**: 560

Scott J, Huskisson EC (1979b) Accuracy of subjective measurements made with or without previous scores: An important source of error in serial measurement of subjective states. *Ann Rheum Dis* **38**: 558–9

Scudds RA (2001) Pain outcome measures. *J Hand Ther* **14**(2): 86–90

Tiplady B, Jackson SHD, Maskery VM, Swift CG (1998) Validity and sensitivity of visual analogue scales in young and older healthy subjects. *Age Ageing* **27**: 63–66

Wewers ME, Lowe NK (1990) A critical review of visual analogue scales in the measurement of clinical phenomena. *Res Nurs Health* **13**: 227–36

The size of the hand can give valuable information on the patient's condition. Wasting will result from disuse, which can be due to a variety of causes—from neurological (Malick and Kasch, 1984) to psychologically-induced disuse (Brand, 1988). Repeated measurement will indicate if muscles are increasing or decreasing in size. Trauma or surgery will inevitably lead to an abnormal accumulation of interstitial fluid in the tissue spaces, resulting in increased hand size and restricted range of movement. If oedema is not reduced, this can result in fibrosis, which glues the tissues together, and movement loss becomes permanent (Lamb, 1980). Consequently, the hand must be measured to ascertain if the therapist is succeeding in the vital battle to reduce and prevent oedema. This chapter considers two methods of doing this, using the volumeter and the tape measure.

The most popular method is undoubtedly the use of a tape measure (Bradley, 1993; Murray *et al*, 2000). However, the volumeter produces good measurements of oedema. Inserting the finger into a system of rings has been recommended (Salter, 1987; Bear-Lehman and Abreu, 1989; Bexon and Salter, 2000). This method is believed to reduce measurement error, although it does not appear popular and the calibrated rings are not readily available. Prior to measuring, the area and type of oedema should be noted.

Volumeter

The volumeter was first described by Eccles (1956) and is based on the Archimedes Principle; 'A body partly or completely immersed in a fluid displaces an amount of fluid equal to the apparent loss of weight' (Hogben, 1938). This method is recommended by the American Society of Hand Therapists (ASHT) (Jaffee and Farney-Mokris, 1992) to evaluate oedema.

When to use the volumeter

- to assess the effects of medical or therapy treatment on oedematous or inflamed hands (Eccles, 1956; Plewes, 1956)
- to assess lymphoedema (Swedborg, 1977)
- to measure the effects of medication in acute synovitis, due to rheumatoid arthritis and gout (Smyth *et al*, 1963)
- to evaluate bier block exsanguination (Mabee and Orlinsky, 2000)

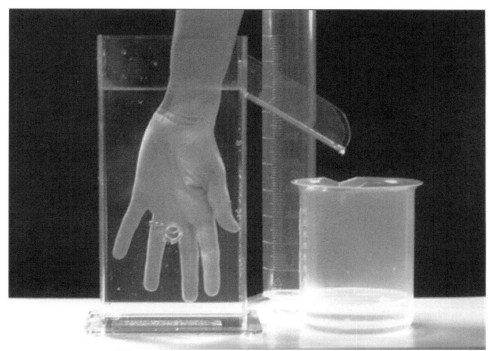

Plate 5.1: The volumeter in use. The hand is pronated, with the thumb towards the spout, viewed from behind the patient

- to ascertain the amount of exercise repetitions or resistance which can be applied without increasing swelling
- to assess progress where there is gross forearm wasting.

Do not use the volumeter

- where immersion in water is contra-indicated; this includes the presence of open wounds, dressings, casts and external fixators (Jaffee and Farney-Mokris, 1992)
- when the patient has an unstable vascular state
- where wasting and oedema are present together.

How to measure

- choose the correct volumeter for your requirements (i.e. hand or arm). A commercial measure should be used rather than a homemade device and the manufacturer's instructions read prior to use, and followed (Jaffee and Farney-Mokris, 1992). Volumeters using the displacement method (i.e. the water is displaced into a measure) are more accurate than those where the change of level in the tank is observed. The tank should have a transverse stop rod to ensure that the immersion point is always the same (Brand and Hollister, 1999).

- assemble all equipment needed: volumeter, beaker, measure, paper and pen
- explain to the patient the purpose of the test and how it will be carried out. Eccles (1956) recommends one or two practice runs so that the patient can learn the procedure and eliminate errors
- place the volumeter on the same level surface, at the same angle for each test. It is possible to mark the position on a table using coloured tapes or stickers. Place the collection beaker by the spout
- prepare the volumeter by filling with water that is at room temperature; this is to ensure patient comfort and a constant hand volume. Fill the volumeter until the water overflows into the beaker (Waylett-Rendall and Seilby, 1991). When the drips have stopped throw away the water in the beaker
- remove any jewellery from the patient's hand and arm; rings should not be worn at all when oedema is present
- take the patient's arm so that the affected palm is toward the patient, with the thumb towards the spout of the volumeter. The tester's hand must not enter the water
- slowly and smoothly lower the patient's hand into the volumeter, keeping the hand as vertical as possible, with the thumb towards the spout and away from the sides. Use the same immersion point on each occasion, the web space of the middle and ring fingers straddling the stop rod ensures this. Do not apply force to the stop rod or this will alter results (Waylett and Seibly, 1981; Waylett-Rendall and Seilby, 1991)
- hold this position until the overflow of water into the collection beaker is complete
- remove the beaker before removing the hand
- measure the displaced water into the graduated cylinder and document the amount displaced in millimetres on the patient record. If more than 500ml of water is collected, measure the contents of the beaker in stages and add the measures together (Waylett-Rendall and Seilby, 1991).
- document any deviation from the protocol
- if measuring both hands, top up the tank with room temperature water before measuring the second hand. Use a beaker rather than a hose (Waylett-Rendall and Seilby, 1991)

- if possible, subsequent tests should be carried out by the same therapist at the same points in the assessment/ treatment session, e.g. do not compare a measure before elevation at one session with a measure taken after elevation on another
- wash and dry the volumeter after use.

Interpretation

No norm values exist; therefore, sequential results should be compared. It is useful to compare measurements with the opposite hand, although this must be done with caution as there may be a degree of asymmetry in hand sizes (Bear-Lehman and Abreu, 1989). Eccles (1956) reported that the dominant hand would tend to be 10–15mls larger. If both hands show a tendency to increase in size this can be indicative of systemic disease rather than an isolated incident (Jaffee and Farney-Mokris, 1992) and should be reported to the referring practitioner.

Reliability

Waylett and Seibly (1981), having tested 20 normal and 20 oedematous hands, showed an intra-rater variation of 10mls and a median inter-rater variation of 10 and 15mls. Further work by Waylett-Rendall and Seilby (1991) on 13 oedematous hands, 16 normal hands and a rubber model demonstrated an intra-rater coefficient of variation of 0.55% (rubber hand), 0.74% (oedematous hands) and 0.83% (normal hands). Inter-rater coefficients were 0.83% (rubber hand), 0.98% (oedematous hands) and 1.08–1.28% (normal hands, divided into groups). These results show that, when one tester is used, a change in hand volume with this measuring device must be 10 ml for a normal hand and 12 ml for an oedematous hand to be considered significant.

To facilitate the comparison with the unaffected hand, Smyth *et al* (1963) showed an overall insignificant change of less than 1% between morning and afternoon measurements, when measuring 36 normal individuals, morning and afternoon. Six normal women tested morning and afternoon on five successive days showed a variation of 1.5% (Smyth *et al*, 1963). These slight variations in the normal can be largely attributed to activity and changes in atmospheric pressure.

Reproducibility tests, measuring six normal individuals ten times in rapid succession, showed a variation of 1% (Smyth *et al*, 1963).

Tape measure

The simplest, quickest and cheapest method of measuring hand size is to take a circumferential measurement using a tape measure. This method is less sensitive (Fess, 2000) and less accurate (Brand and Hollister, 1999). Accuracy will be improved by careful use, which includes calibration of the tape measure and the use of anatomical landmarks to ensure consistent placement of the tape measure (Bear-Lehman and Abreu, 1989).

When to use the tape measure

- when testing in the ward or patient's home (Brand and Hollister, 1999)
- where immersion is contra-indicated
- where swelling is isolated to one joint or digit (Nicholson, 1992)
- where there is wasting with or without oedema.

Do not use the tape measure

- do not use to measure lymphoedema of the hand. Swedborg (1977) advised against the use of this method in all cases of lymphoedema, arguing that the irregularity in arm shape between individuals (both before and after treatment) prevents the degree of oedema being accurately inferred. The British Lymphology Society (2001) recommends calculating limb volume by taking circumferential measurements at 4cm intervals from wrist to axilla, as the method is reliable, reproducible and accurate (Woods, 1994). The hand is not cylindrical and should be excluded from limb volume calculations (Woods, 2001). The methods of calculating volume from circumferential measurements and formulae are well detailed by Sitzia (1995).

Before measuring

- calibrate the tape measure regularly by measuring it against a steel ruler. Variations of up to 1% (3 millimetres on 300 millimetres) have been recorded over a 22-week period (Heck *et al*, 1999)
- select a tape measure that measures in millimetres
- clean the tape using a small alcohol wipe. If measuring an open wound, use a disposable or sterile tape measure.

How to measure

- assemble the equipment needed—tape measure, paper and pen
- explain to the patient the purpose of the test and what will happen
- select the points that will be measured and carry out the measurements below on both hands
- if oedema has obliterated creases, palpate to ensure that a bony landmark is used
- always state the measurement point on the patient's record.

Distal wrist crease

- ask the patient to place the hand palm down on the table and slip the tape measure over the hand to the level of the distal wrist crease. Tighten the tape until there is no slack, but it does not cut into the skin. Turn the palm upwards to check that it is at the level of the distal wrist crease; adjust if necessary. Note the measurement in millimetres on the patient's record.

Metacarpophalangeal (MCP) joints

- it is difficult to detect changes in oedema at this level as the swelling can lie below the level of the MCP joints
- ask the patient to place the hand palm down on the table and slip the tape measure over the hand to the level of the MCP joints. Tighten the tape until there is no slack, but it does not cut into the skin. Turn the palm upwards to check that it is at the level of the distal palmar crease at the little finger MCP joint and the proximal palmar crease at the index finger MCP joint; adjust if necessary. Note the measurement in millimetres on the patient's record.

Proximal interphalangeal (PIP) joint

- ask the patient to place the hand palm down on the table and slip the tape measure over the finger to the level of the selected PIP joint, centred on the corresponding dorsal digital creases. Tighten the tape until there is no slack, but it does not cut into the skin. Turn the palm upwards to check that it is at the level of the intermediate volar digital crease; adjust if necessary. Note the measurement in millimetres on the patient's record.

Distal interphalangeal (DIP) joint

- ask the patient to place the hand palm down on the table and slip the tape measure over the finger to the level of the selected DIP joint, centred on the corresponding dorsal digital crease. Tighten the tape until there is no slack, but it does not cut into the skin. Turn the palm upwards to check that it is at the level of the distal volar digital crease; adjust if necessary. Note the measurement in millimetres on the patient's record.

Thumb metacarpophalangeal (MCP) joint

- ask the patient to place the hand palm down on the table and slip the tape measure over the thumb to the level of the thumb MCP joint, centring on the joint. Palpate to ensure this is correct. Tighten the tape until there is no slack, but it does not cut into the skin. Turn the palm upwards to check that it is centred at the level of the proximal volar thumb crease; adjust if necessary. Note the measurement, in millimetres, on the patient's record.

Forearm

- the measurement of muscle bulk at the forearm can give useful insight into the amount of activity the hand has been performing and may be of particular interest in cases involving insurance or legal claims

- the patient is seated. Ask the patient if you may place a pen mark on his/her arm. Palpate the olecranon process with the elbow extended by the patient's side. Measure down perpendicularly 250mm and make a 10mm mark in washable pen on the patient's forearm. Keep the arm extended and measure the circumference of the forearm, keeping the top edge of tape measure against the distal side of the pen mark. Ensure the tape goes evenly round the forearm. Note the measurement in millimetres on the patient's record.

Interpretation

No norm values exist for these measurements, therefore they should be compared with the opposite hand and subsequent results.

Reliability

Intra-rater variation in a tester measuring 21 normal subjects, on two occasions, showed a mean difference of -0.14mm on the index PIP joint using the method described above (Heck *et al*, 1999). Inter-rater variation in two testers measuring six subjects on the same occasion showed a mean difference of 1mm on the index PIP joint using the same method (Heck *et al*, 1999).

King (1993) compared circumferential measurements of the middle of the proximal phalanx using a tape measure and a tape incorporating a torque meter, which allowed the tension of the tape to be controlled. The coefficient of variation was lower (0.75) for the torque device than the traditional measure (2.92).

Further work should be undertaken by those using the tape measure method alone, to establish its reliability.

The next step

When this part of the assessment is complete the therapist should have a complete record of the extent of any oedema or wasting. Further work may be needed to ascertain the cause. Depending on the cause and the patient's needs, the therapist must consider ways of decreasing oedema, which could include elevation, contrast bathing, ice, massage or compression, unless contraindicated. In the event of wasting, the therapist must consider the cause and the appropriateness of strengthening strategies or electrical stimulation.

To summarise

- the volumeter is the only method recommended by ASHT
- the tape measure can give reliable measurements when a standardised protocol is carried out

---

References

Bradley A (1993) An evaluation of the current methods used in the assessment of outcomes in hand surgery. *Br J Hand Ther* 1(7): 4–7

Bear-Lehman J, Abreu BC (1989) Evaluating the hand: Issues in Reliability and Validity. *Phys Ther* **69**(12): 1025–33

Bexon C, Salter M (2000) Assessment. In: Salter M, Cheshire L, eds. *Hand Therapy Principles and Practice*. Butterworth Heinemann, Oxford: 51–57

Brand PW (1988) The mind and spirit in hand therapy. *J Hand Ther* **July–Sept**: 145–47

Brand PW, Hollister A (1999) *Clinical Mechanics of the Hand*, 3rd edn. CV Mosby, St. Louis: ch 12

British Lymphology Society (2001) Clinical Definitions. British Lymphology Society, 1 Webb's Court, Buckhurst Avenue, Sevenoaks, Kent:5: *http://www.lymphoedema.org/bls*

Eccles MV (1956) Hand volumetrics. *Br J Physic Med* **Jan**: 5–8

Fess EE (2000) *Keynote Lecture*. Annual Conference of British Association of Hand Therapists. Edinburgh, 16th October 2000

Hogben L (1938) *Science for the Citizen*. George Allen & Unwin: ch vii; 371–4

Heck H, Simpson C, Murray K, Smith J, Alcock S, Fathmann M (1999) HATS Evaluation Study. Workpackage 13. Staffordshire University

Jaffee R, Farney-Mokris S (1992) *Clinical Assessment Recommendations*. American Society of Hand Therapists, Philadelphia: 13–19

Lamb DW (1980) The hand—management after injury and operation. *Physiother* **66**(11): 367–8

King TI (1993) Circumferential finger measurements utilizing a torque meter to increase reliability. *J Hand Ther* **6**(1): 35–6

Mabee J, Orlinsky M (2000) Bier Block exsanguination: A volumetric comparison and venous pressure study. *Acad Emer Med* **72**: 105–13

Malick M, Kasch M (1984) *Manual on Management of Specific Hand Problems*, Series 1. Aren Publications, Pittsburgh: 80

Murray K, Topping M, Simpson C (2000) Investigation of the hand assessment techniques used within the United Kingdom. *Br J Hand Ther* **5**(4): 125

Nicholson B (1992) Clinical evaluation. In: Stanley BG, Tribuzi SM, eds. *Concepts in Hand Rehabilitation*. FA Davis, Philadelphia: 59

Plewes LW (1956) Sudeck's atrophy in the hand. *J Bone Joint Surg* **38B**(1): 195–203

Salter MI (1987) *Hand Injuries: A Therapeutic Approach*. Churchill Livingstone, Edinburgh

Sitzia J (1995) Volume measurement in lymphoedema treatment: examination of formulae. *Eur J Cancer Care* **4**: 11–16

Smyth CJ, Velayos EE, Hlad CJ (1963) A Method for measuring swelling of the hands and feet. *Acta Rheum Scand* **9**: 293–305

Swedborg I (1977) Voluminometric estimation of the degree of lymphoedema and its therapy by pneumatic compression. *Scand J Rehab Med* **9**: 131–35

Waylett J, Seibly D (1981) A study to determine the average deviation accuracy of a commercially available volumeter. *J Hand Surg* **6**: 300

Waylett-Rendall J, Seilby DS (1991) A study of accuracy of a commercially available volumeter. *J Hand Ther* **Jan–Mar**: 10–13

Woods M (1994) An audit of swollen limb measurements. *Nurs Stand* **9**(5): 24–26

Woods M (2001) Personal Communication 9/4/01

Chapter 6
Range of movement I: Goniometry

Range of movement has been defined as the available arc of motion within a joint that is assessed by goniometric measurements (Adams *et al*, 1992) and is one of the most frequently used evaluations made in hand assessment. Despite its popularity, goniometry is not the only method available to therapists for measuring range of movement, and alternatives are described in *Chapter 7*. The current chapter considers the background to goniometry, describes how to use it to measure range of movement (active then passive), how to calculate total range of movement and, finally, the use of the goniometer in torque angle measurements. Two methods of recording are described and the reliability of goniometry is addressed.

In obtaining range of movement measurements there are several things to consider. What is to be measured—active movement, passive movement, total movement or individual joint range? It is recommended that assessment starts with the active range and is followed by the passive range of individual joints (Salter, 1987; Bexon and Salter, 2000).

Background

In the biomechanical laboratory, there are a number of accurate methods to measure range of movement, from single joints to the limb as a whole. These include multiple exposure photography, video, opto-electronic methods and electro-goniometers. In 1955, Salter recommended radiographic means as the preferred method. This is no longer acceptable due to the exposure to radiation, however, at the time of writing, children's footwear was routinely assessed for fit using radiography in the pedioscopes in shoe shops.

Methods used in the clinical setting must be safe, quick, cheap and portable. Goniometry meets these requirements and is reported to be the most popular method used (Bradley, 1993 ; Ellis *et al*, 1997; Murray *et al*, 2000; Bucher, 2003). To obtain the best results from all available methods of measuring range, it is important that therapists maximise and maintain their skills; therefore, protocols, training and regular departmental standardisation sessions are needed.

The first known British reference to finger goniometry was made by R Fortescue Fox (1917) who illustrated a French device called 'the Fleximeter' for measuring the MCP joints dorsally, and which could also be used for measuring the wrist and finger joints. Fox stated 'I do not want it understood that we claim absolute accuracy of record by these means, but we are getting on towards some accuracy'. Today the position has changed little, both in goniometer design and reliability of results.

Goniometers currently in clinical use continue to follow the principles Fox learned from Professor Camus and Professor Amar in Paris. Typically, goniometers consist of a protractor with a central point or axis and two measurement arms of varying length. One of these arms remains stationary while the other moves. Today there are a plethora of goniometers available on the market (see *Plate 6.1*). However, no one goniometer is suitable for measuring all joints in the upper limb. A robust goniometer, which can be easily cleaned and read without strain should be selected, depending on the size and natural range of the part to measured. At least three goniometers are usually necessary for the upper limb:

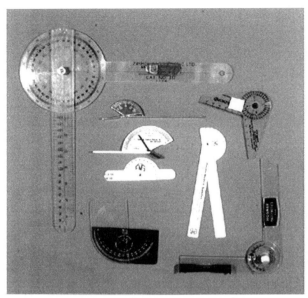

Plate 6.1: A selection of goniometers used to measure joint range in the upper limb

- a large universal goniometer that will read through 360° for the shoulder, elbow, and measuring supination at the wrist

- a smaller goniometer with arms long enough to measure wrist flexion and extension

- a finger goniometer with small arms that will measure hyperextension, for the finger joints.

In addition, specialist devices exist to measure supination and pronation, such as the PROsupinator (North Coast Medical). Preliminary work on an offset goniometer with a plumb line indicates it is reliable (Flowers *et al*, 2001). Such equipment has a useful place, but the decision to purchase may be affected by departmental budgets, the type of patients seen, information on reliability and personal preferences. The only additional equipment needed is a chart or paper and a pen.

Good practice

Goodwin *et al* (1992) studied three very different types of goniometer (the universal, the electrogoniometer and the fluid goniometer) and concluded that they were not interchangeable. Therefore, it is recommended that different models of protractor type goniometers be regarded as not interchangeable. Consequently, it is important to be consistent in the type of goniometer used on each patient (Burk *et al*, 2003), and document this in the notes. If there are several goniometers of the same type in one department, it is best to number them, as one may become loose, stiff or bent and they will not necessarily be interchangeable. Goniometers can be quickly calibrated by placing them on a flat, level surface (this should measure 180°) and measuring the right angle on a setsquare. This should be done weekly and recorded in a logbook. Some plastic goniometers are relatively fragile and metal ones can bend if dropped, so they should be handled with care.

Consistency is also needed in the point selected to read the goniometer, i.e., the side of the pointer is smooth or rounded. If a goniometer with a line is used, e.g. the Devore Pocket Goniometer (North Coast Medical via Promedics UK), consistency in rounding up or down is required. Departmental protocols clarify this and aid consistency.

Ideally, the measurements should be recorded at the same time of day (Salter, 1987; Bexon and Salter, 2000) due to circadian variations in flexibility (Gifford,1987). Although this is not always possible, the same point in the session and the same posture should be used (Salter, 1955). Posture variables include: the height of table, chair and position of the upper limb, particularly the wrist.

When to test

Goniometric measurements should be taken when:

- a loss of active range is observed in a joint or joints
- the patient has a condition that might be expected to result in a change of range or where maintenance of range is a treatment aim (such as, rheumatoid arthritis)
- pre-surgery to evaluate the results of surgery (e.g., fasciectomy)
- measurements should be repeated at intervals that are relevant to the progress expected of the individual patient (see *Chapter 1*).

Always check that other joints of the upper limb are not restricted, as this may reflect a pre-existing problem or one recently acquired relating to the injury or to disuse.

Do not test

- do not attempt to measure range of movement if active movement of the part is contra-indicated
- problems may be encountered in patients with rheumatoid arthritis where joint shape prevents correct alignment, or where pain hampers repeated movements. If many joints are involved measurement may take considerable time. If these two problems are encountered other methods can be useful (see *Chapter 7*).

How to test active range of movement

The same principles apply for testing every joint:

- assemble equipment needed—goniometer, paper/chart and pen
- before beginning, always explain to the patient the purpose of the test and what will happen
- position the patient for the test
- locate the non-moving part of the body
- align the goniometer by placing the axis of the goniometer over the joint, using bony landmarks to ensure the arms are in the correct plane of motion
- ask the patient to move. Ensure the goniometer is correctly aligned, by re-identifying the landmarks (Nicol, 1989)
- take the reading.

This sequence is detailed below for the wrist and hand; the starting positions and goniometer placement used are those recommended by ASHT (Adams *et al*, 1992) unless otherwise stated.

Supination

- select a goniometer with arms that rotate through 360° (e.g. the small universal goniometer)
- seat the patient with the shoulder adducted and the elbow flexed to 90° and the ulnar border of the forearm on a table, with the hand over the edge
- place the axis of the goniometer on the palmar surface, proximal to the ulna styloid
- place the stationary arm parallel to the anterior midline of the humerus
- place the moving arm across the palmar surface of the forearm just proximal to the radial and ulna styloid processes (Stanley and Tribuzi, 1992)
- ask the patient to turn his/her palm upwards
- check that the axis and arms are still properly aligned before the taking the reading.

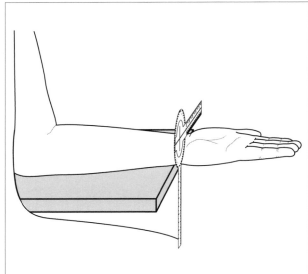

Figure 6.1: Measurement of supination

Pronation

- select a goniometer with arms that rotate through 360°

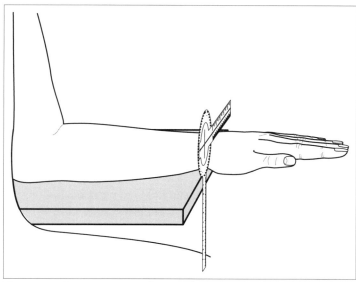

Figure 6.2: Measurement of pronation

- seat the patient with the shoulder adducted and the elbow flexed to 90° and the ulnar border of the forearm on the table, with the hand over the edge

- place the axis of the goniometer on the dorsal surface, proximal to the ulnar styloid

- place the stationary arm parallel to the anterior midline of the humerus

- place the moving arm across the dorsal surface of the forearm just proximal to the radial and ulna styloid processes (Stanley and Tribuzi, 1992)

- ask the patient to turn his/her palm downwards

- check that the axis and arms are still properly aligned before the taking the reading.

Wrist extension

Figure 6.3: Measurement of wrist extension

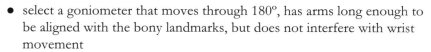

- select a goniometer that moves through 180°, has arms long enough to be aligned with the bony landmarks, but does not interfere with wrist movement

- place the patient's elbow on a table with forearm and wrist in neutral

- place the axis of the goniometer on the proximal end of the thenar crease

- place the stationary arm on the palmar surface of the forearm, parallel to the longitudinal axis of the radius

- place the moving arm on the palmar surface of the forearm, parallel to the longitudinal axis of the third metacarpal

- ask the patient to bend his/her wrist backwards, without moving the forearm

- check that the axis and arms are still properly aligned before taking the reading

- in some cases it may be necessary to align the goniometer with the ulnar border of the hand and forearm.

Wrist flexion

- select a goniometer that moves through 180°, has arms long enough to be aligned with the bony landmarks, but not interfere with wrist movement
- place the patient's elbow on a table with forearm and wrist in neutral
- place the axis of the goniometer dorsally, just distal and radial to the ulna styloid
- place the stationary arm dorsally, parallel to the longitudinal axis of the radius
- place the moving arm dorsally, parallel to the longitudinal axis of the third metacarpal
- ask the patient to bend his/her wrist forwards without moving the forearm
- check that the axis and arms are still properly aligned before taking the reading
- in some cases it may be necessary to align the goniometer with the ulnar border of the hand and forearm.

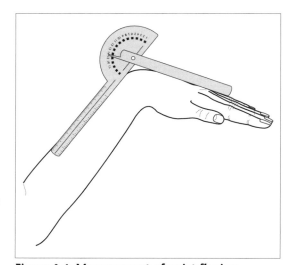

Figure 6.4: Measurement of wrist flexion

Ulnar deviation

- select a goniometer that moves through 180° and has arms long enough to be aligned with the bony landmarks
- place the pronated forearm and hand on a table with the wrist in neutral
- place the axis of the goniometer over the intercarpal joint. Turn the goniometer sideways so that it lies flat against the forearm with the protractor towards the thumb
- place the stationary arm dorsally, parallel to the midline of the forearm
- place the moving arm dorsally, parallel to the midline of the third metacarpal
- ask the patient to move their hand sideways, in the direction of the little finger
- check that the axis and arms are still properly aligned before taking the reading.

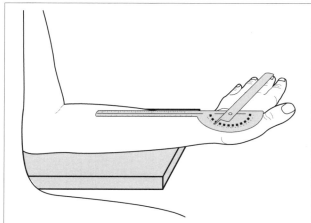

Figure 6.5: Measurement of ulnar deviation

Radial deviation

- select a goniometer that moves through 180° and has arms long enough to be aligned with the bony landmarks

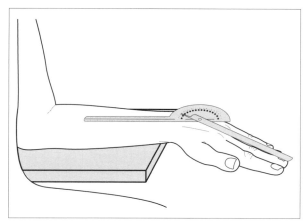

Figure 6.6: Measurement of radial deviation

- place the pronated forearm and hand on a table with the wrist in neutral
- place the axis of the goniometer dorsally, over the intercarpal joint. Turn the goniometer sideways, so that it lies flat with the protractor turning towards the little finger
- place the stationary arm dorsally, parallel to the midline of the forearm
- place the moving arm dorsally, parallel to the midline of the third metacarpal
- ask the patient to move his/her hand sideways, in the direction of their thumb
- check that the axis and arms are still properly aligned before taking the reading.

MCP flexion of the index finger

Figure 6.7: Measurement of flexion of the index finger MCP joint

- select a goniometer that measures at least 30° hyperextension, is divided into 1° increments, has arms short enough to permit full movement and with a broad, smooth surface in contact with the patient (finger goniometer)
- place the elbow on the table with the wrist, forearm and MCP joints in neutral and the IP joints extended
- place the axis of the goniometer dorsally over the index MCP joint
- place the stationary arm dorsally, parallel to the index finger metacarpal
- place the moving arm parallel to the index finger proximal phalanx
- ask the patient to curl his/her fingers into a tight fist
- check that the axis and arms are still properly aligned before the taking the reading.

MCP extension of the index finger

- select a finger goniometer
- rest the elbow on the table with the wrist, forearm and MCP joints in neutral and the IP joints extended
- place the axis of the goniometer dorsally over the index MCP joint
- place the stationary arm dorsally, parallel to the index finger metacarpal
- place the moving arm parallel to the index finger proximal phalanx
- ask the patient to stretch his/her fingers out as far as possible
- check that the axis and arms are still properly aligned before taking the reading.

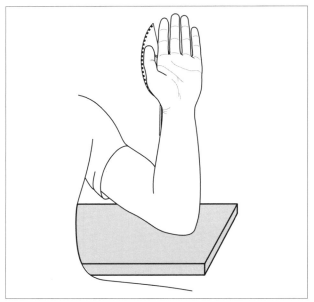

Figure 6.8: Measurement of extension of the index finger MCP joint

PIP flexion of the index finger

- select a finger goniometer
- rest the elbow on the table with the wrist and forearm in neutral. The finger joints are extended (AAOS, 1965)
- place the axis of the goniometer dorsally over the index proximal PIP joint
- place the stationary arm dorsally, parallel to the index finger proximal phalanx
- place the moving arm parallel to the index finger middle phalanx
- ask the patient to curl his/her fingers into a tight fist
- check that the axis and arms are still properly aligned before taking the reading.

Figure 6.9: Measurement of flexion of the index finger PIP joint

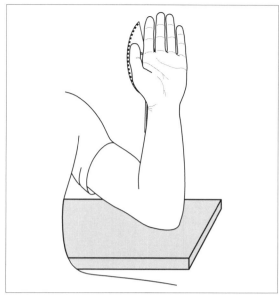

Figure 6.10: Measurement of extension of the index finger PIP joint

PIP extension of the index finger

- select a finger goniometer
- rest the elbow on the table with the wrist, forearm and finger joints in 0° extension
- place the axis of the goniometer dorsally, over the index PIP joint
- place the stationary arm dorsally, parallel to the index finger proximal phalanx
- place the moving arm parallel to the index finger middle phalanx
- ask the patient to stretch his/her fingers back as far as possible
- check that the axis and arms are still properly aligned before taking the reading.

DIP flexion of the index finger

- select a finger goniometer
- rest the elbow on the table with the wrist, forearm and fingers extended (AAOS, 1965)
- place the axis of the goniometer dorsally, over the index DIP joint
- place the stationary arm dorsally, parallel to the index finger middle phalanx
- place the moving arm parallel to the index finger distal phalanx
- ask the patient to curl all his/her fingers into a tight fist
- check that the axis and arms are still properly aligned before taking the reading
- this measures composite flexion—the DIP joints can be measured with the MCP joints extended and the PIP joints flexed. The method used should be noted.

DIP extension of the index finger

- select a finger goniometer
- rest the elbow on the table with the wrist, forearm and fingers in neutral
- place the axis of the goniometer dorsally, over the index DIP joint
- place the stationary arm dorsally, parallel to the index finger middle phalanx
- place the moving arm parallel to the index finger distal phalanx
- ask the patient to stretch out his/her fingers as much as possible
- check that the axis and arms are still properly aligned before taking the reading.

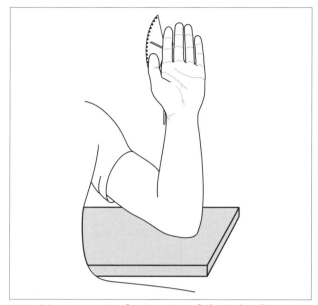

6.11: Measurement of extension of the index finger DIP joint

The finger measurements are repeated for each finger joint in turn, aligning the axis of the goniometer with each finger joint, the stationary arm with the corresponding proximal bone and the moving arm with the distal bone.

Radial abduction of thumb

- select a goniometer that moves through 360° and has arms long enough to be aligned with bony landmarks
- rest the pronated forearm on a table, with the wrist and the thumb IP joint in neutral
- place the axis of the goniometer dorsally, over the intersection of lines parallel to the first and second metacarpals
- place the stationary arm dorsally, along the second metacarpal
- place the moving arm parallel to the radial aspect of the first metacarpal

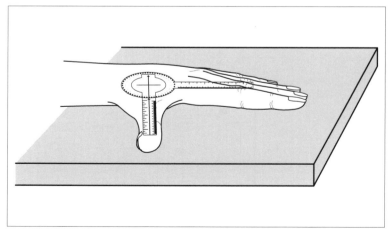

Figure 6.12: Measurement of radial abduction of the thumb

- ask the patient to move his/her thumb sideways, as far away from his/her index finger as possible, to make a right angle
- check that the axis and arms are still properly aligned before taking the reading
- alternatively, this can be measured using a ruler (see *Chapter 7*).

Palmar abduction of thumb

- select a goniometer that moves through 360° and has arms long enough to be aligned with bony landmarks
- the patient rests the elbow on the table with the wrist and the thumb IP joint in neutral

    - place the axis of the goniometer dorsally, over the intersection of lines parallel to the first and second metacarpals
    - place the stationary arm along the radial aspect of the second metacarpal
    - place the moving arm parallel to the radial aspect of the first metacarpal
    - ask the patient to move his/her thumb forward, as far away from the index finger as possible, trying to make it at 90° to the palm
    - check that the axis and arms are still properly aligned before taking the reading.

    Thumb opposition can be measured using the Kapandji Method (see *Chapter 14*).

Thumb MCP flexion

- select a finger goniometer
- rest the elbow on the table, the forearm, wrist and thumb MCP joint in neutral. The IP joint of the thumb is relaxed
- Place the axis of the goniometer dorsally, over the MCP joint
- Place the stationary arm dorsally parallel to the first metacarpal
- Place the moving arm dorsally, parallel to the thumb proximal phalanx
- Ask the patient to bend his/her thumb forward towards the palm, from its bottom knuckle
- Check that the axis and arms are still properly aligned before taking the reading.

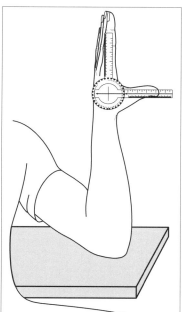

Figure 6.13: Measurement of palmar abduction of the thumb

Thumb MCP extension

- Select a finger goniometer
- Rest the elbow on the table, the forearm, wrist and thumb MCP joint in neutral. The IP joint of the thumb is relaxed
- Place the axis of the goniometer dorsally over the MCP joint
- Place the stationary arm dorsally, parallel to the first metacarpal
- Place the moving arm dorsally, parallel to the thumb proximal phalanx
- Ask the patient to stretch his/her thumb backwards, from its bottom knuckle
- Check that the axis and arms are still properly aligned before taking the reading.

Thumb IP flexion

- Select a finger goniometer
- Rest the elbow on the table, the forearm, wrist and thumb MCP and IP joints in neutral
- Place the axis of the goniometer dorsally over the IP joint of the thumb
- Place the stationary arm dorsally, parallel to the proximal phalanx
- Place the moving arm dorsally, parallel to the distal phalanx
- Ask the patient to bend the thumb at the IP joint
- Check that the axis and arms are still properly aligned before taking the reading.

Thumb IP extension

- Select a finger goniometer
- Rest the elbow on the table, the forearm, wrist and MCP and IP joints of the thumb in neutral
- Place the axis of the goniometer dorsally over the IP joint of the thumb
- Place the stationary arm dorsally, parallel to the proximal phalanx
- Place the moving arm dorsally, parallel to the distal phalanx
- Ask the patient to stretch his/her thumb backwards, as far as possible
- Check that the axis and arms are still properly aligned before taking the reading

How to measure passive range of movement

Using the same starting position and alignment points given above, the therapist moves the patient's joint through its available range. Care should be taken not to force joints through painful range. The measurement is taken in the same way. When testing the finger joints through passive range, the other joints should be relaxed (Adams *et al*, 1992).

Accessory movements should be tested as part of the passive range in the wrist and hand. These movements are small joint movements that cannot be performed voluntarily or in isolation by the patient (Corrigan and Maitland, 1994). These movements are essential to achieve full active and passive movement and there are 33 such movements in the wrist and hand. These should be tested in a position where the surrounding tissues are relaxed, the proximal bone is fixed, and the distal bone is moved (Corrigan and Maitland, 1994). Well detailed by Corrigan and Maitland, these movements cannot be measured; therefore, experience and knowledge of the normal are needed for assessment.

Similarly, the 'end feel' of the joint on passive movement can only be learned by clinical experience and practice on the norm (Corrigan and Maitland, 1994). The type of 'end feel' may be of significance in assessing the cause of loss of range:

- Abrupt and hard may indicate a bony block
- Less abrupt may indicate a restriction of the joint capsule
- Increased elasticity and increased range may indicate swelling around the joint (Nicholson, 1992)
- Extreme elasticity may indicate ligament laxity
- The inability to reach a definite end feel may be due to irritability of the soft tissues or joint capsule (Nicholson, 1992).

It is difficult to standardise the amount of pressure applied passively and, despite experience, 'end feel' is subjective. This has led to the development of the torque range of movement or TROM (see below).

Total active motion

The total active movement (TAM) of a digit is defined as the sum of active flexion measurements of the MCP and IP joints, when making a fist, minus the sum of the active extension deficits for each finger (Macey and Burke, 1995). It is useful for stiff hands in that the total active movement can be expressed as a single figure. This method will not show small changes in an isolated joint, pathological hyperextension (Adams *et al*, 1992), or indicate range if deformities are present.

This figure does not reflect function (Ellis and Bruton, 1998), but the single digit score can be useful for statistical purposes; it might, therefore, be useful as an overall assessment of digital motion (Macey and Burke, 1995). There is an impression that this method is used more frequently for audit and research purposes.

This might be because therapists often use data to plan and evaluate treatment to individual joints.

To calculate for an index finger that has 90° flexion in all joints, but is lacking 30° extension in all joints, the calculation is carried out as follows:

$$TAM = [Flexion\ MCP + PIP + DIP] - [Deficit\ of\ Extension of\ MCP + PIP + DIP]$$
$$= [90 + 90 + 90] - [30 + 30 + 30]$$
$$= [270] - [90]$$
$$= 180$$

Total passive motion

The total passive movement (TPM) of a digit is defined as the sum of passive flexion measurements of the MCP joints and IP joints when making a fist, minus the sum of the passive extension deficits (Macey and Burke, 1995). The calculation is made in the same way as for total active motion and the same restrictions and advantages apply.

Recording

Many units have their own assessment forms or use the form advocated by Robins (1986). These usually provide a table for the completion by the therapist. Care should be taken to place entries in the correct space, as it is very easy to misplace items and this can result in misleading data or numerous crossings out that do not help legibility. It can be helpful to record passive movement in another colour, traditionally red (Bexon and Salter, 2000). Unfortunately, red does not photocopy well and notes are frequently photocopied for the patient's personal use, and legal or insurance purposes. Current recording requirements demand that, when the preferred colour (black) is not used, there must be consistency throughout an organisation of the colour, style and occasions in which it is used (CNST, 2000).

If the patient is unable to achieve the correct starting position, this should be noted, as should a change of placement of the goniometer due to the patient's condition (for example, medial placement of the goniometer, if the joints are excessively swollen) (Adams et al, 1992).

If the patient suffers from early morning stiffness, this could affect findings and it is relevant to note the time of treatment. The notes should also record at which point(s) in the treatment session they were made, i.e. at the start or end of treatment. These will affect the results and can give a misleading impression if not performed consistently (Adams et al, 1992). Two principle methods exist to record movement:

1. The first is to record extension over flexion and to count hyperextension as a positive (+) and loss of movement as a negative (-). Hence, loss of 30° extension, with 90° flexion at the PIP would be recorded as -30/90. Conversely, a PIP joint with 30° hyperextension and 90° would be recorded as +30/90. This is the style advocated by ASHT (Adams et al, 1992).

2.   An alternative method frequently used in Europe (Debrunner and Hepp, 1994) incorporates three figures, inserting the neutral score to give clarification. Extension is measured first, then flexion and the position of the neutral score (recorded as 0) indicates where movement is lacking.

Thus the PIP joint with the loss of extension of 30° and 90° flexion is recorded as 0/30/90. Where:

0	=	Neutral position
30	=	Loss of 30° extension
90	=	Maximum flexion

This indicates that the neutral position cannot be achieved. A joint with 30° hyperextension and 90° flexion is recorded as 30/0/90. Where:

30	=	Maximum extension
0	=	Neutral position
90	=	Maximum flexion

This indicates that the joint passes through the neutral position. Consequently, a PIP joint that extends to the neutral position, but flexes to 90°, would be recorded as 0/0/90.

Whichever method is used, it should be standardised within the department and the record should use a key to indicate that extension is recorded before flexion. If range has not been measured because it is full, this should be noted.

Reliability

Norm values do exist for joint range, however, Salter (1955) recommended that the contra-lateral hand be used for comparison, as there is usually only a mean difference of 3% between left and right, while individual subjects can vary up to 20%. A great deal of work has been done since 1917 looking at the reliability of methods and the instrumentation used. These are difficult to compare and results are not consistent and would vary for each joint. It is, generally, agreed that the goniometer is ±5° accurate (Smith, 1982; Adams *et al*, 1992; Groth *et al*, 2001).

Ellis *et al* (1997) carried out a study where 40 therapists repeatedly measured one subject's digit held first in a flexed and then in extended position. This showed higher intra-rater repeatability than inter-rater repeatability, as illustrated in *Table 6.1*. The repeatability coefficient is in direct proportion to the variability. Burr *et al* (2003) confirmed that this was the case for DIP flexion but not for DIP extension.

These results show that goniometry is less reliable distally than proximally in the hand.

Reliability tests on the PIP and DIP of an impaired subject showed high inter-rater reliability (intraclass correlation coefficients of 0.99 for dorsal placement and 0.86 for lateral placement). Interestingly, these also showed no

Table 6.1: Repeatability coefficients for goniometry (using data extracted from Ellis *et al*, 1997)

	Intra-rater repeatability coefficient	Inter-rater repeatability coefficient
MCP	3.8°–4.3°	4.4°–5.9°
PIP	4.7°–4.3°	7.2°–6.0°
DIP	6.4°–6.1°	9.8°–9.9°

NB: The first figure represents flexion and the second extension.

correlation between goniometric and radiographic measurements (Groth *et al*, 2001). Gajdosik and Bohannon (1987) conclude that goniometry is a valid measure of range of movement, but not of factors affecting range of movement.

When this part of the assessment is complete, the therapist has a record of the deficits or hypermobility of active and passive range of movement.

Torque range of movement

Wright and Johns (1960) developed torque angle measurements to quantify and qualify joint stiffness. When measuring passive range, it can be tempting to consciously or unconsciously increase the amount of force applied, leading to an apparent increase in range. Torque angle measurements can present a solution to this problem and Brand and Hollister (1999) argue that this should be used routinely to measure passive range. This is referred to as torque range of movement (TROM).

Torque is the name given to the moment of force (Brand and Hollister, 1999). A moment is defined as a force multiplied by the perpendicular distance from the line of action of the force to the centre of rotation of the object (Nicol, 1996). Moment of force is the tendency to turn, produced at the axis (joint) when a force (a muscle) is applied to a lever (the bone). Torque is usually measured in Newton metres:

$Torque = Force\,[i.e.\ weight \times gravity] \times perpendicular\ distance$

$= Newtons \times Metres$

$= Nm$

The basis of torque angle measurements is the application of a known force (weight x gravity) at a known distance to move the joint passively to its limits of movement.

Torque angle measurements have two principle advantages. First, objectivity is given to what therapists refer to as the 'end feel' (Macey and Burke, 1995).

Secondly, it is impossible to remember exactly how much force was applied to here on previous occasions and it avoids the temptation by the therapist to apply just a little more force to gain increased passive range (Breger-Lee *et al*, 1990). It has been used to evaluate treatment for contractures of the PIP joints (Brand, 1999), the effects of mobilisations (Randall *et al*, 1992), flexor tendon tightness (Breger-Lee *et al*, 1990) and has been used in a computer-controlled form to measure MCP stiffness in an evaluation of physiotherapeutic techniques (Bromley *et al*, 1994).

Interestingly, the method is not widely used in daily clinical practice in the UK and it is unclear why. Measurement can be undertaken quickly and cheaply, but does at first seem to require an extra set of hands, which could be provided by an assistant. Furthermore, for clinical work, if the force and distance are used consistently, there is no need for complicated calculations.

There are several devices to measure torque angle clinically; these include a spring scale, which is easily obtainable, or more specialised devices, such as the Haldex orthotic gauge (Breger-Lee *et al*, 1990; 1993). The simplest, easiest and cheapest way is to suspend a small weight from the finger or hand.

Do not test

Do not test if:

- the joint is unstable, for example in some patients with rheumatoid arthritis

- there is any reason why force should not be applied, e.g. non-united fracture, tendon repairs of less than 10 weeks

- approach with extreme caution if the joint is painful or lax.

How to test (torque angle extension of the PIP joint)

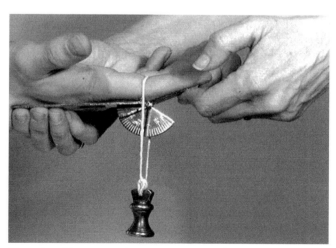

- assemble equipment needed—a small weight, string, finger goniometer, paper and pen

- choose a suitable, standard weight, depending on the size of the hand and the patient's condition. It is not advised to exceed 600 grams for a small hand (Breger-Lee *et al*, 1990). Two hundred and fifty grams could be a safe starting point, although this will have no effect on a powerful hand

- the finger goniometer should have one arm longer than the other

Plate 6.2: Torque angle measurement of extension of the PIP joint

- explain to the patient the purpose of the test. Seat the patient at a table. The therapist stands facing the patient
- these instructions assume the right hand is to be measured by a right-handed therapist
- take the weight of choice and tie a piece of string (about 30 centimetres) through a hole in the top; knot it so that it forms a loop and can be suspended from the finger. Ensure the knot is at the edge of the weight. Slip the loop around your right hand at the level of the thumb
- ask the patient to hold the supinated right hand out above the table, keeping the joints relaxed. Gently, but firmly, hold the wrist and the MCP joint in neutral with the left hand. Continue to support the wrist with the index finger, whilst the heel of your hand supports the MCP joint
- using the right hand, apply the goniometer so that the axis is over the dorsal surface of the PIP joint. Insert the long arm proximally, down the proximal phalanx and under your left hand. Hold the distal arm of the goniometer with the fingers of the left hand
- using your right thumb, slip the weight on to the patient's finger. Centre the string over the flexor crease of the DIP joint. Release the weight slowly and gently. Ensure that the string is at 90° to the proximal phalange
- read the range of movement on the goniometer
- when repeated, always ensure that the same weight and surface markings are used
- this method can be altered depending on the joint involved and the movement measured; it can be adapted for flexion
- torque can be applied, constantly or increasingly over a 20-minute period (Flowers and Pheasant, 1988).

Recording

Always record the weight used, the range obtained and the surface markings used, to facilitate repetition. Also note if the measurement is taken after a given period. To correctly record the force applied, multiply the weight by 9.81 and record force in Newtons. This is not strictly necessary for clinical work.

A series of measurements employing different forces can be used to give a torque angle curve. On a graph, the force is plotted against the range obtained. Flowers and Pheasant (1988), in a study of healthy subjects immobilised in plaster for a one–six week period, demonstrated the use of torque angle curves as an objective measure of quantity and quality of stiffness.

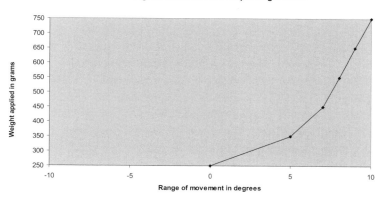

Figure 6.15a Normal Torque Angle Curve

The greater the force, the greater the expected range and, thus, the type of curve obtained can indicate the mechanical quality of the tissues which are preventing free motion.

Conventionally, flexion torques are recorded as negative and extension as positive (Breger-Lee *et al*, 1990). Normal tissues shortened through disuse give a gentle curve, while damaged tissues or adherent scars give a very steep curve (Brand and Hollister, 1999). In clinical practice, these can be used to determine the need for surgery for patients with contractures secondary to median and ulnar

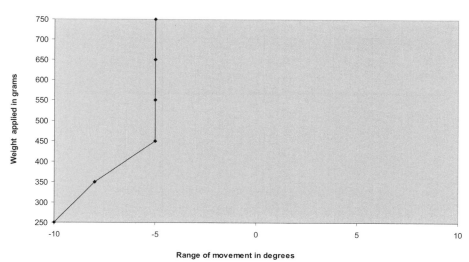

Figure 6.15b Torque Angle Curve Showing Extreme Block to Movement

nerve palsy. Torque angle curves can indicate when therapy has given maximum benefit (Breger-Lee *et al*, 1993).

Reliability

Breger- Lee *et al* (1993) compared intra and inter-rater reliability using the Haldex orthotic gauge with dial goniometer and a cantilever-beam force transducer and electro-goniometer, when assessing extension forces (ranging from 200–800 grams) in 56 normal PIP joints. This showed moderate intra-rater reliability that improved at the higher levels of force (600grams and 800grams). All were significant at the $P<0.05$ using the Pearson Correlation Analysis. Inter-rater reliability was lower than intra-rater reliability. The majority of testers and weights were significantly correlated at the $P<0.05$ level. Further research using the simple weight method would be beneficial.

The next step

When this part of the assessment is completed, the therapist should have an accurate measurement of the active and passive joint range and start to consider the reasons for any deficit. If passive range of individual joints is full, assessment of the composite range from flexion to extension and web spaces should be measured and the causes of any loss considered (see *Chapter 7*).

To summarise

- be consistent in the choice and use of a goniometer
- be consistent and explicit in recording
- record active and passive range and assess accessory movements
- consider the use of torque angle measurement.

References

Adams LS, Greene LW, Topoozian E (1992) Range of motion. In: *Clinical Assessment Recommendations*, 2nd edn. American Society of Hand Therapists, Chicago: 55–69

American Academy of Orthopedic Surgeons (1965) *Joint Motion Method of Measuring and Recording*. Reprinted by The British Orthopaedic Association (1966). Churchill Livingstone, Edinburgh: 26–28

Bexon C, Salter M (2000) Assessment. In: Salter M, Cheshire L, eds. *Hand Therapy: Principles and Practice*. Butterworth-Heinemann, Oxford: 51–57

Bradley A (1993) An evaluation of the current methods used in the assessment of outcomes in hand surgery. *Br J Hand Ther* 1: 74–9

Brand PW, Hollister A (1999) *Clinical Mechanics of the Hand*, 3rd edn. CV Mosby, St Louis: ch1; ch12

Breger-Lee D, Bell-Krotoski J, Brandsma JW (1990) Torque range of motion in the hand clinic. *Hand Ther* **Jan–Mar**: 7–90

Breger-Lee D, Voelker ET, Giurintano D, Novick A, Browder L (1993) Reliability of torque range of motion. A preliminary study. *J Hand Ther* **4**: 29–34

Bromley J, Unsworth A, Haslock I (1994) Changes in stiffness following short- and long-term application of standard physiotherapeutic techniques. *Br J Rheumatol*. **33**: 555–61

Bücher C (2003) A survey of current hand assessment practice in the UK. *Br J Hand Therapy* **8**(3): 102–109

CNST (2000) *Clinical Risk Management Standards*, Version 01. NHS Litigation Authority. June 2000, Standard 6: Health Records: 65–82

Corrigan B, Maitland GD (1994) *Practical Orthopaedic Medicine*. Butterworth-Heinemann, Oxford: 12–15; 87–90

Debrunner HU, Hepp WR (1994) *Orthopädisches Diagnostikum*. Thieme Verlag, Stuttgart

Ellis B, Bruton A, Goddard J (1997) Joint angle measurement: A comparative study of the reliability of goniometry and wire tracing for the hand. *Clin Rehab* **11**: 314–20

Ellis B, Bruton A (1998) Clinical assessment of the hand—A review of joint angle measures. *Br J Hand Ther* **3**(2): 5–8

Flowers KR, Stephans-Chisar J, LeStayo P, Galante B-L (2001) Intrarater reliability of a new method and instrumentation for measuring passive supination and pronation. *J Hand Ther* **14**(1): 30–35

Flowers KR, Pheasant SD (1988) The use of torque angle curves in the assessment of digital joint stiffness. *J Hand Ther* 1: 69–74

Fox RF (1917) Demonstration of the Mensuration Apparatus in Use at the Red Cross Clinic for the Physical Treatment of Officers, Great Portland Street, London, W. *Proc Roy Soc Med* **10**: 63–69

Gajdosik RL, Bohannon RW (1987) Clinical measurement of range of movement review of goniometry emphasising reliability and validity. *Physical Ther* **67**(12): 1867–72

Gifford LS (1987) Circadian variation in human flexibility and grip strength. *Aus J Physiother* **33**(1): 3–9

Goodwin J, Clark C, Deakes J, Burdon D, Lawrence C (1992) Clinical methods of goniometry: A comparative study. *Disabil Rehab* **14**(1): 10–15

Groth GN, VanDeven KM, Phillips EC, Ehretsman RL (2001) Goniometry of the proximal and distal interphalangeal joints, Part II. *J Hand Ther* **14**(1): 23–9

Macey AC, Burke FD (1995) Outcomes of hand surgery. *J Hand Surg* **20B**(6): 841–55

Murray K, Topping M, Simpson C (2000) Investigation of the hand assessment techniques used within the United Kingdom. *Br J Hand Ther* **5**(4): 125

Nicol AC (1996) *Introductory Mechanics, Course Book 1*, Postgraduate Diploma in Biomechanics. University of Strathclyde, Glasgow: 31–41

Nicol AC (1989) Measurement of joint motion. *Clin Rehab* **3**: 1–9

Nicholson B (1992) Clinical evaluation. In: Stanley BG, Tribuzi SM, eds. *Concepts in Hand Rehabilitation*. FA Davis, Philadelphia: 59

Randall T, Portney L, Harris BA (1992) Effects of joint mobilisation on joint stiffness and active motion of the metacarpal-phalangeal joint. *J Orthopaed Sports Physic Ther* **16**(1): 30–6

Robins RHC (1986) Hand assessment charts. *J Hand Surg* **11B**(2): 287–98

Salter MI (1987) *Hand Injuries: A Therapeutic Approach*. Churchill Livingstone, Edinburgh: 24–29

Salter N (1955) Methods of measurement of muscle and joint function. *J Bone Joint Surg* **37B**(3): 474–90

Smith DS (1982) Measurement of joint range: An overview. *Clinics Rheum Dis* **8**(3): 523–31

Stanley BG, Tribuzi SM, eds (1992) *Concepts in Hand Rehabilitation*. FA Davis, Philadelphia: Appendix B, 527–8

Wright V, Johns RJ (1960) Observations on the measurement of joint stiffness. *Arthritis Rheumatism* **3**: 328–40

Chapter 7
Range of movement II—Other methods

While goniometry is the most commonly used method of assessing joint range other clinical methods exist and are in widespread use. These include visual estimation, wire tracings, measurement of composite flexion and span.

Visual estimation

Visual estimation was the first method to be used and remains popular (Salter, 1955; Ellis *et al*, 1997; Murray *et al*, 2000; Bücher, 2003), but it is entirely subjective. It is a quick, easy method to assess joint angle, requires no tools and can be used on all joints. The therapist looks at joint range and visualises it against an imaginary protractor and the range expected in a healthy joint. It is, therefore, highly subjective, although published results on reliability are equivocal (Ellis and Bruton, 1998).

There are many potential sources of error when using this method. If the estimator is inconsistent and views the joint from different angles, results may be misleading; this makes it unsuitable for multiple observers. Furthermore, there may be a preference for a certain end digit—either 0 or 5 (Ellis and Bruton, 1998). Generally, the method lacks precision and fails to meet the basic requirements of measuring. For these reasons, this method is not recommended, and should only be used when other methods are unavailable and to establish full range.

Wire tracing

Glanville (1964) and Barron developed this method to measure joint range at the Odstock Hand Unit in Salisbury (Bexon, 1993). Robins (1986) recommended that wire tracings and goniometry be used on a hand assessment chart. These can provide useful information about total active and passive finger movement (Hage and de Groot, 1996). This method is particularly useful for painful hands as there is less need to repeat movements, unlike measuring with a goniometer. It is also useful for very deformed hands where swellings and nodules make goniometry difficult. Furthermore, this method can indicate where there is an extension lag. Wire tracing is cheap, the whole hand can be recorded on one sheet of A4 paper, and the patient can see at a glance if there is improvement (Glanville, 1964). A disadvantage of this method is that the required size of solder wire can be difficult to obtain in D-I-Y stores. Also, it cannot be used easily in audit as an end stage measure (Macey and Burke, 1995), as this would involve comparison of individual tracings, which cannot easily be entered on a spreadsheet.

How to test

- collect equipment needed— Flexicurve or 21 centimetres of 16SWG multi-core solder wire, catheter, A4 paper, and coloured pens

- explain the purpose of the test to the patient and what will happen

- insert solder wire into a clear plastic flexible tube or catheter (Roberts, 1989; Bexon, 1993; Bexon and Salter, 2000) or wrap in clingfilm. Solder contains tin and lead, and care should be taken, as some therapists and patients may develop an allergy to it. Alternatively, use a Flexicurve, a flexible measure often used to assess the lumbar spine

Plate 7.1: Using a Flexicurve to record index finger flexion

- sit the patient comfortably at a table with the elbow supported and the wrist in neutral or slight extension. Ask the patient to extend all the fingers

- place the wire along the dorsum of the index finger. Start with the end of the wire at the tip of the finger. If using solder wire, without a plastic sleeve, make a hook over the tip of the finger. If using the Flexicurve, pinch it and use this point to mark the end of the finger tip (not the nail). Gently mould the wire or Flexicurve down the finger and hand (Roberts, 1989). This should extend at least five centimetres down the metacarpals (Hage and de Groot, 1996). If the finger is painful, bend the wire, without making skin contact, so that it exactly matches the contour of the finger and hand. Check it is correct by placing the bent wire on the finger (Salter, 1987)

- carefully remove the wire and place on the upper quarter of a piece of A4 paper, which is in the portrait position (i.e. with the short side horizontally, at the top). Ensure that the MCP joint is at the left of the page. Trace a solid line along the underside (i.e. that surface which was against the skin of the finger), mark the joints and label each joint and the finger (Salter, 1987; Roberts, 1989; Bexon, 1993)

- repeat this for each finger on the same piece of paper

- keep the elbow and wrist in the same position and ask the patient to make a fist and again place the wire against the dorsum of the index finger. Repeat for flexion using the same approach

- superimpose the new shape on the corresponding tracing of extension, ensuring that the wire is orientated correctly, with the joints aligned. There will be an apparent lengthening of the proximal phalanx (Roberts, 1989). Using the proximal phalanx as a baseline (Salter, 1987; Roberts, 1989), trace in a broken line from the underside of the wire onto the first tracing in the same coloured ink. Hage and de Groot (1996) recommend using the metacarpal as a baseline; the choice will be dependent on the patient's amount of movement and the therapist's preference. The evidence is not clear about which bone is the most suitable baseline; however, while the angles may be the same, they will appear very differently (Beresford, 1993)

- subsequent measurements can be superimposed using different coloured inks

- to measure total passive movement this method can be repeated, and the therapist passively puts the fingers into maximum extension and flexion. This should be recorded on either a separate sheet or in another colour.

Recording

- ensure that the wire tracing report sheet contains the patient's name, unit number or date of birth; number it as a continuation sheet and attach to the record, this will prevent losing it in the short or long term

- ensure that there is a key. The key should clarify the colour used on each date and the movement represented by a solid or broken line. It must be clear whether active or passive movement is recorded and the type of wire/Flexicurve should be recorded. The record should be signed on each occasion

- it has been mentioned previously that coloured inks (see *Chapter 6*) can be a problem, therefore use must be consistent within the organisation and colours that will photocopy should be selected.

Reliability

In a study (Ellis *et al*, 1997), 40 therapists were asked to carry out repeated readings for goniometry and wire tracing on the DIP, PIP and MCP joints of the finger in two different, controlled positions. Repeatability coefficients (see *Table 7.1*) were higher than for goniometry for both intra and inter-rater reliability and are particularly high at the DIP Joint, showing less reliability than goniometry. Not unexpectedly, it was found that, like goniometry, wire tracing has better intra-rater reliability than inter-rater reliability.

Table 7.1 Repeatability coefficients for wire tracings extracted from Ellis and Bruton 1997

	Intra-Rater Reliability Coefficient	Inter-Rater Repeatability Coefficient
MCP	8.9° –8.0°	10.3°–10.4°
PIP	10.9°–8.1°	12.3°– 9.5°
DIP	9.8°–10.5°	11.9°–13.2°

NB: The first figure represents flexion and the second extension.

Composite finger flexion or pulp to palm measure

This is a quick, cheap method, providing easy feedback to the patient. It is particularly useful to assess total active movement and the ability, or progress toward, fist making; however, it fails to give an indication of extensor lag (Chiu 1995).

How to test

- collect equipment needed—ruler, paper/chart and pen
- explain the purpose of the test to the patient
- seat the patient comfortably, with the hand supinated on a table
- place the zero end of the ruler perpendicular to an imaginary line, joining the distal palmar crease on the ulnar side of the hand and the proximal palmar crease on the radial side (Macey and Burke, 1995)

- ask the patient to flex the index finger to the ruler and slide the finger down the ruler towards the palm (Macey and Burke, 1995)

- measure from the point where the nail becomes white

- note distance from the measuring point to the palm in millimetres and record with the landmarks used

- repeat passively, if appropriate, by moving the patient's fingers into maximum flexion.

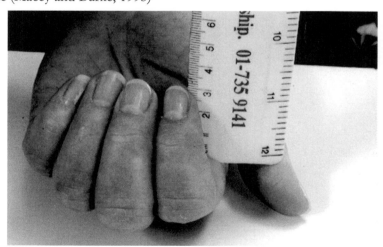

Plate 7.2 Using a ruler to measure composite flexion

Reliability

Ellis and Bruton (2000) compared goniometry with composite finger flexion measurement. Fifty-one therapists assessed three fingers of a normal subject using a standardised protocol. Results showed intra-rater variability was greater than for goniometry, but the two methods had equal inter-rater reliability. These results indicate that composite finger flexion has a place in the assessment of multiple joint problems or where goniometry is impracticable. Composite finger flexion measurements are not interchangeable with total finger flexion measured (MacDermid *et al*, 2001).

Span

A vital part of function is the ability to stretch out the fingers to enable a grasp to be taken on objects of various sizes and to manipulate them. To do this the two transverse arches, the oblique arch and the five longitudinal arches of the hand (Tubiana *et al*, 1996), flatten and reform. This involves movement at the carpal, CMC joints, extension and abduction at the MCP joints and extension of the IP joints. It is a complex activity, occurring in three dimensions.

When to test

- it is useful to measure when there is an apparent loss of span, either for the whole hand or abduction of individual fingers
- where passive movements are full, but function appears to be affected
- the patient has a condition where it can reasonably be expected to affect span (e.g. rheumatoid arthritis)
- the patient reports difficulty with function, e.g. they are unable to hold large objects such as a jam jar.

Measurement using a ruler is in widespread use and has been recommended over a considerable period of time (Boscheinen-Morrin *et al*, 1987; Salter, 1987; Bexon and Salter, 2000; Boscheinen-Morrin and Conolly, 2001). It has the following advantages:

- it is quick
- no special equipment is required
- a variety of measures can be taken (thumb to little finger, thumb to index finger, index finger to little finger and the distance between each finger)
- results provide comprehensible feedback to the patient on progress (Ellis and Bruton, 1998)

These have to weighed against the disadvantages, which are:

- reliability is poor or unknown
- the artificiality of the testing position

- the lack of standardised starting position. Bexon and Salter (2000) recommend measuring span on the palmar surface; however, the dorsal method has been selected here, as measuring points can be more easily identified

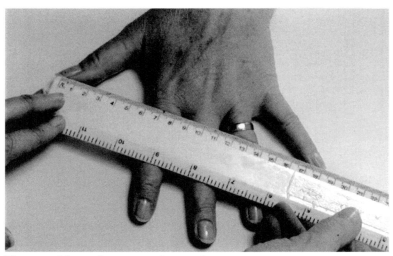

Plate 7.3: Measuring span using a ruler

- there is no standardised tool; a tape measure or ruler have been used. A ruler is preferred, as tape measures may stretch and are calibrated less consistently than a ruler (Heck *et al*, 1999).

How to test (thumb to little finger)

- gather equipment needed—ruler, paper or chart, and pen
- sit opposite the patient at a narrow table
- ask the patient to place the pronated hand and forearm on the table (so that the wrist is in neutral) with the IP joints of the fingers and thumb extended
- ask the patient to stretch the thumb and fingers as far apart as possible
- place the ruler across the top of the fingers, lining up the zero with the medial nail bed of the thumb (i.e. the point where the white of the nail begins). This point is discernible in nail biters. Measure diagonally to the lateral nail bed of the little finger, across the top of the fingers
- measure the distance in millimetres and record it.

Other measures can be taken using exactly the same method, but altering the measurement points:

- thumb to index finger—the medial thumb nail bed to the lateral nail bed of the index finger. This can be used to quickly measure radial abduction of the thumb.
- index to little finger—the medial nail bed of the index finger to the lateral nail bed of the little finger
- abduction of the MCP finger joints—the distance between fingers is measured using adjacent nail beds (Adams *et al*, 1992).

Recording

It is important to specify the span measured, the tool used, the measuring points and if the hand is pronated or supinated. This will ensure subsequent measures are made in the same way. When using pre-printed forms it is recommended that there is a space to record span when appropriate (Robins, 1986).

Reliability

Heck *et al* (1999) found this method unacceptable, measuring thumb to little finger showing intra-rater limits of agreement of -4.95–7.29 on one tester and -49.46–79.46 on another. Inter-rater reliability was also unacceptable with limits of agreement of -52.49–39.39. It has been argued that, by placing the hand flat on a table and fixing a digit, passive movement can occur. The position of the wrist cannot be controlled in the unsupported hand and this can affect span. Simpson (2000), measuring thumb to little finger on the right hand of 50 normal subjects, demonstrated a significant difference between the two positions, with a lower incidence of variability when the hand was supported ($p<0.001$). This study noted that there was variability in the normal of +/- 16 millimetres and, therefore, any significant clinical change must exceed 16 millimetres.

No normative values exist for this method; therefore, the results should either be compared with the opposite hand or with subsequent measures. There is scope for further research on measuring span to establish its usefulness as a measure.

Interpretation of findings

When the range of movement measurements are complete, consider possible causes for the pattern of results; a subjective assessment is needed to compliment and interpret objective findings. It may be that range is limited by swelling or pain, in which case active and passive movements are likely to be equal. Differences between active and passive movements should be investigated. If passive movement exceeds active movement, this may reflect weakness or a disruption of the tendon gliding mechanism. The latter may be identified if adjacent joints are placed so that the tendons are not stretched and the passive range of movement of the joint becomes equal to active range. Differences between isolated and composite movements can indicate tendon shortening or tethering. If passive range is less than active, results should be checked.

It is also important to establish if loss of range is due to extrinsic or intrinsic tightness (see *Chapter14*). A deficiency of span may be due to loss of joint range, loss of length or active muscle power (in the abductors of the thumb and little finger and the dorsal interosseus muscles), loss of skin elasticity or restricted by oedema. Further tests are needed to ascertain the causes and effects on function of findings.

To summarise

- avoid visual estimation if possible
- select the most appropriate tool and system for your purposes and patient
- be consistent in all recording and subsequent measures
- compare with the unaffected hand if possible.

References

Adams LS, Greene LW, Topoozian E (1992) *Range of Motion in Clinical Assessment Recommendations*, 2nd edn. American Society of Hand Therapists, Chicago

Beresford K (1993) Odstock wire tracings—introduction. *Br J Hand Ther* 1(6):10

Bexon C (1993) Odstock wire tracings. The correct method. *Br J Hand Ther* 1(6): 10–12

Bexon C, Salter M (2000) Assessment. In: Salter M, Cheshire L, eds. *Hand Therapy Principles and Practice*. Butterworth-Heinemann, Oxford; 51–57

Boscheinen-Morrin J, Conolly WB (2001) *The Hand Fundamentals of Therapy*. Butterworth-Heinemann, Oxford

Boscheinen-Morrin J, Davey V, Conolly WB (1987) *The Hand Fundamentals of Hand Therapy*. Butterworths, Sevenoaks: 8

Bücher C (2003) A survey of current hand assessment practice in the UK. *Br J Hand Therapy* 8(3): 102–109

Burr N, Pratt A, Stott D (2003) Inter-rater and intra-rater reliability when measuring interphalangeal joints. *Physiotherapy* 89(11): 641–51

Chiu H-Y (1995) A method of two dimensional measurement for evaluating finger motion impairment. *J Hand Surg* 20B(5): 691–95

Ellis B, Bruton A (2000) A study to compare the intra and inter-rater reliability of composite finger flexion measurement with goniometry. *Br J Hand Ther* 5(4): 122

Ellis B, Bruton A (1998) Clinical assessment of the hand—A review of joint angle measures. *Br J Hand Ther* 3(2): 5–8

Ellis B, Bruton A, Goddard J (1997) Joint angle measurement: A comparative study of the reliability of goniometry and wire tracing for the hand. *Clinical Rehab* 11(4): 314–20

Glanville H (1964) Objective treatment of hand injuries: A new method of measurement. *Ann Physical Med* vii(8): 304–6

Hage JJ, de Groot PJM (1996) Letters to the editor. *J Hand Surg* 21B(4): 564–5

Heck H, Simpson CS, Murray K, Smith J, Alcock S, Fathmann M (1999) HATS Evaluation Study Workpackage 13. Staffordshire University, Staffs

Macey AC, Burke FD (1995) Outcomes of hand surgery. *J Hand Surg* **20B**(6): 841–55

MacDermid JC, Fox E, Richards RS, Roth JH (2001) Validity of pulp-to-palm distance as a measure of finger flexion. *J Hand Surg* (British and European) **26B**(5): 432–35

Murray K, Topping M, Simpson C (2000) Investigation of the hand assessment techniques used within the United Kingdom. *Br J Hand Ther* **5**(4): 125

Roberts C (1989) The Odstock hand assessment. *Br J Occ Ther* **52**(7): 256–61

Robins RHC (1986) Hand assessment charts. *J Hand Surg* **11B**(2): 287–98

Salter MI (1987) *Hand Injuries: A Therapeutic Approach*. Churchill Livingstone, Edinburgh: 24–29

Salter N (1955) Methods of measurement of muscle and joint function. *J Bone Joint Surg* **37B**(3): 474–90

Simpson C. (2000) Measure for measure. *Br J Hand Therapists* **5**(4): 122

Tubiana R, Thomine J-M, Mackin E (1996) *Examination of the Hand and Wrist*. Martin Dunitz, London: 7–21;168–9 325–6

Chapter 8
Grip strength

Isometric grip strength is generally regarded as the best indication of upper limb health (Skelton *et al*, 1994); in the clinical setting it is usual to measure maximum grip, not how long grip is sustained. This chapter considers the uses and indications for testing, the background, and describes three methods of measuring grip strength.

Uses

Grip strength can be used:

- to evaluate the sensorimotor status of the upper limb
- to evaluate the progress of disease or outcome of treatment. It is particularly useful following carpal tunnel release and healed wrist fractures
- as part of general fitness studies, for example it forms part the armed forces' fitness test
- where symptoms may be vague or there are complaints of weakness or pain; for example, it can be used to indicate internal wrist pathology, which can be confirmed by diagnostic testing (Czitrom and Lister, 1988; Cooney, 1994). Grip strength will be reduced in osteoarthritis (Labi *et al*, 1982)
- to predict functional outcome following stroke (Sunderland *et al*, 1989).

When not to test grip strength

Do not test grip strength:

- until 12 weeks after tendon repair. Active remodelling continues for 12–16 weeks post surgery (Smith, 1992). Although it is unusual for tendon repairs to fail after nine weeks post surgery (Harris *et al*, 1999), it is inadvisable to demand maximum effort before the 12-week stage is reached
- where tissue healing is incomplete and a demand would cause damage or pain, e.g. unhealed finger fractures or skin grafts
- if effort increases pain to levels unacceptable to the patient
- to monitor disease activity in rheumatoid arthritis, as grip strength has been shown to be a poor indicator of this (Deodhar *et al*, 1973; Spiegel *et al*, 1987; Dixon *et al*, 1988)

- if the patient must wear a glove, as this will affect results (Rock *et al*, 2001).

Background

The first hand grip dynamometer is believed to have been developed by Regnier in 1807 (Salter, 1955). This dynamometer was an oval spring type and was subsequently refined. Measuring strength against a spring, either by compression or extension, involves increased resistance towards the end of range of movement. In 1875, Hamilton designed a rubber bulb which, when compressed, caused coloured liquid to rise in a tube (Salter, 1955). Fox (1917) described the 'Dynamographic Pear', developed by Professor Amar, to measure 'the very slightest movement of a paralysed hand day by day, or week by week'. The device was an india-rubber ball connected to an air chamber. Pressure exerted on the air when the ball was squeezed, pressed on water in a U-tube causing a float to rise. Further development has continued and there are now over 22 different devices for testing grip strength.

There are three main types used in clinical practice; these are the hydraulic dynamometers (Jamar/Baseline), Martin Vigorimeter and the sphygmomanometer. Each method has its place depending on the aims of the assessment and the patient.

The hydraulic dynamometer

The hydraulic dynamometer is the most common and reliable method used to measure grip strength (Mathiowetz *et al*, 1984;1985; Hamilton *et al*, 1994). The Jamar was first described by Bechtol (1954) and measures maximum voluntary contraction in a transverse volar grasp. The Jamar dynamometer (Asimov Engineering) has five grasp settings, set at 1.0, 1.5, 2.0, 2.5 and 3 inch spacings (Hamilton, 1994), and is the method for assessing grip strength recommended by the American Society of Hand Therapists (Fess, 1992) and the American Society for Surgery of the Hand (1990).

Uses

This method is best used for adult hands, especially those with grip strength of at least 80 pounds. It should be used where there is no inflammation of the PIP or MCP joints and where large changes can be expected.

Before testing

- assemble equipment needed—a straight-backed chair 46 centimetres high with no arms, dynamometer, paper/chart and pen

- always use the same dynamometer (Mathiowetz *et al*, 1985). In departments where there are more than one, each dynamometer should be numbered

- dynamometers should be calibrated regularly by placing a known weight on them (Bohannon, 1991). Calibration should be done on each handle setting using weights from 5 kilograms to 55 kilograms in 5 kilogram increments (Fess, 1987; 1992). It may be necessary to return the dynamometer to the makers for recalibration if there is an unacceptable inaccuracy (i.e. the dynamometer does not consistently measure the known amount)

- if the dynamometer appears to have a smell or feels sticky, this is probably a sign that the hydraulic system is leaking. This will substantially affect results and the dynamometer should be returned to the manufacturer

- always handle the dynamometer with care. If it is dropped it can be seriously damaged and will need to be returned to the manufacturer for repair/recalibration. Always ensure that it is kept in the carrying case and that the catch is secure

- check that the pointer and the red peak hold indicator are at zero before testing. The peak hold indicator can be returned to zero by turning the central knob on the dial, anticlockwise. If the pointer is above the zero mark, this can be corrected by pulling on the sprung palm piece, i.e. apply force in the opposite direction to that applied to grip

- choose the grasp setting(s) to be used. The second setting gives maximal contraction (Firrell, 1996), as there is full function of profundus, superficialis and interossoeus muscles. The fifth position (widest) uses mostly the profundus muscles. The first position (narrowest) uses the profundus and superficialis through maximum length and adds little to grip strength (Stokes, 1983). Furthermore, it shows the lowest test-retest reliability (Hamilton, 1994). The choice of setting(s) will depend on the nature of the injury and the size of the hand

- test the unaffected hand first or, in bilateral problems, the dominant hand.

Positioning the patient

Seat the patient in a straight backed chair (46 centimetres high with no arms) with the shoulder adducted and neutrally rotated, elbow flexed at 90°, the forearm in a neutral position, the wrist between 0° and 30° extension and between 0° and 15° ulnar deviation. Lightly hold the readout dial and place a supporting hand under the dynamometer to prevent it being dropped inadvertently; the dynamometer weighs 22.6 ounces/638 grams and may be difficult for patients to hold (Mathiowetz *et al*, 1984;1985; 1985A; Fess, 1992).

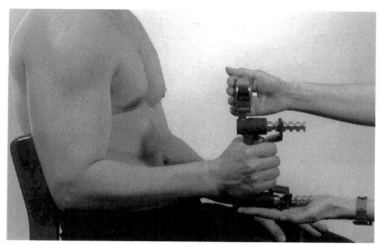

Plate 8.1: The hydraulic dynamometer in use

How to test

- explain the purpose of the test to the patient

- give the patient the following instructions, 'I want you to hold the handle like this and squeeze as hard as you can'

- demonstrate and then give the dynamometer to the patient, positioned as described above

- ask 'Are you ready? Squeeze as hard as you can'. As the patient begins to squeeze, say 'Harder! …Harder…Relax'. Record the score

- repeat three times on each hand, and calculate the mean

- take the reading from the peak hold indicator needle and return to zero between each attempt

- a short, sub maximal rehearsal, used as warm up, has been shown to give a higher reading for maximum grip (Rodger and Neibuhr, 1992)

- take subsequent readings at a consistent point of the assessment/treatment session, e.g. always measure on arrival or on completing the session.

Recording

The following information should be recorded: date and time of the test, the dynamometer used, each reading for each hand, and the mean. Where the patient is unable to achieve the starting position, this should be noted. The measurement can be taken in pounds or kilograms, the choice is a matter of preference, but should be consistently used and be recorded unambiguously.

Interpretation

Data collected in exactly this method can be compared with the published norm values for these tests. Those produced by Mathiowetz *et al* (1985) used the Jamar on an American population. The manufacturer (Fabrication Enterprises Incorporated) of the Baseline dynamometer state that results can be regarded as equivalent to the Jamar (Mathiowetz, 1995). Mathiowetz (1985) did not use a warm up period; therefore, when comparing results with norms, do not incorporate a warm up period.

Gilbertson and Barber-Lomax (1994) have produced norm values for the second setting of the dynamometer in the United Kingdom; however, results

Table 8.1: A method of recording grip strength

Date	Dyn No	Right Hand = Dominant			Mean Rt	Left Hand			Mean Lt
		Test 1	Test 2	Test 3		Test 1	Test 2	Test 3	
1/1/00 10.00	3 Setting 2	35 lbs	40 lbs	35 lbs	36.6 lbs	70 lbs	75 lbs	75 lbs	73.3 lbs

should always be compared with norm values for the appropriate handle setting, carried out with correctly calibrated dynamometers. Normative values exist for children aged 6–19 years (Mathiowetz *et al*, 1985B). It is useful to compare with the value for contra lateral hand or earlier values for the hand. The choice of comparator will depend on the reason for the assessment.

Variables affecting grip strength include: time of day, sex, age, hand size, hand dominance, motivation, intramuscular temperature, and upper limb position (Desrosiers *et al*, 1995). Physical activity from occupation and leisure activities will also affect grip strength (Harth and Wetter, 1994) and these factors should be borne in mind when evaluating results.

Reliability

There are many good reports of reliability. When correctly calibrated, it has a minimum selection criteria of +0.9994 correlation coefficient (Fess, 1992). Mathiowetz *et al* (1984) report a significant correlation co-efficient of 0.97 or above for inter-rater reliability and correlation coefficient of 0.85 for test-retest reliability. MacDermid *et al* (1994) have demonstrated almost perfect levels of inter-rater reliability; testing 38 patients with cumulative trauma disorder, they conclude that grip strength tests by different therapists can be regarded as inter-changeable. This is particularly important in clinical practice where it is not always possible for the same therapist to assess on every occasion.

Ng and Fan (2001), testing 30 healthy subjects on the Jamar with the elbow at 0°, 30°, 60°, 90°and 120° flexion, at sessions one week apart, demonstrated that 90° flexion was the position of choice. Very little difference in grip was demonstrated between 0° and 90°, but results taken at 120° showed a significant decrease ($p < 0.001$). This study also confirmed that the test is reproducible when a standard protocol is followed.

Sincerity

As this test involves maximal effort from patients it is not fully objective, and occasionally clinicians may feel that a low effort is being made. If this occurs, then further tests can be made. This could be particularly useful in assessing for legal or insurance purposes. However, before proceeding with sincerity testing, it is wise to ensure that this meets professional and workplace guidelines on informed consent. Sincerity testing involves many repetitions and, therefore, may not be possible in conditions such as carpal tunnel syndrome and tendinitis, where symptoms can be aggravated. Two methods have been described, both of which are reported to help detect when a maximal voluntary effort was not made.

Five grip analysis

This analysis is sometimes known as the five-rung test. The patient is tested with the dynamometer used as described above on each of the five handle settings, starting first with the unaffected hand. The scores are then plotted on a graph. A normal hand should show a slightly skewed, bell-shaped curve (see *Figure 8.1a*). The patient who is exerting maximum effort and has a weakness of grip will demonstrate a diminished bell-shaped curve. The patient making a low effort will show a flat line (Stokes *et al*, 1995) (see *Figure 8.1b*).

Figure 8.1a Normal Curve

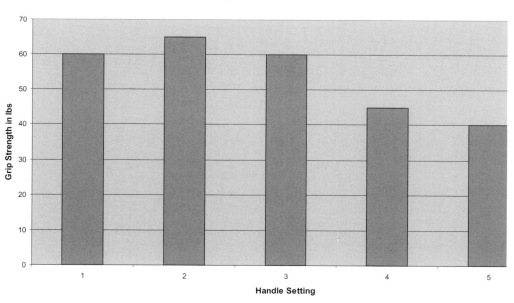

It has been shown that genuinely weak patients will produce a flattened curve and, therefore, this method must be treated with caution when used in isolation (Hamilton, 1994).

Rapid exchange grip

A scribe is needed to record the scores. The dynamometer is set on the handle position where the maximum static score was achieved. The dynamometer is

Figure 8.1b Low Effort Curve

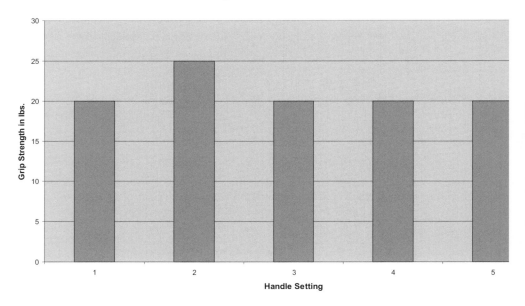

held by the tester as near as possible to the recommended position in the midline of the patient. A metronome is set to a rate of 1.5 seconds. The patient is asked to grip as hard as possible using alternate hands until told to stop. The patient should practice touching, but not squeezing the dynamometer until the rhythm is established. The sequence is repeated, squeezing five times on each hand, starting on the right (Taylor and Shechtman, 2000).

Results from the rapid exchange grip must be compared with static grip. However, there is no recommended method of doing this, either comparing with five rung test or the maximal static grip test (Shechtman and Taylor, 2000).

Hildreth *et al* (1989) compare the peak rapid exchange grip with the peak score on the five rung test. If the rapid exchange grip is the greater, the test is positive and it is deemed that the patient is making insincere efforts. Stokes *et al* (1995) also compared these two tests and calculated a critical range for the test to be positive. If the difference between the peak score on the five rung test and the peak score on the rapid exchange grip is more than 12 pounds (5.45 kilograms), it is deemed positive, and a low effort is being made.

Shechtman and Taylor (2000) point out that Hildreth *et al* have a narrow criteria that could give a false negative, where an insincere patient is regarded as sincere. This could result in unnecessary treatment and a frustrated therapist as the patient fails to recover. Conversely, the method used by Stokes *et al* could give a false positive, where a sincere patient is labelled insincere. This could result in the patient not receiving necessary treatment.

This issue is very significant in the United States of America, where Worker's Compensation calculation involves grip strength. In the United Kingdom it has less significance, but occasionally patients may feign weakness. Research on this topic has not been thorough as researchers have used different protocols (Shechtman and Taylor, 2002). Until further work is completed, it cannot be regarded as hard evidence. However, this method does give an indication of sincerity, especially if viewed in the context of other abnormal clinical findings. Accusations of insincerity are not to be made lightly, and the therapist must eliminate measuring faults and ensure that every effort has been made to motivate the patient to maximal effort.

Another commonly used method of judging sincerity is to use the coefficient of variation (CV).

$$\textit{The Coefficient of Variation}\,[CV\,]=[\,\textit{Standard}\,\frac{\textit{Deviation}}{\textit{Average}}\,\textit{of at least 3 trials}\,]\times 100$$

Box 8.1: Calculation of the coefficient of variation

The higher the coefficient of variation, the greater the variability and the smaller the consistency. This method is not suitable for determining sincerity, as injured patients with compromised hand strength may have inflated coefficient of variation values (Shechtman, 2000).

The Martin Vigorimeter

The Martin Vigorimeter measures grip strength in terms of air pressure, i.e. the intensity of force over a specific area. It measures spherical grip, a precision grasp that is capable of being powerful, but allows for object manipulation (Napier, 1956). The equipment consists of three graded rubber bulbs attached by a rubber tube to a manometer, which measures grip strength in kilopounds per square centimetre. It has the advantage of being very light (6 ounces) but, due to its rubber composition, it can perish over time, unlike the hydraulic dynamometer.

Uses

This method is best used for children, whose hands are too small to use the dynamometer optimally or comfortably or where spherical grip is needed (Robertson and Deitz, 1988. Link *et al* 1995). Elderly patients have expressed a preference for the vigorimeter, finding it more comfortable (Desrosiers *et al*, 1995). As the vigorimeter measures pressure, i.e. the force applied over a particular area, the growth of the hand in small children could affect the results if monitored over a prolonged period (Richards and Palmiter-Thomas, 1996).

Plate 8.2: Martin vigorimeter in use

The vigorimeter measures smaller increments than the hydraulic dynamometer. This can be useful when small changes are anticipated; however, the dial lacks the clarity of the hydraulic dynamometers.

How to test

- assemble equipment needed—straight-backed chair, vigorimeter, paper/chart and pen
- seat the patient in the chair, with feet firmly on the floor, with the shoulder adducted and neutrally rotated, the elbow flexed at 90°, the forearm in a neutral position, the wrist between 0° and 30° extension and between 0° and 15° ulnar deviation
- ensure that the red needle is at zero
- place the bulb in the patient's hand, with the tube extending out between the thumb and index finger. Allow the hand to rest on a table
- instruct the patient to 'Squeeze the ball as hard as you can. Harder! Harder! Let go! Good Job!' (Link *et al*, 1995)
- return the red needle to zero
- three readings are taken on alternate hands, and the mean for each calculated.

Reliability

Although some authors have found excellent test-retest and inter-rater reliability, this is not universally the case. High correlation coefficients can be seen between values for the Jamar (0.89) and the Martin Vigorimeter (0.90) (Desrosiers *et al*, 1995). It has been argued that this is a misleading method of comparing statistics (Bland and Altman, 1986). The vigorimeter and dynamometer cannot be regarded as interchangeable as they measure different types of grasp and different things, i.e. force and pressure. Norms exist for children as young as three years (Link *et al*, 1995) and adults (Thorngren and Werner, 1979; Desrosiers *et al*, 1995).

The sphygmomanometer

A sphygmomanometer, or blood pressure measuring device, is generally available in most clinical settings and can be easily adapted to measure grip pressure. It has the advantage that it is light for the patient to hold.

Uses

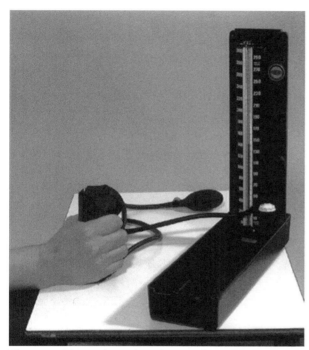

Plate 8.3: Measuring grip using a sphygmomanometer

This method is frequently recommended for patients with rheumatoid arthritis as it is softer for them to grip and, therefore, less painful, particularly where there is inflammation of the MCP or IP joints (Melvin, 1989). Furthermore, those with severe hand deformities cannot achieve the starting position for the hydraulic dynamometer (Richards and Palmiter-Thomas, 1996). It has been used primarily for this purpose (Deodhar *et al*, 1973; Spiegel *et al*, 1987; Dixon *et al*, 1988; Roberts, 1989). However, despite its softness, it is not the automatic choice of this group of patients (Helliwell *et al*, 1987).

The size of the scale limits it to 300 millimetres of mercury, so it can only be used for grips of under 70lbs. It is useful where small changes are expected, as the gradations are smaller than the hydraulic dynamometer (Richards and Palmiter-Thomas, 1996). Like the vigorimeter, it measures pressure rather than force, so hands of different sizes and the same strength will have different scores (Bohannon, 1991; Richards and Palmiter-Thomas, 1996). Furthermore, air is not an ideal medium for transmitting pressure due to its compressibility (Bohannon, 1991).

If selecting this method, ensure the sphygmomanometer has been internally cleaned and calibrated.

How to test

- collect equipment needed—sphygmomanometer, small bag/tape, paper/chart and pen
- roll up the cloth cuff and secure it by stitching, taping or placing in a bag, so that when inflated to its starting point an even circumference is maintained. An inflation pressure of 20–40 millimetres of mercury and 13–20 centimetres in circumference (Melvin, 1989; Bohannon, 1991; Richards and Palmiter-Thomas, 1996).

- seat the patient with the forearm and hand unsupported and neutrally rotated
- inflate the sphygmomanometer to its starting point
- ask the patient to grip the cuff as hard as possible, and repeat this on alternate hands three times. Ensure that the mercury is returned to the starting point each time
- take the mean of the three trials (Melvin, 1989)
- the patient may or may not be allowed to see the score, depending on the purpose of the test; therefore, the choice must be consistent (Melvin, 1989).

Reliability

Information on reliability is conflicting (Richards and Palmiter-Thomas, 1996); however, as many different forms of testing and modification exist, this is not surprising. Furthermore, temperature can affect air compressibility. Nevertheless, this method can be useful in certain clinical settings. Results are not interchangeable with the vigorimeter or the hydraulic dynamometer.

The next step

When this part of the assessment is complete, the therapist will have an accurate measure of grip strength, should have formed an impression of the cause of weakness, and be in a position to consider means of strengthening grip if necessary or appropriate.

To summarise

- decide what is the purpose of testing grip strength
- pick a method suitable for that purpose and the patient
- always use the same method and equipment
- always follow the protocol or note any deviations.

References

American Society for Surgery to The Hand (1990) *The Hand Examination and Diagnosis*, 3rd edn. Churchill Livingstone, Edinburgh: 9;13; 45–46

Bechtol CD (1954) Grip test: use of a dynamometer with adjustable spacing. *J Bone Joint Surg* **36A**(4): 820–24; 835

Bland MJ, Altman DG (1986) Statistical methods for assessing agreement between methods of clinical measurement. *Lancet* **i**: 307–10

Bohannon R (1991) Hand grip dynamometers: Issues relevant to application. *J Hum Muscle Perf* **1**(2): 16–36

Cooney WP (1994) Hand strength: Normative values. Letter. *J Hand Surg* **20**(6): 1057–8

Czitrom AA, Lister GD (1988) Measurement of grip strength in the diagnosis of wrist pain. *J Hand Surg* **13A**(1): 16–18

Deodhar SD, Dick WC, Hodgkinson R, Buchanan WW (1973) Measurement of clinical response to anti-inflammatory drug therapy in rheumatoid arthritis. *Q J Med* New Series **XLII**(166) 387–401

Desrosiers J, Hébert R, Bravo G, Dutil É (1995) Comparison of the Jamar Dynamometer and the Martin Vigorimeter for grip strength measurements in a healthy elderly population. *Scand J Rehab Med* **27**: 137–43

Dixon JS, Hayes S, Constable PDL, Bird HA (1988) What are the 'best' measurements for monitoring patients during short-term second line therapy? *Br J Rheumatol* **27**: 37–43

Fess EE (1992) *Grip Strength In Clinical Assessment Recommendations*, 2nd edn. American Society of Hand Therapists, Philadelphia: 41–5

Fess EE (1987) A Method for checking Jamar dynamometer calibration. *J Hand Ther* **Oct–Dec**: 28–32

Firrell JC (1996) Which setting of the dynamometer provides maximal grip strength. *J Hand Surg* **21A**: 397–401

Fox RF (1917) Demonstration of the mensuration apparatus in use at the Red Cross Clinic for the physical treatment of officers, Great Portland Street, London, W. *Proc R Soc Med* **10**: 63–9

Gilbertson L, Barber-Lomax S (1994) Power and pinch grip strength recorded using the hand held Jamar dynamometer and B&L hydraulic pinch gauge. British normative data for adults. *Br J Occup Ther* **57**(12): 483–8

Hamilton A, Balnave R, Adams R, (1994) Grip strength testing reliability. *J Hand Ther* **7**: 163–70

Harris S, Harris D, Foster A, Elliot D (1999) The aetiology of the acute rupture of flexor tendons in zones 1 and 2 during early mobilisation. *J Hand Ther* **24B**(3): 275–80

Harth A, Vetter WR (1994) Grip and pinch strength among selected occupational groups. *Occup Ther Int* **1**: 13–28

Helliwell P, Howe A, Wright V (1987) Functional assessment of the hand: Reproducibility, acceptability, and utility of a new system for measuring strength. *Ann Rheumat Dis* **46**: 203–8

Hildreth D, Lister GD (1989) Detection of submaximal effort by the use of the rapid exchange grip. *J Hand Surg* **14A**: 742–45

Labi MLC, Gresham GE, Rathey UK (1982) Hand function in osteo-arthritis. *Arch Physic Med Rehab* **63**: 438–40

Link L, Lukens S, Bush M (1995) Spherical grip strength in children 3 to 6 years of age. *Am J Occup Ther* **49**(4): 318–26

MacDermid JC, Kramer JF, Woodbury MG, McFarlane RM, Roth JH (1994) Interrater reliability of pinch and grip strength measurements in patients with cumulative trauma disorders. *J Hand Ther* **Jan–Mar**: 10–14

Mathiowetz V (1995) Letter to Fabrication Enterprises Incorporated

Mathiowetz V, Kashman N, Volland G, Weber K, Dowe M, Rogers S (1985) Grip and pinch strength: normative data for adults. *Arch Physic Med Rehab* **66**: 69–74

Mathiowetz V, Rennells C, Donahoe L (1985A) Effect of elbow position on grip and key pinch strength. *J Hand Surg* **10A**: 694–97

Mathiowetz V, Wiemer DM, Federman SM (1985B) Grip and pinch strength norms for 6- to 19-year-olds. *Am J Occup Ther* **40**(10): 705–11

Mathiowetz V, Weber K, Volland G, Kashman N (1984) Reliability and validity of grip and pinch strength evaluations. *J Hand Surg* **9A**: 222–26

Melvin J (1989) *Rheumatic Disease in the Adult and Child: Occupational Therapy and Rehabilitation*. 3rd edn. FA Davis Company, Philadelphia: 352–55

Napier JR (1956) The prehensile movements of the normal hand. *J Bone Joint Surg* **38B**(4): 902–13

Ng GYF, Fan ACC (2001) Does elbow position affect strength and reproducibility of power grip measurements. *Physiotherapy* **87**(2): 68–72

Roberts C (1989) The Odstock hand assessment. *Br J Occup Ther* **52**(7): 256–61

Robertson A, Deitz J (1988) A description of grip strength in preschool children. *Am J Occup Ther* **42**(10): 647–52

Rodger M, Neibuhr BR (1992) Effect of warm-up prior to maximal grip contractions. *J Hand Ther* **Jul–Sept**: 143–6

Richards L, Palmiter-Thomas P (1996) Grip strength measurement: A critical review of tools, methods and clinical utility. *Crit Rev Phys Rehab Med* **8**(1&2): 87–109

Rock KM, Mikat RP, Foster C (2001) The effects of gloves on gripstrength and three-point pinch. *J Hand Therapy* **14**(4): 286–90

Salter N (1955) Methods of measurement of muscle and joint function. *J Bone Joint Surg* **37B**(3): 474–90

Shechtman O (2000) Using the coefficient of variation to detect sincerity of grip strength: A literature review. *J Hand Ther* **13**(1): 25–32

Shechtman O, Taylor C (2002) How do therapists administer the rapid exchange test? A survey. *J Hand Therapy* **15**(1): 53–61

Shechtman O, Taylor C (2000) The use of the rapid exchange grip test in detecting sincerity of effort, part II: Validity of the test. *J Hand Ther* **13**(3): 203–10

Skelton DA, Greig CA, Davies JM, Young A (1994) Strength, power and related functional ability of healthy people aged 65–89 years. *Age Ageing* **23**: 371–77

Smith K (1992) Tendon healing. In: Stanley BG, Tribuzi SM, eds. *Concepts in Hand Rehabilitation*. FA Davis, Philadelphia: 59

Spiegel JS, Paulus H, Ward N, Spiegel T, Leake B, Kane RL (1987) What are we measuring? An examination of walk time and grip strength. *J Rheumatol* **14**(1): 80–86

Stokes HM (1983) The seriously uninjured hand—weakness of grip. *J Occup Med* **25**(9): 683–4

Stokes HM, Landrieu KM, Domangue B, Kunen S (1995) Identification of low-effort patients through dynamometry. *J Hand Surg* **20A**(6): 1047–56

Sunderland A, Tinson D, Bradley L, Langton Hewer R (1989) Arm Function after stroke. An evaluation of grip strength as a measure of recovery and a prognostic indicator. *J Neurol Neurosurg Psychiatry* **52**: 1267–72

Taylor C, Shechtman O (2000) The Use of the rapid exchange grip test in detecting sincerity of effort, part I: Administration of the test. *J Hand Ther* **13**(3): 195–202

Thorngren KG, Werner CO (1979) Normal grip strength. *Acta Orothopaed Scand* **50**: 255–59

Pinch strength gives a good indication of functional strength and acknowledges the role of the thumb as arguably the most important digit.

This chapter considers the variables affecting pinch grip, describes how to measure, record and interpret data, and looks at the reliability of the method.

There is considerable debate about the terminology related to types of pinch grip and it is, therefore, important to be clear about the definition when recording. Three types of pinch grip can be tested: tip pinch grip, tripod (also known as palmar or three jaw chuck) grip and key grip or lateral pinch grip. There are several types of pinch gauge, which can be used to measure the force of these grips; however, the B&L pinch gauge (B&L Engineering) has attracted the most research and calibration accuracy has been demonstrated (Mathiowetz *et al*, 1984). Whichever gauge is selected the principles of testing remain the same, unless the manufacturer gives other instructions.

The variables are fewer than for grip strength; Young *et al* (1989) demonstrated no significant difference in the time of day, and wrist deviation has no significant effect on tip and key grip (Lamoreaux and Hoffer, 1995). Mathiowetz *et al* (1985A) have shown that elbow flexion has a significant affect on key grip. The position of the IP joint of the thumb is a crucial variable of key grip; Apfel (1986) demonstrated an increase of between 28% and 38% when the IP joint of the thumb is flexed. Gilbertson and Barber-Lomax (1994) have shown that pinch grip in women stays relatively constant until 70 years of age, after which it declines rapidly, while in men there is a more gradual decline.

When to test

- where pinch grip can reasonably be expected to be weak; for example, following a de Quervain's release or a healed fractured scaphoid
- where a problem with pinch is highlighted during functional reporting or testing.

Do not test

- where there are tendon replacements of less than 12 weeks
- in any other case where maximal effort may be contraindicated; for example, collateral ligament repairs
- if excessive pain is caused
- if the patient is unable to oppose the thumb to the first finger
- where there are inflamed MCP and IP joints of the fingers or thumb, as the maximum force exerted can cause damage (Melvin, 1989)

- if the patient must wear a glove, as this will affect results (Rock et al, 2001)
- if lack of range makes it physically impossible to exert pressure on the gauge.

Before testing

- collect equipment needed; a straight-backed chair (46 centimetres high with no arms), pinch gauge, paper/chart and pen
- always select the same pinch gauge (Mathiowetz *et al*, 1985; 1985B). In departments with multiple gauges, each one should be numbered
- calibrate the pinch gauge regularly, by suspending a known weight from the finger grooves (Mathiowetz *et al*, 1984). Return the pinch gauge to the makers for recalibration if there is an unacceptable inaccuracy (i.e. the pinch gauge does not consistently measure the known amount)
- always handle the pinch gauge with care. If it is dropped it can be damaged and will need to be returned to the manufacturer for repair/recalibration. Keep it in the manufacturer's box; it will be vulnerable to damage if put in a pocket
- check that the pointer and peak hold indicator are at zero before testing. Return the red peak hold indicator to zero by turning the central knob on the dial anticlockwise
- ask the patient which is the dominant hand and test it first
- explain to the patient the purpose of the test and what will happen.

Tip pinch grip

In this grip, the thumb pulp or pad is pinched against the pulp or pad of the index finger, and the remaining fingers are flexed (Gilbertson and Barber Lomax,1994); the movement mimics the grip needed to pick up a small object such as a piece of paper or a marble.

How to test

- seat the patient and ensure that the shoulder is adducted and neutrally rotated, elbow flexed at 90°, the forearm is in a neutral position, the wrist between 0° and 30° extension and between 0° and 15° ulnar deviation (Mathiowetz *et al*, 1984)
- place the cord loop over your own wrist to prevent inadvertent dropping
- tell the patient, 'I want you to place the tip of your thumb on this side and the tip of your index finger to make an O. Curl your other fingers in the palm as I am doing.' Demonstrate this position. Turn the opposite

end of the pinch gauge towards the patient with the narrowest side uppermost for the patient to pinch (Mathiowetz *et al*, 1984; 1985)

- check that this position is satisfactory. Ask 'Are you ready? Pinch as hard as you can.' As the patient begins to squeeze say, 'Harder!…Harder!…Relax' (Mathiowetz *et al*, 1984; 1985)

- correct the patient if the position is not maintained, for example, the thumb/index finger hyperextends or the fingers slip. Record if it is impossible to achieve the standardised position and the modified position adopted

Plate 9.1: Measuring tip pinch grip, viewed from above

- read the score on the needle side of the red readout marker and record (Mathiowetz *et al*, 1985; 1985B). Return the readout marker to zero

- repeat this sequence three times. Record each reading and the mean

- to gain an indication of the strength of each of the fingers and the thumb in each of the positions, repeat the process measuring the thumb against each finger in turn (Roberts, 1989).

Tripod pinch grip

Tripod pinch grip, or palmar pinch, is where the thumb pulp or pad is opposed to the pads or pulp of the index and middle fingers, while the remaining fingers are flexed. This grip can be used for writing.

How to test

- seat the patient with the shoulder adducted and neutrally rotated, elbow flexed at 90°, the forearm in a neutral position, the wrist between 0° and 30° extension and between 0° and 15° ulnar deviation (Mathiowetz *et al*, 1984)

- place the cord loop over your wrist to prevent inadvertent dropping

- tell the patient, 'I want you to place the tip of your thumb on this side and your first two fingers on this side as I am doing.' Demonstrate this position. Turn the opposite end of the pinch gauge towards the patient with the narrowest side uppermost for the patient to grip (Mathiowetz *et al*, 1984)

Plate 9.2: Measuring tripod pinch grip

- check the position is correct and ask, 'Are you ready? Pinch as hard as you can.' As the patient begins to squeeze say, 'Harder!...Harder!...Relax' (Mathiowetz et al, 1984; 1985)

- correct the patient if the position is not maintained. Record if it is impossible to achieve the standardised position and the modified position adopted

- read the score on the needle side of the red readout marker and record (Mathiowetz et al, 1985;1985B). Return the readout marker to zero

- repeat the sequence three times and record each reading and the mean.

Key pinch

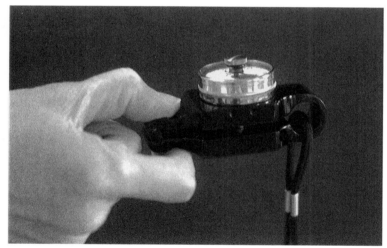

Plate 9.3: Measuring key pinch

Key pinch, or lateral pinch, occurs where the thumb pulp or pad is opposed to the lateral aspect of the PIP joint of the index finger. The remaining fingers are flexed. As its name implies, this is the position used for a door or car ignition key.

How to test

- seat the patient with the shoulder adducted and neutrally rotated, elbow flexed at 90°, the forearm in a neutral position, the wrist between 0° and 30° extension and between 0° and 15° ulnar deviation (Mathiowetz et al, 1984; 1985)

- place the cord loop over your wrist to prevent inadvertent dropping

- tell the patient, 'I want you to place your thumb on top and your index finger below as I am doing and pinch as hard as you can.' Demonstrate this position. Turn the opposite end of the pinch gauge towards the patient with the dial side uppermost for the patient to grip (Mathiowetz *et al* 1984; 1985)

- check the position and ask, 'Are you ready? Squeeze as hard as you can.' As the patient begins to squeeze say, 'Harder!…Harder!…Relax' (Mathiowetz *et al*, 1984; 1985)

- correct the patient if he/she cannot maintain the position; for example, if the thumb is extended or excessively flexed. Record if it is impossible to achieve the standardised position and the modified position adopted

- read the score on the needle side of the red readout marker and record (Mathiowetz *et al*, 1985;1985B). Return the readout marker to zero

- repeat the sequence three times and record each reading and the mean.

Recording

The following should be recorded: date and time of the test, the pinch gauge used, the grip(s) tested, each reading for each grip, hand, and the mean. Ensure the record is signed and the therapist's name printed underneath. Where the patient is unable to achieve the starting position, this should be noted. The measurement can be taken in pounds or kilograms, it is a matter of preference, but choice should be consistent and recorded unambiguously.

Table 9.1 A method of recording pinch grip

Patient Name———————————————— Patient Number————————— Sheet————

	Gauge No	Left 1	Left 2	Left 3	Mean Left	Right 1	Right 2	Right 3	Mean Right	Comment
Tip-l										
Tip-m										
Tip-r										
Tip- l										
Tripod										
Key										

Tested by Name————————————Signature———————————————— Date————

Interpretation

Norm values exist for the B&L pinch gauge with children (Mathiowetz *et al*, 1985B) and adults (Mathiowetz *et al* 1985). These were produced using an American population; however, Harth and Vetter (1994) demonstrated little difference between samples in the United States of America and Germany. Gilbertson and Barber-Lomax (1994) have produced norms for all three pinch grips in adults in the United Kingdom and these are lower than those produced by Mathiowetz *et al*. Young *et al* (1989) warn that, due to the large span of values given in the norms, they are not suitable for predicting outcomes. Scores can usefully be compared with the opposite hand and with subsequent recordings. Only results obtained using the B&L gauge can be compared with the published norm values; these are enclosed in the box when purchased. It is interesting to note that recent work on inter-instrument reliability has shown that normative data for the B&L gauge is interchangeable with two computerised pinchmeters (MacDermid *et al*, 2001).

Reliability

Inter-rater reliability on all three types of pinch grip had a correlation coefficient of 0.97 or above when tested by Mathiowetz *et al* (1984) on normal subjects, which indicates that results can be compared with those of a trained tester using the same protocol. Test-retest correlation on the mean of three trials for all types of pinch grip range from 0.812 (right tripod grip) to 0.870 (left key grip).

Validity

The B&L pinch gauge had an accuracy of +/- 1% (Mathiowetz *et al*, 1984).

The next step

When this part of the assessment is complete, the therapist will have an objective measure of the patient's pinch strength, and it is necessary to consider the following in the light of findings of other parts of the assessment:

- if the muscles of the thumb or opposing finger are weak, consider the cause and if strengthening is possible or appropriate.
- if the thumb flexes excessively on key grip, this could indicate that the 1st palmar interosseous is weak, possibly due to ulnar nerve damage. Confirm by testing for Froment's sign (see *Chapter 14*)
- if pain is preventing maximal contraction, quantify pain and select the most appropriate pain relief measure(s) available
- if the thumb CMC joint is unstable, consider appropriate splinting.

To summarise

- always be sure of which pinch grip you are testing
- always use the same gauge and method for subsequent retests
- take care of the gauge and calibrate it regularly.

References

Apfel E (1986) The Effect of thumb interphalangeal joint position on strength of key pinch. *J Hand Surg* **11A**(1): 47–51

Gilbertson L, Barber-Lomax S (1994) Power and pinch grip strength recorded using the hand held Jamar dynamometer and B&L hydraulic pinch gauge. British normative data for adults. *Br J Occup Ther* **57**(12): 483–8

Harth A, Vetter WR (1994) Grip and pinch strength among selected occupational groups. *Occup Ther Int* **1**: 13–28

Lamoreaux L, Hoffer MM (1995) The effect of wrist deviation on grip and pinch strength. *Clin Orthopaed Rel Res* **314**: 152–55

MacDermid JC, Evenhuis W, Louzon M (2001) Inter-instrument reliability of pinch strength scores. *J Hand Ther* **14**(1): 36–42

Mathiowetz V, Weber K, Volland G, Kashman N (1984) Reliability and validity of grip and pinch strength evaluations. *J Hand Surg* **9A**: 222–6

Mathiowetz V, Kashman N, Volland G, Weber K, Dowe M, Rogers S (1985) Grip and pinch strength: normative data for adults. *Arch Physic Med Rehab* **66**: 69–74

Mathiowetz V, Rennells C, Donahoe L (1985A) Effect of elbow position on grip and key pinch strength. *J Hand Surg* **10A**: 694–7

Mathiowetz V, Wiemer DM, Federman SM (1985B) Grip and pinch strength norms for 6- to 19-year-olds. *Am J Occup Ther* **40**(10): 705–11

Melvin J (1989) *Rheumatic Disease in the Adult and Child: Occupational Therapy and Rehabilitation*, 3rd edn. FA Davis Company, Philadelphia: 352–55

Roberts C (1989) The Odstock hand assessment. *Br J Occup Ther* **52**(7): 256–61

Rock KM, Mikat RP, Foster C (2001) The effects of gloves on gripstrength and three-point pinch. *J Hand Therapy* **14**(4): 286–90

Young VL, Pin P, Kraemer BA, Gould RB, Nemergut L, Pellowski M (1989) Fluctuation in grip and pinch strength among normal subjects. *J Hand Surg* **14A**: 125–9

Chapter 10
Muscle testing

'No man is an Island, entire of itself; every man is a piece of the Continent, a part of the main, if a clod be washed away by the sea, Europe is the less"

(John Donne, *Meditation* XV11).

This passage really sums up the way in which muscles work, always as part of the whole, never in isolation. If one muscle is not functioning, others working in relation to it will have diminished function.

Muscular activity is essential to movement, strength and function; therefore, it is necessary to establish if muscles are working and how effectively and efficiently this happens. This can be done in the clinical setting by manual muscle testing. The principle of manual muscle testing is that individual muscles (or muscle groups) are tested to ascertain if they are contracting voluntarily and, if so, whether they are able to work against gravity and a manually applied resistance. Brandsma *et al* (1995) recommend the use of the title 'movement testing', however, the term 'manual muscle testing' sums up the therapist's actions and is used here.

This chapter looks at the background to testing, indications for testing, principles of testing, how to test and record individual muscles and the assessment of muscle tone.

Background

The origins of manual muscle testing, using five grades and gravity, lie in the United States following the poliomyelitis epidemics in the early twentieth century. Dr Robert Lovett (1916) is credited as the originator of manual muscle testing (Salter, 1955; Lacôte *et al*, 1987). It should be noted that Lovett states in the foreword of his book that he is indebted to the senior assistant in his private practice, Wilhelmine Wright, who had 'devoted practically her whole time to this department of physical therapeutics—formulating for me the exercise tests', (Lovett, 1916). In her paper, Wright (1912) defined five classes of strength and gave directions for progressive exercise and testing. Her paper demonstrated that testing was an integral part of the treatment, not a separate entity.

The advantages of this method are that no specialised equipment is required, it is quick to administer as part of the treatment programme, and is relatively simple to score, while providing valuable information on the tissues. Its prime disadvantage is that, at grade 5 level, a manual worker or sportsman will easily cope with the maximum resistance offered by a therapist, but may not be strong enough to resume his or her normal activities. Furthermore, it can be very difficult to standardise the resistance given, and it lacks the sensitivity of more sophisticated methods, such as a myometer (Herbison *et al*, 1996). If not as sensitive, it is an intensely practical guide, as any grade less than a full contraction against gravity, with the ability to hold at the end of range, must affect function. It is argued that this method is largely subjective (Salter, 1955), open to error, and it is difficult to distinguish between the different grades (Oldham *et al*, 1992). However, skill can be developed. The therapist requires experience testing normal subjects and patients of all ages, a thorough knowledge of anatomy, and an awareness of trick movements to carry out manual muscle testing well (Kendall, 1991).

Several scales have been devised in attempts to grade muscles more finely. Shultis-Keirnan (1992) points out that no one method has been proven to be superior to other methods; therefore, those proposed by the Medical Research Council (1943) are probably the simplest to use (see *Box 10.1*).

Departments should have a testing protocol defining the grade, or the record must include an explanatory key. This ensures that like is compared with like.

Grade 0	No contraction
Grade 1	Flicker or trace of a contraction
Grade 2	Active movement, with gravity eliminated
Grade 3	Active movement against gravity
Grade 4	Active movement against gravity and resistance
Grade 5	Normal power

Box 10.1 Medical Research Council (1943) manual muscle testing scale

When to test

Manual muscle testing can be used to identify muscles not working, or working sub-maximally, to assess nerve function. It is also useful in the differential diagnosis of peripheral nerve lesions (Brandsma *et al*, 1995); for example, it can be used to distinguish between type 3 and 4 low ulnar palsy (Brandsma, 1995) and to monitor nerve regeneration (Boscheinen-Morrin *et al*, 1987; Brandsma 1995; Brandsma and Schreuders, 2001). It can also be used to identify and monitor myopathies and neuropathies, particularly entrapment neuropathies, which may have an origin proximal to the hand, and it has been extensively used for assessment in poliomyelitis and leprosy, (Brandsma *et al*, 1995). Other applications for use include: Guillain-Barré syndrome, quadriplegia (Shultis-Keirnan,1992), muscular dystrophy (Kilmer *et al*, 1993), to give data on individual patients that can be compiled for research purposes and give information on the pattern of disease (Kilmer *et al*, 1993), to evaluate potential muscles for tendon transfer preoperatively (Boscheinen-Morrin *et al*, 1987), and assess success postoperatively (Shultis-Keirnan,1992).

It can be a useful tool to distinguish between loss of muscle function following spontaneous or traumatic tendon rupture, which may have been missed by other clinicians, or gross weakness following immobility. A good example of this is flexor pollicis longus, which may be ruptured when the lower third of the forearm is fractured. However, following a period of immobility, it may be so weak that it can only contract with gravity counterbalanced. Correct identification of the problem at the outset of therapy is helpful to all involved.

It is rarely necessary to test all the muscles of the hand and arm; a selection should be carefully made depending on the patient's condition and muscle innervations. Brandsma and Schreuders (2001) are a selection of tests for the intrinsic muscles of the hand.

When not to test

Testing should not be carried out:

- if active movement is contra-indicated (e.g. immediately following a secondary tendon repair)
- if resisted movement only is contraindicated, the muscle should be tested only with gravity counterbalanced (Shultis-Keirnan,1992)
- if spasticity is present. The muscles are working hard, but involuntarily (Shultis-Keirnan,1992), invalidating the test. In these circumstances, a test of spasticity should be used (See muscle tone below)
- if the patient is unable or unwilling to co-operate fully (Shultis-Keirnan,1992), or follow the detailed instructions, testing is pointless
- if the patient is cold. The Medical Research Council (1943) recommended that when testing power and sensation, the patient must be thoroughly warm for 15–30 minutes before testing. In 1943, fuel was in short supply and wards heated by a stove; therefore, this was excellent advice. Today, centrally heated hospitals and efficient car heaters minimise this problem, making it easy to overlook. If a patient attends on an exceptionally cold day, or has had a lengthy wait for public transport, this advice is relevant, as results will be reduced, giving a false impression.

How to test

Practical skills are sometimes difficult to learn from static media, such as books. The development of video and information technology has greatly helped this and manual muscle testing has been demonstrated on video (Kendall, 1987) and CD ROM (Epier and Wainwright, 1999). Overall, there are several principles to this form of testing. The therapist must consider positioning, palpation, pressure, consistency, and avoidance of fatigue.

- the patient and the part tested should be comfortably and properly positioned with the proximal or adjacent parts stabilised so that multi joint muscles are not forced to contract or lengthen over all joints (Kendall 1991). These factors enable the patient to make a maximal effort
- palpation is essential to detect a contraction flicker and ensure that the muscle tested is actually producing the movement

- when applying pressure to resist movement, placement of the therapist's hand must be consistent. Pressure should be applied gradually, directly opposite the movement requested (Kendall, 1991). Resistance should be applied in the shortened position and given for 2–3 seconds on the small muscles of the hand (Brandsma *et al*, 1995)

- the testing sequence should be the same on every occasion to compare reactions and fatigue. Testing should be done at the same time of day, preferably in the morning to decrease fatigue (Lacôte *et al*, 1987). Whenever possible, the same examiner should repeat the tests (Lacôte *et al*, 1987) and be vigilant in case trick movements are being used. Recovering muscles are very weak; therefore, repeated attempts at testing a particular muscle causes fatigue, giving an erroneous impression.

Many manuals exist for muscle testing and sometimes these give conflicting advice. Below are some suggestions for positioning, and instructions to be given to patients. The nerve supply and nerve root are included to facilitate the identification of the source of any problems. 'P' represents the point of palpation and 'R' the point at which resistance is applied. An arrow shows the direction of movement.

Extensor carpi radialis longus (radial nerve C6, C7)

The dual actions of this muscle, extending and radially deviating the wrist, make it difficult to isolate and test.

- grade 1–2: sit the patient at a table, with the elbow flexed at 90°. The hand is pronated, the fingers relaxed. Ask the patient to move the hand in the direction of the thumb, i.e. radial deviation

- palpate for a flicker dorsally at the base of the second metacarpal, or at the lateral aspect of the elbow above extensor carpi radialis brevis

- grade 3: place the hand and relaxed fingers, with the ulnar border downwards, over the edge of the table. Ask the patient to lift the hand up

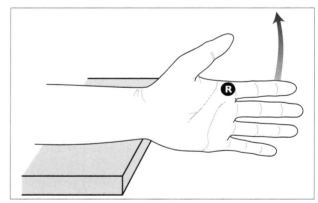

Figure 10.1: Starting position for testing extensor carpi radialis longus grade 3

- grade 4–5: apply resistance at the upper third of the second metacarpal, in an ulna direction. Do not allow the patient to extend the fingers when resistance is applied.

Extensor carpi radialis brevis (radial nerve C6, C7)

Lying in the second dorsal wrist compartment, with extensor carpi radialis longus, it extends the wrist.

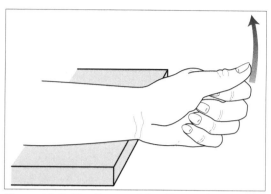

Figure 10.2: Starting position for testing extensor carpi radialis brevis gravity counterbalanced

- grade 1–2: the patient places the ulnar border of his/her fisted hand on the table. Ask the patient to move the wrist backwards (into extension), without moving the forearm
- palpate for a flicker over the base of the third metacarpal.
- grade 3: place the pronated fisted hand over the edge of a table. Ask the patient to lift the hand upwards without moving the forearm
- grade 4–5: apply resistance at the upper third of the third metacarpal. Do not allow the patient to extend the fingers when resistance is applied.

Extensor digitorum (radial nerve C7)

Lying in the fourth dorsal wrist compartment it extends the MCP joints of the fingers.

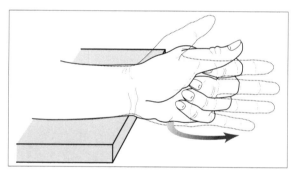

Figure 10.3: Testing for extensor digitorum gravity counterbalanced

- grade 1–2: place the ulnar border of the fisted hand on a table. Ensure the wrist is passively extended, to prevent automatic MCP extension, by a tenodesis effect. Ask the patient to straighten the fingers without moving the wrist
- palpate for a flicker over each metacarpal
- grade 3: place the pronated fisted hand on a table, so that the fingers are over the edge. Ask the patient to straighten his/her fingers without moving the wrist
- grade 4–5: apply resistance to the proximal phalanges in turn.

Extensor digitorum indices (radial nerve C7)

Lying with extensor digitorum in the fourth compartment of the wrist; it acts to extend the MCP joint of the index finger in isolation. The starting positions and resistance points remain as for extensor digitorum. Ask the patient to straighten his/her index finger, while keeping the other fingers bent. Palpate over the second metacarpal, just ulnar to the extensor digitorum.

Extensor digiti minimi (radial nerve C7)

Lying in the fifth dorsal compartment of the wrist, it extends the MCP joint of the little finger. Disruptions can easily be overlooked. Starting positions, palpation, and resistance points remain as above for the finger extensors. Ask the patient to extend his/her little finger, while keeping the other fingers flexed.

> **The patient is asked to extend the little and index finger while keeping the ring and middle fingers flexed. This is a useful test to establish how well extensor digiti minimi and extensor digitorum indices are working, as extensor digitorum augments their action.**

Box 10.2: Horns of the bull sign

Extensor carpi ulnaris (radial nerve C7)

Lying in the sixth dorsal compartment of the wrist, it has dual actions of extending the wrist in supination and ulnar deviation in pronation. When the wrist is extended in supination, it naturally tends to ulnar deviation.

- grade 1–2: place the fisted hand in pronation Ask the patient to move the hand into ulnar deviation
- palpate for a flicker under the styloid process of the ulna.
- grade 3: place the hand, with the fingers relaxed, over the edge of a table. Ask the patient to lift the wrist up and out, towards the little finger
- grade 4–5: apply resistance to the fourth and fifth metacarpals, against the direction of the movement.

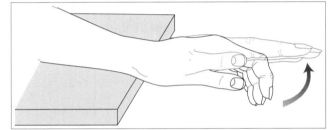

Figure 10.4: Testing for extensor carpi ulnaris against gravity

Flexor carpi radialis (median nerve C6, C7)

Flexor carpi radialis inserts into the base of second and third metacarpals and flexes the wrist against a resistance.

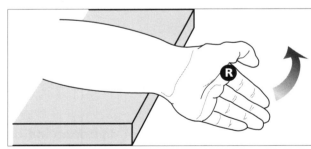

Figure 10.5: Testing for flexor carpi radialis against gravity

- grade 1–2: place the ulnar border of the hand, with the wrist extended on a table. The fingers should be relaxed, not flexed. Ask the patient to flex the wrist in slight radial deviation
- palpate on the volar surface of the wrist, just radial to the midline

- grade 3: place the supinated hand over the edge of the table, with the wrist extended. Ask the patient to flex the wrist in slight radial deviation
- grade 4–5: apply resistance to the head of the second metacarpal, in the direction of extension and ulnar deviation. Do not allow the patient to flex the fingers.

Palmaris longus (median nerve C6)

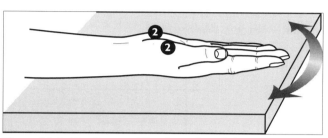

Figure 10.6: Starting position for palmaris longus grade 3–5

The clinical significance of testing palmaris longus is that, when present, it can be used for tendon transfers. It lies centrally on the volar aspect of the wrist and inserts into the palmar fascia.

- grade 1–2: place the ulnar border of the hand, with the wrist in neutral on a table. Ask the patient to flex the wrist. Very little movement occurs; therefore, it should be sufficient to observe the tendon in this position
- palpate just ulnar to flexor carpi radialis.
- grade 3: place the supinated hand on a table. Repeat the instruction above
- grade 4–5: apply resistance to the hypothenar and thenar eminences.

Flexor carpi ulnaris (ulnar nerve C8, TI)

Inserting into the pisiform, it is the strongest flexor of the wrist. In conjunction with extensor carpi ulnaris it is also an ulnar deviator.

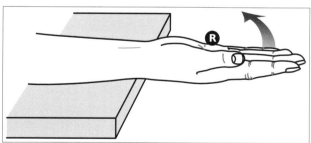

Figure 10.7: Testing for flexor carpi ulnaris against gravity

- grade 1–2: place the ulna border of the hand, with the wrist extended, on a table. The fingers should be relaxed, not flexed. Ask the patient to flex the wrist and draw the hand towards the forearm, i.e. the little finger attempts to touch the ulna border of the forearm
- palpate on the volar surface of the wrist, just proximal to the pisiform
- grade 3: place the supinated hand, with the wrist and fingers extended, over the table edge. Ask the patient to flex the wrist and move it in the direction of the little finger

- grade 4–5: apply resistance to the head of the fifth metacarpal bone, in the direction of flexion and radial deviation. Do not allow the fingers to flex.

Flexor digitorum superficialis (median nerve C7, C8, T1)

Flexor digitorum superficialis inserts into the sides of the middle phalanx of each finger and acts to flex the PIP joints. Patients sometimes have difficulty isolating the required movement. It has been suggested that by moving the PIP joint passively a few times, this will facilitate understanding (Daniels and Worthingham, 1972). Alternatively, the movement can be demonstrated (Brandsma *et al*, 1995). Each finger should be tested individually and it is important to prevent substitution of flexor digitorum profundus.

- grade 1–2: place the hand with the ulnar border on a table. Stabilise the wrist in neutral and hold the fingers not being tested in extension. Ask the patient to flex a PIP joint

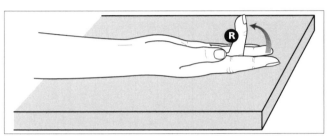

Figure 10.8: Testing for flexor digitorum superficialis against gravity

- palpate, using your other hand, at the wrist, medial to palmaris longus. Palpation alone is insufficient to confirm activity, as flexor digitorum profundus may be felt. The ability to flex the PIP joint when the DIP joint is flaccid confirms activity (Medical Research Council, 1943).

- grade 3: place the supinated hand on a table, with the wrist in neutral and fingers not being tested, held in extension. Ask the patient to bend the finger at the proximal phalanx

- grade 4–5: apply resistance in the direction of extension, to the middle phalanx.

Flexor digitorum profundus (median nerve-volar interosseous branch C8,T1)

Inserting into the base of the distal phalanx of each finger, flexor digitorum profundus flexes the DIP joints. If the wrist is extended, the tenodesis effect means that the fingers appear to flex, this also applies when testing flexor digitorum superficialis (Nicholson, 1992). Test each finger individually.

- grade 1–2: place the ulnar border of the hand on a table. Hold the wrist and PIP joints in neutral throughout the test. Ask the patient to flex the DIP joint

- palpate at the middle phalanx of the finger being tested

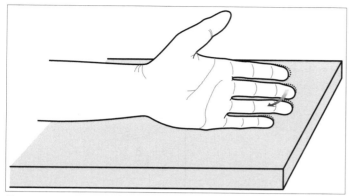

Figure 10.9: Testing for flexor digitorum profundus gravity counterbalanced

- grade 3: place the hand in supination on a table, with the wrist in neutral. Hold the fingers not tested and the PIP joint of the finger tested in extension

- grade 4–5: apply resistance in the direction of extension, to the palmar surface of the distal phalanx of the finger tested.

Lumbricals (first and second, median nerve, C6, C7, third and fourth ulnar nerve, C8)

The lumbricals arise from the tendons of the flexor digitorum profundus and insert into the tendinous expansions of extensor digitorum of the corresponding finger. They act to flex the MCP joints through 90°. Their dual nerve supply often necessitates testing as a group and individually.

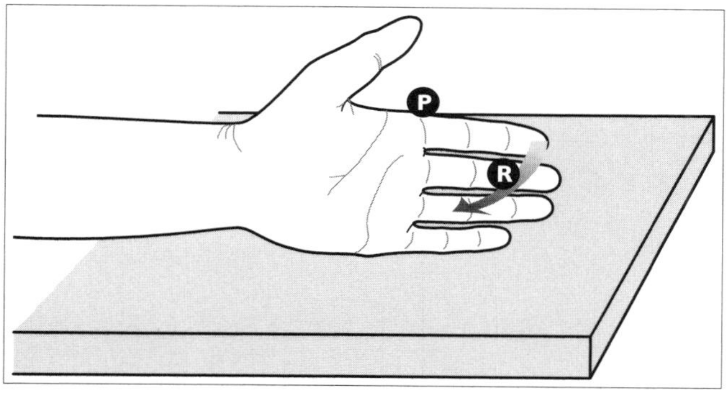

Figure 10.10: Palpation and resistance points for lumbricals; the fingers are shown extended to permit viewing.

- grade 1–2: place the ulnar border of the hand on a table, the wrist in neutral. Stabilise the metacarpals so that the proximal phalanges are in extension. Ensure the middle and distal phalanges are in flexion. Ask the patient to flex at the MCP joints and extend the IP joints

- palpate at the radial border of the proximal phalanx. This is a difficult, even impossible, muscle to palpate; therefore, it may be impossible to detect at grade 1

- grades 3–5: apply graded resistance in the final position in direction of extension, at the volar surface of the proximal phalanges, minimum for grade 3 and maximum for grade 5.

Dorsal interossei (ulnar nerve C8)

These muscles lie deep between the metacarpals, arising from adjacent sides of the metacarpals and inserting into the base of proximal phalanges of three fingers. (The first and second into the radial side of the index and middle fingers and the third and fourth into the ulna side of the middle and ring fingers.) They also insert into the aponeurotic expansions of the corresponding extensor digitorum tendons. They assist the lumbricals and palmar interossei to flex the MCP joints, while extending the IP joints; however, their distinguishing function is the abduction of the fingers (other than the little finger) from midline. The first dorsal interosseous, the easiest to palpate and test, is described here.

- grade 1–2: rest the pronated hand on a table, with the IP joints extended and the fingers adducted. Ask the patient to abduct the index finger, keeping it straight

- palpate at the first web space, against the first metacarpal

- grades 3–5: apply graded resistance, in the direction of adduction, to the radial border of the proximal phalanx of the index finger.

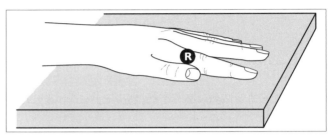

Figure 10.11: Testing for the first dorsal interosseous muscle

Palmar interossei (ulnar nerve C8, T1)

These arise from the entire length of the volar surface of the second, fourth and fifth metacarpal bones and insert into the side of the base of the proximal phalanx of the corresponding finger and the aponeurotic expansion of extensor digitorum. They adduct the fingers to midline.

- grade 1–2: support the patient's pronated hand, with the fingers neutrally extended and abducted. Ask the patient to bring his/her straight fingers together

- palpate in the second, third and fourth web spaces sequentially. However, they are deep and, therefore, difficult to palpate

- grades 3–5: apply graded resistance on the sides of each distal phalanx in turn

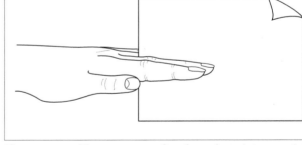

Figure 10.12: The paper test for the palmar interossei

- a quick test for the palmar interossei is to place a piece of paper in the web spaces and ask the patient to hold it there. Normally, the paper should be held against a resistance; compare with the unaffected hand.

Abductor digiti minimi and flexor digiti minimi (ulnar nerve C8)

These muscles abduct the little finger and flex the MCP joint, and are tested as for the dorsal interossei. Palpate at the ulnar border of the hand and apply resistance at the ulna border of the proximal phalanx. Differentiation between the two is difficult.

Opponens digiti minimi (ulnar nerve C8)

Flexes the fifth metacarpal.

- grade 1–2: support the hand with the forearm in neutral. Ask the patient to cup the palm and bring the little finger in front of the others
- it can only be palpated if the overlying muscles are not functioning
- grades 3–5: apply graded resistance on the sides of the distal phalanx.

Extensor pollicis longus (radial nerve C7)

Extensor pollicis longus primarily extends the MCP and IP joints of the thumb and lies in the third dorsal compartment of the wrist.

- grade 1–2: place the ulnar border of the hand on a table. Ask the patient to lift the thumb behind the hand. This brings the CMC joint into the plane of the palm

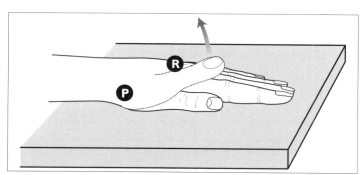

- palpate at the ulnar border of the anatomical snuffbox
- grade 3: place the pronated hand flat on a table. Ask the patient to lift the straight thumb up
- grade 4–5: apply resistance to the medial dorsal border of the proximal phalanx of the thumb.

Figure 10.13: Testing for extensor pollicis longus against gravity

Extensor pollicis brevis (radial nerve C7)

Extensor pollicis brevis lies in the first dorsal wrist compartment and extends the MCP joint of the thumb.

- grade 1–2: place the ulnar border of the hand on a table. Stabilise the first metacarpal, in radial abduction. Ask the patient to extend the proximal phalanx of the thumb, the IP joint remaining relaxed
- palpate at the lateral margin of the anatomical snuffbox posterior and medial to abductor pollicis longus
- grade 3–5: apply graded resistance to the proximal phalanx in the direction of flexion of the MCP joint.

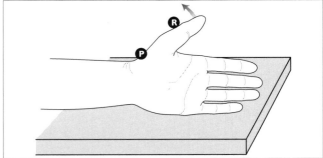

Figure 10.14: Testing for extensor pollicis brevis

Abductor pollicis longus (radial nerve C7)

Lying in the first dorsal compartment of the wrist and inserting into the dorsal base of the first metacarpal, it radially abducts the thumb.

- grade 1–2: place the pronated hand on a table. Ask the patient to radially abduct the thumb (i.e. make a right angle with the index finger)
- palpate at the base of the thumb metacarpal, on the medial border of the anatomical snuffbox
- grade 3: place the ulnar border of the hand on a table. The forearm is in neutral. Ask the patient to radially abduct the thumb
- grade 4–5: apply resistance at the distal phalanx, in the direction of flexion of the IP joint.

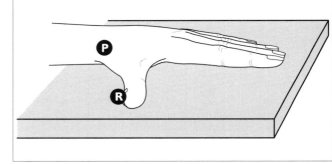

Figure 10.15: Testing for abductor pollicis longus gravity counterbalanced

Flexor pollicis longus (median nerve C8, T1)

Inserting into the volar base of the distal phalanx of the thumb, it flexes the thumb IP joint.

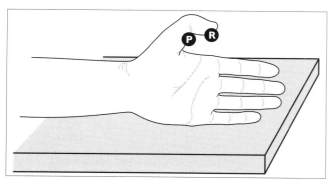

Figure 10.16: Testing for flexor pollicis longus gravity counterbalanced

- grade 1–2: place the ulnar border of the hand on a table, with the wrist in neutral. Stabilise the proximal phalanx of the thumb and the first metacarpal, with the MCP joint in extension. Ask the patient to flex the thumb at the IP joint

- use the finger stabilising the proximal phalanx to palpate the tendon on the volar aspect of the IP joint of the thumb

- grade 3: hold the supinated hand, with the wrist in neutral and the MCP joint of the thumb in extension, as above. Ask the patient to flex the thumb

- grade 4–5: apply resistance in the direction of extension, to the volar aspect of the distal phalanx.

Flexor pollicis brevis (median nerve C6, C7; ulnar nerve C8, T1)

The relationship with the long flexor of the thumb and dual innervation make it difficult to test. It flexes the MCP joint of the thumb.

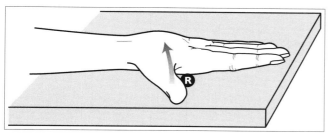

Figure 10.17: Testing for flexor pollicis brevis against gravity

- grade 1–2: place the ulnar border of the hand on a table, with the wrist stabilised and the IP joint of the thumb in extension. Ask the patient to flex the thumb at the metacarpal joint

- palpate in the thenar eminence medial to abductor pollicis brevis.

- grade 3: hold the hand as above, in supination. Repeat the instructions

- grade 4–5: apply resistance to the volar surface of the proximal phalanx of the thumb.

Abductor pollicis brevis (median nerve C6, C7)

This muscle brings the metacarpal joint of the thumb into palmar abduction (i.e. the thumb is at 90° to the palm), accompanied by pronation and radial deviation.

- grade 1–2: supinate the hand, with the wrist and the IP joint of the thumb in extension. The thumb is adducted. Ask the patient to move the thumb away from the side of the hand, to a point vertically above the original position. The thumbnail maintains its position in a plane at right angles to the palm

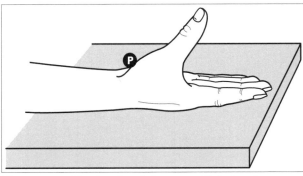

Figure10.18: Testing for abductor pollicis brevis

- palpate at the bottom of the thenar eminence, medial to the MCP joint of the thumb

- grade 3–5: apply graded resistance in the direction of adduction, to the lateral border of the proximal phalanx of the thumb.

Adductor pollicis (ulnar nerve C8)

This muscle brings the first metacarpal towards the second metacarpal.

- grade 1–2: supinate the hand on a table, with the wrist and the IP joint of the thumb extended. Ask the patient to bring the straight thumb towards the index finger

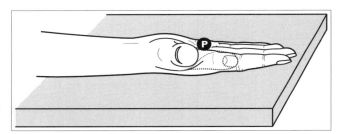

- palpate dorsally in the first web space, proximal to the first dorsal interosseus

- grade 3–5: apply graded resistance to the medial border of the thumb.

Figure 10.19: Testing for adductor pollicis

Opponens pollicis (median nerve C6, C7)

- grade 1–2: place the ulnar border of the hand on the table, with the forearm and wrist in neutral. Ask the patient to touch the base of the little finger with the thumb. The thumbnail stays parallel to the palm throughout. This position is gravity assisted

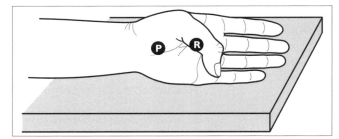

- palpate in the thenar eminence, radial to the abductor pollicis brevis; however, it can be palpated only if the other thenar muscles have atrophied

Figure 10.20: Testing for opponens pollicis, gravity assisted

- grade 3: place the supinated hand on the table and follow the instructions above
- grade 4–5: apply graded resistance at the proximal phalanx.

Recording

Recording results in tabular form will quickly indicate trends (Brandsma, 1995). A basic chart with space at the left to name the selected muscles gives flexibility. It can aid clarification to record grades 1–2 in a different colour from the stronger grades, provided it is used consistently and photocopies well (see *Chapter 6*).

Patient Name————————————————————— Number—————Date—————————

Muscle Tested	Right				Left				Comments
	1/9/00	5/9/00	14/9/00	21/9/00	1/9/00	5/9/00	14/9/00	21/9/00	
FDS Median	1	2	3	4	5				
FDPMedian	0	0	1	2	5				
APL Radial	3	4	5	5	5				
FPL Median	0	0	1	2	5				Unable to take up testing position
Signature									
Name of Therapist									

Figure 10.21: Suggested method for recording manual muscle testing

Reliability

Brandsma *et al* (1995) demonstrated intra-rater and inter-rater reliability by experienced testers, of 28 patients with leprosy neuropathy, following a standardised protocol. Movements tested were abduction of the little finger, adduction of the little finger, abduction of the index finger, abduction of the thumb, thumb opposition and MCP flexion with the IP joints extended (intrinsic plus position). Results showed intra-rater reliability coefficients ranged from 0.71 to 0.96 and inter-rater reliability coefficients were slightly lower at between 0.72 and 0.93. It has been shown that reliability is greatest for Grade 0 and Grade 5 (Brandsma and Schrenders, 2001).

Interpretation

Scores represent an isolation of something which Donne, Milch (1943) and Brandsma (1995) remind us are part of a whole. Therefore, it is always necessary to consider the wider picture. Schreuders and Stam (1996) tested the lumbrical muscles using a hand held dynamometer and compared this to manual muscle testing using the Medical Research Council scale. They found that grade 3 correlates with about 0.8 kg and grade 5 with about 6.5 kg of MCP flexion strength, even when testing shows the maximum grade function in the form of grip strength can continue to improve (Brandsma, 1995). If the problem is unilateral, results can be compared with the opposite hand; if the problem is bilateral, it must be compared with knowledge of what constitutes normal resistance. Results taken over a period will indicate trends (deterioration or improvement) or no change, giving an opportunity to evaluate treatment.

Having established the areas of weakness and bearing in mind the nerve/nerve root supply, it is possible to distinguish between weakness caused by a peripheral problem (and the level of lesion), or a nerve root problem. If pain is reproduced when resistance is applied to muscle that is contracting strongly, it can be indicative of a problem, such as tenosynovitis. If pain is reproduced and contraction is weak, more serious damage may be indicated (Corrigan and Maitland, 1994). Consideration of the cause of the problem makes it is possible to plan treatment accordingly:

- weak innervated muscles require facilitation and strengthening of the contraction, unless exercise is contraindicated (as in acute poliomyelitis)
- denervated muscles require that steps be taken to maintain muscle length and condition, by stretching and neuromuscular stimulation
- pain relief and stretching may be indicated in cases of tenosynovitis.

Muscle tone

Spasticity has been defined as, 'a velocity-dependent response of muscle to passive stretching' (Bohannon and Smith, 1987), and occurs as part of an upper motor neuron lesion. When this increase in muscle tone is present in the upper limb, the therapist will usually wish to reduce it; therefore, spasticity should be clinically assessed using a simple measure. Electrophysiologic quantification is reliable (Sehgal and McGuire, 1998), but currently not practicable in most clinics.

Several scales exist to measure spasticity, but the Ashworth scale (Ashworth, 1964) is regarded as the scale of choice (Vattanasilp and Ada,1999). The therapist moves the part, or limb, and the tone graded as described in *Box 10.3*.

Box 10.3: The Ashworth scale (Ashworth, 1964)

0	No increase in tone
1	Slight increase in tone giving a 'catch' when the limb was moved in flexion or extension
2	More marked increase in tone, but limb easily flexed
3	Considerable increase in tone, passive movements are difficult
4	Limb rigid in flexion or extension

The modified Ashworth scale was developed as many patients were found to be scoring at the lower end of the scale and grade 1 was indiscrete (Bohannon and Smith, 1987). Consequently, this scale may be more precise for grades 1 and 2, where increases in tone are slight. It is defined in *Box 10.4* (Bohannon and Smith, 1987). Muscle tone changes with:

- positioning
- health and well-being of the patient
- Efforts made elsewhere in the body

Box 10.4: The modified Ashworth scale (Bohannon and Smith, 1987)

0	No increase in muscle tone
1	Slight increase in muscle tone, manifested by a catch and release or by minimal resistance at the end of range of motion when the affected part(s) is moved in flexion or extension
1+	Slight increase in muscle tone, manifested by a catch, followed by minimal resistance throughout the remainder (less than half) the range of movement
2	More marked increase in tone through most of the range of movement, but affected part(s) easily moved
3	Considerable increase in muscle tone, passive movement is difficult
4	Affected part(s) rigid in flexion or extension

Consequently, assessment is subjective, but is of some use when looking at the spastic hand. Efforts must be made to assess consistently in position and the start/finish of treatment.

Spasticity can be complicated by sensory and cognitive losses and therefore, if present, cannot be considered in isolation, and a selection of specialist neurological tests will be needed.

Reliability

Skold *et al* (1998) showed a significant correlation ($p<0.05$) between the modified Ashworth scale and electromyographic recordings in 15 tetraplegic patients on all grades. Bohannon and Smith (1987) found that the results of two testers on 30 patients, using the modified Ashworth scale, were significantly correlated ($p<0.001$). Gregson *et al* (1999) demonstrated very good reliability of the modified Ashworth scale on 32 stroke patients examined by two raters. This applied to intra-rater (kappa=0.84) and inter-rater reliability (kappa= 0.83).

A theoretical analysis of 40 papers by Pandyan *et al* (1999) confirmed that the Ashworth scale was an ordinal measurement of resistance to passive movement and that reliability is better in the upper limb.

> ## To summarise
>
> - manual muscle testing, although subjective, is a useful tool
> - be consistent in procedure, positioning, grading and resisting movements
> - be selective in what is tested
> - no muscle works in isolation
> - the Ashworth/modified Ashworth scale can be used to assess spasticity.

References

Ashworth B (1964) Preliminary trial of carisoprodol in multiple sclerosis. *Practitioner* **192**: 540–2

Bohannon RW, Smith MB (1987) Inter-rater reliability of a modified Ashworth scale of muscle spasticity. *Physic Ther* **67**(2): 206–7

Boscheinen-Morrin J, Davey V, Conolly WB (1987) *The Hand Fundamentals of Therapy*. Butterworth, Sevenoaks: 13–14

Brandsma JW (1995) Manual muscle testing and dynamometry for bilateral ulnar neuropraxia in a surgeon. *J Hand Ther* **8**(3): 191–4

Brandsma JW, Schreuders TAR (2001) Sensible manual muscle strength testing to evaluate and monitor strength of the intrinsic muscles of the hand: A commentary. *J Hand Therapy* **14**(14): 273–78

Brandsma JW, Schreuders TAR, Birke JA, Piefer A, Oostendorp R (1995) Manual muscle testing: intraobserver and interobserver reliabilities for the intrinsic muscles of the hand. *J Hand Ther* **8**(3): 185–90

Corrigan B, Maitland GD (1994) *Practical Orthopaedic Medicine*. Butterworth-Heinemann, Oxford: 13

Daniels L, Worthington C (1972) *Muscle Testing Techniques of Manual Muscle Examination*. 3rd edn. WB Saunders, Philadelphia: 114–37

Epier M, Wainwright S (1999) *Manual Muscle Testing—An Interactive Tutorial*. Slack Incorporated, New Jersey

Gregson JM, Leathley M, Moore AP, Sharma AK, Smith TL, Watkins CL (1999) Reliability of the tone assessment scale and modified Ashworth scale as clinical tools for assessing poststroke spasticity. *Arch Phys Med Rehab* **80**(9): 1013–6

Herbison GJ, Isaac Z, Cohen ME, Ditunno JF, Jr (1996) Strength post-spinal cord injury: Myometer vs, manual muscle test. *Spinal Cord* **34**(9): 543–8

Kendall F (1987) *Florence Kendall's Muscle Testing Video Library. Williams & Wilkins Electronic Media*. Distributed by Lippincott Williams & Wilkins, Baltimore. MD

Kendall FP (1991) Manual muscle testing: There is no substitute. *J Hand Ther* **4**(4): 159–61

Kilmer DD, Abresch RT, Fowler WM, Jr (1993) Serial manual muscle testing in Duchenne muscular dystrophy. *Arch Phys Med Rehab* **74**(11): 1168–71

Lacôte M, Chevalier AM, Miranda A, Bleton JP, Stevenin P (1987) *Clinical Evaluation of Muscle Function*, 2nd edn. Churchill Livingstone, Edinburgh, London, Melbourne and New York

Lovett RW (1916) *The Treatment of Infantile Paralysis*. William Heinemann, London

Medical Research Council (1943) *Aids To the Investigation of Peripheral Nerve Injuries*. War Memorandum Number 7, Revised 2nd edn. Reprinted 1972

Milch H (1943) Measurement of muscle strength. *J Bone Joint Surg* **XXVII**(1): 137–41

Nicholson B (1992) Clinical evaluation. In: Stanley BG, Tribuzi SM, eds. *Concepts in Hand Rehabilitation*. FA Davis, Philadelphia: 76–85

Oldham J, Tallis R, Howe T, Smith G, Petterson T (1992) Objective assessment of muscle function. *Nurs Stand* **6**(45): 37–9

Pandyan AD, Johnson GR, Price CIM, Curless RH, Barnes MP, Rodgers H (1999) A review of the properties and limitations of the Ashworth and modified Ashworth scale as measures of spasticity. *Clin Rehab* **13**(5): 373–83

Salter N (1955) Methods of measurement of muscle and joint function. *J Bone Joint Surg* **37B**(3): 474–90

Sehgal N, McGuire JR (1998) Beyond Ashworth: Electrophysiologic quantification of spasticity. *Physical Med Rehab Clin N Am* **9**(4) 949–79

Schreuders TAR, Stam HJ (1996) Strength measurements of the lumbrical muscles. *J Hand Ther* **9**(4): 303–5

Shultis-Keirnan L (1992) Manual muscle testing. In: *Clinical Assessment Recommendations*, 2nd edn. American Society of Hand Therapists, Chicago: 47–53

Skold C, Harms-Ringdahl K, Hulting C, Levi R, Seiger A (1998) Simultaneous Ashworth measurements and electromyographic recordings in tetraplegic patients. *Arch Phys Med Rehab* **79**(8): 959–65

Vattanasilp W, Ada L (1999) The relationship between clinical and laboratory measures of spasticity. *Aus J Physiother* **45**(2): 135–9

Wright WG (1912) Muscle training in the treatment of infantile paralysis. *Boston M & S J* **167**: 567–74

Chapter 11
Sensation and sensibility

A radio programme told the story of a person, blind for many years, having his sight restored. Although he could see, making sense of the new environment was hard; familiar objects, such as a cup, could only be recognised when they were felt. This indicates the difference between sensation and sensibility. Omer (1973) was the first to differentiate between the two. He defined sensation as 'The acceptance and activation of impulses in the afferents of the nervous system' and sensibility as 'The conscious appreciation and interpretation of an external stimulus that produced sensation'. Sensation is interesting, but sensibility enables us to make the most of our environment and our motor abilities.

This chapter describes when to test sensibility, and methods of testing autonomic function, touch threshold and tactile gnosis. Finally, the problem of assessing hypersensitivity is considered.

When to test

Testing will usually be necessary when there has been, or there is a possibility of, neurological damage. Therefore, it may be used in cases of nerve compression (e.g. carpal tunnel syndrome) or neuropathy (e.g. diabetes), following division or repair of a peripheral nerve, or in an upper motor neuron lesion where sensation is primarily affected.

Sensibility testing enables the therapist to determine the extent of the functional loss and recovery. This can be used to diagnose partial or complete lesions, evaluate results of repair, determine the need for neurolysis, determine the level of sensory evaluation and provide objective data in compensation cases (Waylett-Rendall, 1988).

The choice of method will depend on the patient's motor and cognitive abilities, but Yekutiel (2000) describes sensory testing as being in a very crude state. This is true; current clinical tests are simplistic and do not address the complex active process of sensibility.

When not to test

Do not test if there is no suggestion of nerve problems from the history and observations.

Autonomic testing

Peripheral nerve damage almost invariably affects the autonomic system. In the six months following injury or suture, the return of autonomic activity generally indicates some recovery of the sensory function of a peripheral nerve. However, it does not correlate with functional sensation (Edshage, 1980). Despite this, autonomic tests have been recommended for use with suspected malingerers (Waylett-Rendall, 1988). Results should be viewed with caution if malingering is suspected; occasionally, sympathetic function returns in isolation (Bell-Krotoski, 1991). Therefore, results should be considered in the context of other suspect tests, e.g. sincerity testing of grip. Autonomic function can be performed in two ways: the O'Riain wrinkle test and the Ninhydrin sweat test.

O'Riain wrinkle test

This method was devised in 1973 by O'Riain and is based on the fact that a normal hand, immersed in water for any period of time, becomes wrinkled. A mother reported that this was absent in her child, following a nerve repair, and that the phenomenon gradually returned (O'Riain, 1973). This is a wonderful illustration of how, by listening to patients, we can progress our knowledge and effectiveness. The test can be used to assess sympathetic nerve function, and is particularly useful for young children or adults with a cognitive deficit, in the six months following a complete peripheral nerve lesion.

Do not test if placing the hand in water is contraindicated.

How to test

- assemble the equipment needed—large bowl, thermometer, pen and chart
- explain the purpose of the test to the patient or accompanying adult
- fill a large bowl or a sink with warm water—warmer than blood heat (about 40°C)
- encourage the patient to immerse both hands in the water. Water toys or some purposeful activity will assist in maintaining immersion
- check hands after 10, 20 and 30 minutes. If wrinkling occurs, cease immersion. Note that there is considerable variance in the immersion time prescribed. ASSH (1990) recommends that this be for 5–10 minutes; however, O'Riain (1973) recommends 30 minutes and ASHT (Stone, 1992) 20–30 minutes
- inspect the fingertips on both hands and mark the wrinkle patterns on a hand sensibility evaluation form. Scored on a scale of 0–3, 0 is no wrinkling and 3 normal wrinkling
- repeat at 4–6 week intervals until either normal wrinkling is resumed or no further change is noted (Stone, 1992).

Recording

Retain the charts, ensuring the patient's name, identification number and numerical score are on them and that they are dated. The scores for 3 and 2 are very subjective, making this the least reliable of the sudomotor tests (Waylett-Rendall, 1988).

Ninhydrin sweat test

This test, described by Moberg (1958), grew out of criminological identification and gives a useful indication of sympathetic nerve function. Sweat contains 10 amino acids and, therefore, fingerprints on paper can be stained by Ninhydrin (2,2 Dihydroxy-1, 3-(2H)-dione) and then fixed (Moberg, 1958). The marks on the paper are directly proportional to the sweating produced. The test is recommended for use on complete nerve injuries that have occurred within the last six months (Stone, 1992). As it is the most reliable test of sudomotor activity, it has been described as useful for suspected malingerers (Waylett Rendall, 1988).

Ninhydrin spray contains hazardous propellants, butan and chlorodifluormethane and should be used in a fume cupboard and with protective equipment (Merck Eurolab, 2000). There are recorded cases of allergic contact dermatitis (Murphy and Gawkrodger, 2000), allergic rhinitis and occupational asthma, even when used in a fume cupboard (Piirilä *et al*, 1997). Consequently, this test should be approached with extreme caution and use made of the clinical chemistry department, where proper facilities exist. Directions for taking the test are readily available (Moberg, 1958; Stone, 1992), but only if absolutely necessary should it be carried out, using directions from the supplier. A risk assessment must be undertaken before use.

Detection touch threshold testing

Monofilament testing

The history of the touch/pressure threshold test is described by Dellon (1981) who translated and appraised the original articles. He reported that, in 1896, Von Frey described the attachment of a straight hair to a candlestick to test touch or pressure. The hair was applied to the skin until it bent and the patient recognised the pressure. Different hair strengths were used progressively, starting with a child's, a woman's, a man's and finally a horse's hair. Von Frey also identified that pressure thresholds are not the same throughout the body. In the 1950s, Dr Josephine Semmes and Dr Sidney Weinstein used the newly invented substance of nylon to make monofilament rods as an alternative to hair. Nylon was better suited to the purpose than hairs and gave a wider range of heavier forces (Bell-Krotoski, 1999). The test, first described by Von Prince and Butler (1967), establishes the pressure needed to detect touch in the hand.

These are now available in a sophisticated kit form of 5 or 20 Semmes-Weinstein Monofilaments. (North Coast Medical vis Promedics in UK; Smith & Nephew) or the Weinstein enhanced sensory test (Rosen and Jerosch-Herold, 2000). The five-rod kit form has the advantage of decreased cost, increased portability and shortens testing time, while producing virtually the same information as the larger set (Bell-Krotoski, 1991). If the department has more than one set of monofilaments, these should be numbered to ensure that the same set is used at each testing of the patient. The fibres are graded by filament number to logarithms of ten times the force needed to bend the fibre in milligrams (Bell-Krotoski and Burford, 1997; Brand and Hollister, 1999). Screening forms can be purchased separately to record information graphically. The monofilaments have been identified by Fess (1998) as one of the four tools that meet all reliability, validity, equipment, administration, scoring, and interpretation requisites.

The test is useful for acute neural compression, chronic neuropathies, and nerve laceration repairs and permits mapping of the areas affected. It has proved useful to screen peripheral nerve problems by site monitoring (Bell-Krotoski, 1991). It should not be used in areas where there is no pinprick sensation (Waylett-Rendall, 1988). When testing for pinprick, always use a sterile needle or a purpose-made disposable tester.

As for all tests of sensibility, except for the autonomous system, test in a quiet, warm area of the department and try to arrange not to be interrupted. The therapist needs to concentrate on technique and the patient on the test; distractions make this harder for everyone. A good light is essential, as it can be hard to see the filaments.

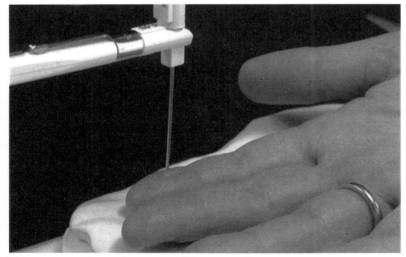

Plate 11.1 Testing using a monofilament rod

How to test

- gather the equipment required—therapeutic putty or rice pillow, or towel, portable screen, monofilaments, chart, and coloured pencils

- explain the purpose of the test to the patient

- seat the patient at a table with the hand supported either on a towel (Stone, 1992), therapeutic putty (Brand and Hollister, 1999) or rice pillow . Support is essential as any movement, even if unseen, will be felt in the forearm muscles and tendons, giving a false positive (Brand and Hollister, 1999)

- demonstrate to the patient the testing method (Von Prince and Butler, 1967) before arranging the portable screen to obscure the hand tested, and prevent the therapist giving visual clues to the patient (Brand and Hollister, 1999)

- start on the volar surface and apply the monofilaments perpendicularly to the skin until the filament bends for 1.5 seconds. Start with the 2.83 filament on the arm and work distally. Select a thinner filament if there is a normal response. Use a thicker filament if there is no response. Ask the patient to state when he/she is being touched

- do not mark a point as sensitive until two positive responses have been given to stimuli. Establish a sensitive area early on and return to it if two insensitive areas have been touched in succession. This prevents the patient becoming tense (Brand and Hollister, 1999)

- return the monofilaments carefully to the box as, if this is done carelessly and the lid closed, the filaments will be damaged and cannot be used

- record threshold monofilament numbers on the diagram of the hand, in the colour advised on the chart. Note any delayed or referred responses. Normative values are available and scores can be interpreted (see *Box 11.1*).

- repeat weekly, initially, and then at 4–6 weeks until fully recovered, or there is no further change

- store the monofilaments in an area with a constant temperature, away from sunlight. Check regularly for any deformation of the filaments and discard if they do not reform (Bell-Krotoski, 1990; 1991). Monofilaments made of polyhexamethylene dodecandiamide (Nylon 612, Du Pont) can be cleaned with alcohol, although they may temporarily become limp (Bell-Krotoski, 1990).

Normal	1.65–2.83
Diminished light touch	3.22–3.61
Diminished protective sensation	3.84–4.31
Loss of protective sensation filament markings	3.84–4.31
Untestable	6.65+

Box 11.1: Monofilament scores and interpretation

Reliability

Tests have shown the filaments to have acceptable intra-rater and inter-rater reliability when calibrated correctly (Bell-Krotoski and Tomancik, 1987) when used in a standardised manner (Novak, 2001). It is recommended that the lengths and diameter of monofilaments be tested, using a micrometer, if they are to be used for research purposes (Bell-Krotoski and Tomancik, 1987). The perpendicular set of the monofilaments ensures that the vibration of the tester's hand is minimised; hence, it is testing touch pressure rather than vibration sense (Bell-Krotoski and Burford, 1997). It is reported that the monofilaments have a reliability coefficient of 0.84 (Bell-Krotoski, 1991). Recent work (Massy-Westrop, 2002) has shown that five smallest monofilaments of the full kit are not reliable. A pilot study has indicated that there is a positive correlation between the results of monofilament testing and sensory discrimination performance (King, 1997).

Other discrimination tests such as hot/cold, blunt and sharp are not included here, as they are a less affective method than touch filaments. Hot/cold discrimination can be tested by asking the patient to close his/her eyes and applying, at random, test tubes containing hot and cold water. A more controlled method is to use Neurotemps (Thames Valley Test Company, 2001); these are rapidly heated or cooled and incorporate a thermometer. Temperature discrimination should be evaluated prior to using any thermal treatment modality, to ensure that the patient will recognise overheating or overchilling. Vibration sense is not included here, as it is possible to transmit the vibration by bone and, therefore, a false result can be obtained.

Tactile gnosis

Tactile gnosis is the functional capacity to interpret sensory input from the hand without using vision (Rosen and Jerosch-Herold, 2000). The concept is usually attributed to Moberg; however, Moberg himself credited it to Broman in 1945 (Moberg, 1958). Bunnell stated that when sensory function is lost, the eyes of the fingers are blind (cited by Dellon, 1981). The fingertips moving over Braille enable the blind to read by recognising the pattern of raised dots. Similarly, by moving the hand lightly over fabric or wood, its texture can be established more accurately than by sight alone. Tactile gnosis enables man to explore, identify, and manipulate unseen objects. To assess tactile gnosis, several methods are available. These include the static and moving two point discrimination tests, Moberg pick-up test, and shape/texture identification test (STI-test).

Two-point discrimination

Weber introduced the static two point discrimination test and a skin deformation test in 1835. However, from as early as 1872, the test was criticised (Dellon, 1981). The moving two point test was developed by Dellon in 1978. Moberg (1991) stated that he devised his own version in the 1940s, but did not write it up. This is a cautionary tale for any therapist with a bright idea! Although Dellon originally used a paper clip and Moberg (1990;1991) continued to advocate this, a paper clip should not be used today. The paper clip was not designed for this purpose and should not be used as a medical device; furthermore, one end is sharp enough to pierce the patient or therapist. Several devices are readily available commercially; these include a disc or callipers.

This test appears very easy to carry out, but there are many sources for potential error, which make it unsuitable for use as a comparator to evaluate surgical or therapeutic techniques (Moberg, 1991). Although ASHT (Stone, 1992) say that no experience is necessary to carry out this test, training and validation are necessary within the department.

When to test

This test can be used to establish the quality of sensation and the ability of the digit to function as a sensory organ, reflecting the quality of nerve ending density in the skin and re-education of the area of recognition in the brain (Dellon, 1981; Brand and Hollister, 1999). Moberg (1990) recommends its use with stroke patients as a reliable quantitative indicator of joint position sense.

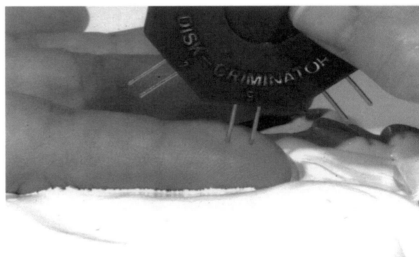

Plate 11.2: Two-point testing using a Disk-Criminator

Do not test

- do not test if there is no sensory return to the hand on the mapping exercise
- do not use this test in isolation.

How to test

- collect equipment needed—portable screen, callipers or disc, towel, therapeutic putty or rice pillow, chart and pen
- explain the purpose of the test
- sit the patient at a table with the hand on putty and the palm upwards (Brand and Hollister, 1999). Alternatively, support the hand on the rice pillow. Place a screen over the patient's hand to prevent visual clues. Place a towel on the table to prevent the patient receiving any auditory cues (Bexon and Salter, 2000). Test both hands for comparison
- orientate the patient by demonstrating on a normally innervated area and reinforce a correct response (Dellon, 1978)
- **to carry out the static test**—using the disc or callipers on a 5mm setting, start distally and work proximally. Randomly place either 1 point or 2 parallel to the long axis of the finger until the skin blanches. Ask the patient how many points he/she can feel. Record the number of correct responses. If 70% are correct the distance is scored. If less than 70%, increase the distance between the points until 70% is achieved. Do not increase more than 15mm and do not measure below the proximal digital crease (Stone, 1992)
- **to carry out the moving test**—start with the disc or callipers on 5–8mm setting. Randomly place either one or two points perpendicular to the skin of the fingertips, parallel to the long axis of the finger. Maintain contact and move the instrument distally (Stone, 1992)
- when touching with two points, ensure that both touch simultaneously
- Pressure must be light (5gm) (Brand and Hollister, 1999); however, this is difficult to judge—a guide is that the skin should only blanch (Stone, 1992). Excessive pressure can give false readings
- ask the patient to say how many points he/she feels. Record the number of correct responses. If 70% are correct, score the distance and move to a smaller distance, but do not use spacing smaller than 2mm. If less than 70%, increase the distance between the points until 70% is achieved (Stone, 1992)
- take care at the edges of the fingers where the dorsal nerve may give a false reading, and on the ring and middle fingers, which may have dual innervation (Brand and Hollister, 1999)
- record the area tested and the scores. This can be done on a diagrammatic representation of the hand
- test again at intervals of 4–6 weeks until either within normal range or there is no progress.

Interpretation

ASSH (1990) state that abnormal results are more than 6mm on the static test and more than 3mm on the moving test, indicating that axonal damage has occurred, due to severe nerve compression or division. If there is mild or moderate nerve compression, the two-point test may well be normal, but other tests will be negative.

Reliability

Bell-Krotoski and Burford (1997) have demonstrated that, even when the blanching point is used as a guide, there are large variations of force, and that the difference in pressure between one point and two could mean that pressure rather than discrimination is being tested. The test lacks sensitivity to change and should not be used alone (Jerosch-Herold, 1999). Bell-Krotoski (1999) noted that patients, whose results on this test were within normal limits, complained of sensory loss. Subsequently, she was able to show, using Semmes-Weinstein filaments, that these patients lacked protective sensation.

The Moberg pick-up test

This test was devised by Moberg (1958) to address a perceived poor correlation between the tests contemporarily in use, and the actual ability of the patient to use the hand. The basis of the test is that the patient is shown a number of small objects on a table and asked to place these in a box using alternate hands. This is repeated and timed with the patient blindfolded, and the patient is also asked to identify the objects. The manner of manipulation can also be illuminating. The test was quantified and refined at the Brooke Medical Centre in the 1960s and a normal result for a male was considered to be 5–8 seconds (Omer, 1980). Dellon (1981) refined the test and recent work has attempted to standardise it further (Ng *et al*, 1999). The test is quick and inexpensive to carry out; however, testing demands repeated exposure to several objects, which may cause discomfort for patients with regenerating nerves (Rosén and Lundborg, 1998). The version given below assesses tactile gnosis and stereognosis. Stereognosis has been defined as the faculty to perceive and understand the form and nature of objects by a sense of touch (Waylett-Rendall, 1988).

When to test

- where the patient has a median or median and ulnar nerve lesion and has good motor return.

Do not test

- where there is no motor function
- should the patient not wish to be blindfolded, do not perform the test unless a screen is available.

How to test

- collect the equipment needed. Select 12 small metal items—a wing nut, screw, key, nail, large nut, large coin, small coin, safety pin, paper clip, square nut, hexagonal nut and a washer. A shallow container (the lid of a 200 gram coffee jar is suitable), chart, blindfold and stopwatch are also needed. It is best to work on a wooden surface (Dellon, 1981)
- standardise the test by marking out a table with tape or paint, so there are two equal A5 rectangles, equidistant from the container. Spread the metal objects on the rectangle on the uninjured side. Seat the patient facing the layout
- explain the purpose of the test, and that it is timed, to the patient

Plate 11.3 The Moberg pick-up test

- ask the patient to place the uninjured hand on the table and, when instructed, place the objects in the central container one at a time, as fast as possible. Time the movement from the word 'Go' and correct any abnormal movements used. Record these
- repeat the test with the opposite hand. Discontinue if the test takes longer than five minutes (Bexon and Salter, 2000)
- repeat this sequence three times
- blindfold the patient. One at a time, randomly select and place each object into the patient's three-point grip on the affected side and ask the patient to identify each item. Time how long is taken to identify each item. Repeat this twice until all the objects are identified, but allow no longer than 30 seconds per object (Dellon,1981)

- do not remove the blindfold. Repeat the timed pick-up sequence three times on both hands. Record the times taken. Divide the time taken on the sighted and blindfolded pick-ups by the time taken for the opposite hand and multiply by 100 to give a percentage of the standard time (Bexon and Salter, 2000)

- when repeating the test always use the same items.

Recording

A small chart can be pre-prepared to record lengths of time taken. The chart below was completed for a male without hand pathology and the score for the right hand score was divided by the score for the left hand.

Table 11.1: Scores of Moberg pick-up test for male without hand pathology

Patient Name: A Bloggs   Identification Number: 6767676   Date: 7/11/00

Test	Right—in secs	Left—in secs	Comment
Sighted test 1	0.1697	0.2272.	
Sighted test 2	0.1947	0.2019	
Sighted test 3	0.1804	0.1553	
Total	**0.5448**	**0.5591**	
Calculation	Time injured hand ÷ Time uninjured hand x100 = 97.5		
Blindfolded test 1	0.4341	0.3597	
Blindfolded test 2	0.4137	0.4122	
Blindfolded test 3	0.3643	0.3419	
Total	**1.2121**	**1.1138**	
Calculation	Time injured hand ÷ Time uninjured hand x100 = 108.9		
Recognition	**Test One**	**Test Two**	
Wing nut	0.031	0.0163	
Screw	0.1681	0.0600	
Key	0.0500	0.0500	
Nail	0.0597	0.0403	
Large Coin £1	0.0832	0.0316	
Small Coin 1p	0.1500	0.0907	
Large Nut	0.1147	0.0375	
Washer	0.0649	0.0669	
Safety Pin	0.0834	0.0159	
Paper Clip	0.0941	0.0490	
Hexagonal Nut	0.0610	0.0431	
Square Nut	0.0282	0.0291	
Total Recognition	**1.0824**	**0.5304**	

Signature————————————————   Name————————————————

Interpretation

The blindfolded pick-up will be much longer than for the sighted pick-up. When recovery is occurring, this will decrease probably to twice the sighted test (Bexon and Salter, 2000). This is illustrated in *Table 11.1*.

Reliability

There are satisfactory reliability studies on the test. Ng *et al* (1999) showed differences between gender and hand dominance. The test's greatest asset is to enable performance to be evaluated over a period of time. Like two-point discrimination, it cannot be used to compare different surgical or therapeutic techniques, as it is not standardised. For this reason, it is probably best to use the coins of the land rather than those used by Dellon and Ng *et al*. A one-pound coin and a five-pence piece could give a useful range.

Shape/texture identification (STI) test

Described by Rosén and Lundborg (1998), this test is a quantitative test for assessing tactile gnosis. It has the advantage of being quick (about 10 minutes), active, but requiring less motor function than the Moberg test. Also, it appears to the patient as a more sophisticated test using an instrument designed for the purpose, rather than a random collection of objects.

The STI-test instrument (Pi Medical, Sweden) is composed of four separate discs. The discs present three different shapes (cube, cylinder, and hexagon); each disc has shapes of different diameters (15, 8 or 5mm). The discs also present raised dots in groups of one, two and three, spaced differently on each disc (15, 8 or 5mm). The discs are slipped onto a base unit and the patient asked to identify them without sight. The test comes with an explicit protocol.

How to test

- gather the equipment needed— STI-test instrument, portable screen, record sheet and pen. Select a quiet area to carry out the test

- explain the purpose of the test to the patient

- seat the patient at a table with the template containing the samples

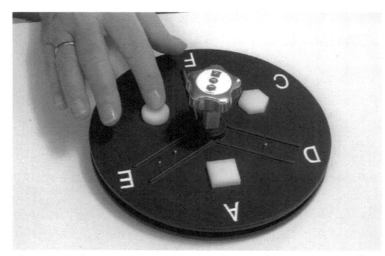

Plate 11.4: The STI-test in use (note: the template is not normally used for identification. It is used here for photographic clarity).

of the shapes and textures in front of him/her. Position the screen between the template and patient

- ask the patient to identify the shapes and textures presented, first with the uninjured hand, using either the index finger or the little finger, depending on the nerve involved
- offer larger shapes first, the choice of three presented randomly by spinning the disc on the base. Repeat with the medium and, finally, the small shapes. Offer each shape once only
- repeat this with the injured hand, using the index or little finger depending on the nerve lesion
- insert the disc with the largest spacing and present the number of dots randomly for identification by the uninjured hand. Repeat with the medium and, finally, the small shapes. Offer each texture once only
- repeat with the textures on the injured hand
- if all three shapes and textures on a disc are correctly identified, the patient scores a point giving a potential range from 0–6 for each hand (Rosén and Lundborg, 1998).

Recording

Scores are recorded for each hand on the patient's record or on the sheet provided by the manufacturer.

Interpretation

The norm is taken to be six, based on the testing of 60 control subjects (Rosén and Lundborg, 1998). An increasing score will reflect recovery.

Reliability

Testing on a variety of patient types showed that the test had higher sensitivity with patients with nerve repair. This was lower for patients with vibration-induced neuropathy and carpal tunnel syndrome. Test/retest results on 52 nerve repair patients, expressed with a weighted kappa value, were good (0.79) (Rosén and Lundborg,1998). Inter-tester reliability is also good. A study carried out on 91 patients with severe nerve injuries demonstrated this with a weighted kappa value of 0.66 (Rosén, 2003). The STI-test has been shown to have superior test responsiveness when compared with the two-point discrimination test (Rosen and Jerosch-Herold, 2000).

Hypersensitivity

Hypersensitivity is defined as a condition of extreme discomfort or irritability in response to normally non-noxious tactile stimulation (Yerxa *et al*, 1983). This can occur in those with scars, amputations, or crush injuries and prevents normal hand use, as they are unable to tolerate contact. This can be assessed using a visual analogue scale (see *Chapter 4*), monofilaments (Hochreiter *et al*, 1983) (see *Chapter 4*) or the Downey Hand Centre Sensitivity Test (Yerxa, 1983; Barber, 1990; Stone, 1992). This test takes between 30 minutes (Stone, 1992) to an hour (Yerxa, 1983) to administer and assesses response to touch, contact and vibration. This test is commercially available in a slightly modified form as the Three-Phase Hand Sensitivity Test (North Coast Medical via Promedica in UK) (Waylett-Rendall, 1995).

Three-phase hand sensitivity test

When to use

- in healed wounds, amputations or crush injuries where the patient reports hypersensitivity or gentle stroking produces an unpleasant re-action (Barber, 1990)
- to establish the level of intervention and evaluate the effects of desensitisation treatment (Barber, 1990).

Equipment

- a simplified home constructed kit will affect reliability and prevents comparison with other centres
- the touch test requires the use of ten dowelling rods, with different textured fabric wrapped around. These are graded from the smoothest to roughest: 1 (moleskin) and 10 (Velcro hooks)
- the contact or immersion phase uses ten large plastic lidded containers, with a variety of substances. These are graded from 1–10, from smoothest to roughest: 1 (cotton scraps) to 10 (plastic cubes)
- the assessment of vibration on the area requires a battery operated vibrator (23–53 cycles per second) and electric vibrator (83–100 cycles per second). These can be applied in a graded manner from lowest exposure to vibration: 1 (83 cycles per second, no actual contact) to 10 (no problems with vibration).

For each phase in the test, the therapist randomly picks a grade and the patient is exposed to it. Another grade is selected and the patient is asked to compare it for irritation until his/her own hierarchy of irritation is formed. The test is repeated weekly throughout the period of treatment, or until there is tolerance of the most irritating stimulus.

Recording

The purchased kit includes directions and record sheets incorporated into the records.

Interpretation

Having identified the most irritating stimuli, a desensitisation programme is devised. It has been recommended that other substances be used for the desensitisation treatment, rather than the test substances, to maintain objectivity (Barber, 1990). However, this may not be possible in daily clinical practice.

Reliability

The Downey Hand Centre sensitivity test was tested on normal hands for test/retest reliability and showed reliability coefficients of between 0.74 (contact particles right hand) and 0.82 (vibration left and right hand). These results were deemed sufficient for research, as well as clinical use (Yerxa, 1983; Barber, 1990; Stone, 1992). The modifications in the three-phase hand sensitivity test will affect the validity of the test.

To summarise

- therapist and patient must concentrate—avoid noise and interruptions
- select the tests appropriate for the patient's abilities and condition.

References

American Society for Surgery to The Hand (1990) *The Hand Examination and Diagnosis*. 3rd edn . Churchill Livingstone, Edinburgh: 43–5

Barber L (1990) Desensitization of the Traumatized Hand. In: Hunter J, Schneider L, Mackin E, Bell J, eds. *Rehabilitation of the Hand*, 2nd edn. CV Mosby, St.Louis: 721–30

Bell-Krotoski J (1999) Research in a clinical testing sensibility: A personal journey. *Br J Hand Ther* **4**(1): 13–22

Bell-Krotoski J (1991) Advances in sensibility evaluation. Frontiers in hand rehabilitation. *Hand Clinics* 7(3): 527–46

Bell-Krotoski J (1990) 'Pocket filaments' and specifications for the Semmes-Weinstein monofilaments. *J Hand Ther* Jan-March: 26–31

Bell-Krotoski J, Buford W (1997) The force/time relationship of clinically used sensory testing instruments. *J Hand Ther* **10**: 297–309

Bell-Krotoski J, Tomancik E (1987) The repeatability of testing with Semmes-Weinstein monofilaments. *J Hand Surg* **12A**: 155–61

Bexon C, Salter M (2000) Assessment. In: Salter M, Cheshire L, eds. *Hand Therapy Principles and Practice*. Butterworth-Heinemann, Oxford: 43–50

Brand PW Hollister A (1999) *Clinical Mechanics of the Hand*, 3rd edn. CV Mosby, St Louis: 340–43

Dellon AL (1981) *Evaluation of the Sensibility and Re-education of Sensation of the Hand*. Williams and Wilkins, Baltimore: 6–9; 99;102–4: 123–39

Dellon AL (1978) The moving two point discrimination test: Clinical evaluation of the quickly-adapting fiber/receptor system. *J Hand Surg* **3**(5): 474–81

Edshage S (1980) Experience with clinical methods of testing sensation after peripheral nerve surgery. In: Jewett DL, McCarroll HR, eds. *Nerve Repair and Regeneration*. Mosby, St Louis: 246

Fess EE (1998) Making a difference: The importance of good assessment tools. *Br J Hand Ther* **3**(2): 3

Hochreiter NW, Jewell MJ, Barber L, Browne P (1983) Effect of vibration on tactile sensitivity. *Physic Ther* **63**(6): 934–7

Jerosch-Herold C (1999) The clinical usefulness of two point discrimination. *Br J Hand Ther* **4**(4): 151

King PM (1997) Sensory function assessment. A pilot comparison study of touch pressure threshold with texture and tactile discrimination. *J Hand Ther* **10**(1) 24–8

Massey-Westropp N (2002) The effects of normal human variability and hand activity on sensory testing with the full Semmes-Weinstein monofilaments kit. *J Hand Therapy* **15**(1): 48–52

Merck Eurolab (2000) *Safety Data Sheet Ninhydrin Spray*. Merck Eurolab Ltd, Merck House, Poole, Dorset, England

Moberg E (1958) Objective methods for determining the functional value of sensibility in the hand. *J Bone Joint Surg* **40B**(3): 454–75

Moberg E (1991) The unsolved problem—how to test the functional value of hand sensibility. *J Hand Ther* **4**: 105–10

Moberg E (1990) Two point discrimination test. *Scan J Rehab Med* **22**: 127–30

Murphy R, Gawkrodger DJ (2000) Allergic contact dermatitis from Ninhydrin in a forensic scientist. *Contact Dermititis* **42**(6): 357

Ng CL, Ho DD, Chow SP (1999) The Moberg Pick up test: results of testing with a standard protocol. *J Hand Ther* **12**: 309–12

Novak CB (2001) Evaluation of hand sensibility: A review. *J Hand Therapy* **14**(4): 266–72

Omer GE (1980) Sensory evaluation of the pick up test. In: Jewett DL, McCarroll HR, eds. *Nerve Repair and Regeneration*. Mosby, St Louis: 250–51

Omer GE (1973) Sensibility of the hand as opposed to sensation in the hand. *Ann Chir* **27**(5): 479–85

O'Riain S (1973) New and simple test of nerve function in hand. *Br Med J* **3**: 615–16

Piirilä P, Estlander T, Hytönen M, Keskinen H, Tupasela O, Tuppurainen M (1997) Rhinitis caused by Ninhydrin develops into occupational asthma. *Eur Respir J* **10**: 1918–21

Rosén B (2003) Inter-tester reliability of a tactile gnosis test: The STI-Test. *Br J Hand Therapy* **8**(3): 98–101

Rosén B, Jerosch-Herold C (2000) Comparing the responsiveness over time of two tactile gnosis tests: Two-point discrimination and the STI–test. *Br J Hand Ther* **5**(4): 114–19

Rosén B, Lundborg G (1998) A new tactile gnosis instrument in sensibility testing. *J Hand Ther* **11**: 251–57

Stone JH (1992) *Sensibility in Clinical Assessment Recommendations*, 2nd edn. American Society of Hand Therapists, Chicago: 71–83

Thames Valley Test Company (2001) *Complete Catalogue of Psychological Tests*. Thames Valley Test Company, Thurston, Bury St Edmunds: http://www.tvtc.com

Von Prince K, Butler B (1967) Measuring sensory function of the hand in peripheral nerve injuries. *Am J Occ Ther* **21**(6): 385–95

Waylett-Rendall J (1995) Desensitization of the traumatised hand. In: Hunter J, Mackin E, Bell J, eds. *Rehabilitation of the Hand*, 4th edn. CV Mosby, St Louis: 693–700

Waylett-Rendall J (1988) Sensibility evaluation and rehabilitation. peripheral nerve problems. *Orthop Clin North Am* **19**(1): 43–56

Yekutiel M (2000) *Sensory Re-education of the Hand After Stroke*. Whurr Publishing, London and Philadelphia: 14–28

Yerxa EJ, Barber LM, Diaz O, Black W, Azen SP (1983) Development of a sensitivity test for the hypersensitive hand. *Am J Occup Ther* **37**(3): 176–81

Chapter 12
Function

Hand function must form the core of therapeutic practice, yet it is difficult to define as it covers purposeful, productive activity as well as mental, emotional and social performance (Fisher, 1992). The function of the hand intricately involves upper limb motion, strength, dexterity, motivation (McPhee, 1987), and sensation and co-ordination (Jebsen, 1969). Patients often describe loss of these in terms of their functional loss, i.e. their disability or handicap (WHO, 1980). Therefore, function must be assessed as part of a comprehensive system and this is generally of great importance to the patient. This chapter examines the uses and role of functional assessment, and describes a variety of methods for doing this, considering their advantages and usefulness.

Background

Strangely, few therapists assess function. Murray *et al* (2000) found 67% therapists tested function and, of these, 54% used their own test (n=122). The reasons given for the use of non-standard tests were lack of equipment, lack of knowledge, irrelevance of standardised measures, and lack of time. This evidence confirms Jeffreson and Hammond's (1997) findings that 81% of rheumatological occupational therapists in the United Kingdom used non-standardised measures (n=62).

There are many tests that may be norm referenced or criterion referenced. In a norm referenced test, the time taken to complete the task is recorded and the score can be compared to published norms. In criterion referenced tests, the task is compared qualitatively to the criterion of normal movements used to complete the task.

There has also been a considerable amount of work done on establishing the effects of function on disability and handicap by the completion of standardised questionnaires, which are used as outcome measures. These can be detailed and use language with which the patient is unfamiliar. Functional literacy is the ability to understand and employ printed information in daily life, at home, at work and in the community. In England, it has been shown that 24% of the population is functionally illiterate, and in some areas this rises to 40% (National Literacy Trust, 2000). Furthermore, tests and instructions translated from one language to another may not be accurate. A test suitable for one culture may not be readily transferable to another, so that questionnaires in English, originating outside the United Kingdom, may be difficult to understand (Kirwan and Reeback, 1986). The available tests range in complexity and detail. The test selected must be applicable to the patient's needs (Fisher, 1992) and abilities, both physical and cognitive, and should represent every day function (McPhee, 1987). The clinical environment where the patient is seen will also have an impact on choice—the test may have to be portable or quick if the patient is seen as part of a busy hand clinic. Cost of equipment can be of significance for many departments, particularly in non-specialised units.

The advantages and disadvantages of a selection of standardised tests are outlined below. These are: Jebsen test of hand function, Purdue pegboard test, Sollerman test, grip ability test, sequential occupational dexterity assessment (SODA), the modified hand assessment questionnaire (MHAQ), arthritis impact measurement scales, the Michigan hand and DASH outcomes. The Odstock functional assessment is also included due to its popularity. It is impossible to describe them all in depth. When using a standardised test of function, it is important to follow exactly the directions given in the original paper or manual. It is necessary to go back to the original paper and work with colleagues in the department to ensure that the test is being carried out in exactly the way recommended, or to use the manual provided by the manufacturer.

When to use functional tests

- to identify and prioritise functional problems that enable these problems to be addressed
- to monitor changes over time, particularly in rheumatoid arthritis
- to evaluate effectiveness of therapy and surgery
- to evaluate need for and effectiveness of splinting.

The Jebsen test

Sometimes known as the Jebsen-Taylor Test of Hand Function (Jebsen *et al*, 1969), the advantage of this test is that it can be carried out quickly (in about 15 minutes). The test uses inexpensive materials; although it may take some persistence to locate these materials in the United Kingdom, once assembled they are ready. The test involves writing a short sentence, turning over cards, picking up small objects, stacking checkers (draughts), simulated eating, moving empty large cans and weighted large cans. The non-dominant hand is always tested first and the test must follow the defined sequence.

For ease of application, a table should be dedicated to this purpose, and the placement of each object involved, marked permanently. If taking the test into the clinic or patient's home, an oilcloth or paper similarly marked could be used, although Jebsen shows clearly that a wooden desk is used. Directions for the therapist, and instructions to be read out to each patient, can be placed on cards and laminated to ensure standardisation is maintained.

The test involves the use of American money (pennies); increased transatlantic travel make these easier to obtain than in 1969 and, fortunately, they closely resemble the size and weight of one penny coins that British patients are more likely to handle.

Jebsen *et al* provided wonderfully detailed descriptions. Although, today, 'the regularly-sized bottle caps (each 1 inch in diameter placed with the cap facing up)' conjures up a plastic screw top to therapists who were possibly not even born in 1969. Careful scrutiny of the pictures indicates metal bottle tops are used and, fortunately, these are readily available again. The cans should be used without labels or plastic coverings. The disadvantages of this test are that the explicit instructions sound a little stilted; first asking the patient if he/she normally wears glasses for reading, when in fact he/she may already be wearing them. Also, the first task, writing with a non-dominant hand, can appear pointless, as it is an infrequently performed task. Finally, the test does not consider the quality of movement, only speed (Sollerman and Ejeskär, 1995).

Jebsen *et al* tested 300 normal subjects, aged 20–94 years, with an even sex/age distribution to produce the norms. Tests on 26 patients showed that the test had test-retest reliability ($p<0.01$) and the practice effect was not significant ($p<0.05$). Test results from 33 patients with hemiparesis, rheumatoid arthritis, and traumatic quadriparesis, compared with those in a normal group, showed that the test had discriminative ability. Since 1969, the test has been used to test patients who had cerebrovascular accidents, spina bifida, wrist arthrodesis, rheumatoid arthritis, osteoarthritis, and radioulnar synostosis (Sharma *et al* 1994).

The Jebsen test is not without its flaws but, when standardised fully, it is a cheap, quick and useful tool in departments where many hand conditions may be seen.

The Purdue pegboard test

The Purdue pegboard test (Tiffin and Asher, 1948) was designed to assist in the selection of employees in industrial jobs requiring manipulative dexterity. It is a test of finger dexterity, involving rapid, skilful, and controlled movements of small objects (Mathiowetz *et al*, 1986). It is quick to administer, taking between 2.5 and 7.5 minutes (Apfel and Carranza, 1992). The test is portable and the manufacturer provides a manual.

Tiffin and Asher (1948) gave specific instructions. The test involves placing as many pins as possible in prepared holes with the right hand, then the left, and, finally, both hands together. A period of 30 seconds is given for each test and practice time is allowed. The number of pins inserted by each hand and the number of paired pins is added together. The final part of the test is the assembly of pin, washer, collar and washer to achieve as many assemblies as possible in one minute. Both hands must move at the same time and, again, a practice time is incorporated. The score for this part of the test is calculated by scoring four for each complete assembly and a point for each item assembled. This gives a total of five scores.

The test was shown to be reliable on intra-rater testing and these reliability coefficients ranged from 0.60 to 0.76. Norm values were produced (Tiffin and Asher, 1948), but these were done on an earlier form of the test and it is recommended that these should no longer be used. Newer, normative values now exist for various age groups (Mathiowetz *et al*, 1986). The test has been shown to be valid provided it reflects the occupation for which it is contemplated. It can be a useful tool for measuring recovering dexterity.

The Sollerman hand function test

Sollerman and Sperling (1978) argued the need for a test of function to assess grip function, based on integrated activities rather than picking up activities. The eight grips most commonly used were identified, and seven of these grips were incorporated into the test. The test is made up of 20 sub-tests using the hands singly and together, each considered to be an activity of daily living; and the patient is scored on a scale of 0–4 according to given guidelines, which incorporate quality and speed. This gives a maximum score of 80. The test equipment is mounted in a box for ease of standardisation (Sollerman and Ejeskär, 1995).

This test is very popular in Scandinavia, where it is often incorporated into research (Rosén *et al*, 2000). This is not surprising as the test was designed for Swedish manners and habits, and is not necessarily immediately transferable to other cultures (Sollerman and Ejeskär, 1995). It is a reliable, valid and standardised test that looks at quality and ability (Sollerman and Ejeskär, 1995), is quick and easy to use in the clinical setting (Hammond, 2000), and takes only 20 minutes. An important aspect is that the elbow and shoulder movement is not evaluated—it is purely a test of hand function (Sollerman and Ejeskär, 1995). However, the commercial test kit is relatively expensive, the positioning of some pieces within the box is not entirely natural, nor is the box readily portable. Furthermore, some training of therapists is necessary to ensure that there is consistency in the interpretation of quality, although Sollerman and Ejeskär state that it can be used by occupational therapists without much experience of the method.

The test was evaluated for reliability and validity by comparing results with those from the Swedish insurance companies' disability rating scale and patients' estimation of hand function. This was performed on 73 arms, of 59 tetraplegic patients, prior to surgery and post surgery. This showed that the results of the Sollerman test correlate well with the disability rating scale, and that inter-rater reliability was high.

Grip ability test

The Sollerman grip function test was developed for use with general populations and it became apparent that there was a need for a shorter, simpler version for clinical use and for an efficient method to test treatment outcome for patients with rheumatoid arthritis (Dellhag *et al*, 1992). This test has only three tasks: putting a tubular stocking over the non-dominant hand, putting a paper clip on an envelope, and pouring water from a 1-litre jug with a handle into a beaker. Precise directions are given (Dellhag and Bjelle, 1995). The individual tasks are timed and discontinued if not performed within 60 seconds. The test is supremely portable, the objects involved are easy to obtain and the test takes five minutes to perform.

The test was evaluated on patients with rheumatoid arthritis and shown to have intra- and inter-rater reliability (n=20; p<0.001) and was sensitive to change (n=24. p<0.05). The validity of the test was established against the health assessment questionnaire (Dellhag and Bjelle, 1995). The grip ability test is very useful for a busy therapist in clinical practice; as with the Jebsen test, the use of laminated cards and a home-prepared kit ensures standardisation is maintained.

SODA

The sequential occupational dexterity assessment (SODA) is a standardised test assessing dexterity, defined as a complex bimanual functional ability in activities of daily living. It was developed in Holland. The test comprises 12 tasks that include writing a sentence, picking up an envelope, picking up coins, holding a telephone receiver to one ear, unscrewing the top of a toothpaste tube, handling a spoon and knife, buttoning a blouse, unscrewing a large bottle, pouring water into a glass, washing and drying hands, The therapist observes and grades the performance on a scale of 0–4, according to guidelines, and the patient is asked to score the difficulty of the task on a scale of 0–2 (van Lankveld *et al*, 1996). These are all described in detail in the manual (SODA, 1995), but the details are complex; training and extreme concentration are needed to carry out the test. The test takes 15–20 minutes (van Lankveld *et al*, 1996; 1999) and is relatively portable (Hammond, 2000). Some of the equipment may not be immediately available in the United Kingdom. The test also exists in a shortened form of six tasks, which is almost equal to the original test (van Lankveld *et al*, 1999).

SODA was evaluated on a group of 109 rheumatoid arthritis patients and was demonstrated to be reliable, with good internal consistency, and to be valid (van Lankveld *et al*, 1996), although the test has not been validated on populations outside Holland (O'Connor *et al*, 1999). Tests on smaller groups of rheumatoid arthritis patients have demonstrated test-retest reliability, sensitivity to change, and inter-rater reliability (van Lankveld *et al*, 1996). It has been shown that there is a good correlation with the Sollerman test (p<0.01); however, the SODA has better correlation with measures of impairment and is slightly quicker to administer. (O'Connor *et al*, 1999).

The Odstock hand function assessment

The Odstock hand function assessment (Roberts, 1989; Bexon and Salter, 2000) is the most popular test used in the United Kingdom, either in its published form or in departmental modification (Hammond, 1996). The chart forms a basis for analysing how patients use their hand and identifies and prioritises their problems (Bexon and Salter, 2000). The chart lists 39 everyday tasks that involve single or bilateral manual involvement, and the patient is asked to rate these as easy, fair, difficult, or impossible. Where tasks are described as difficult or impossible, the therapist and patient together analyse the reason for this, using a 10-point problem index report. When completed, the number of difficult or impossible tasks, and the reasons for their creating problems are totalled, creating a priority problem list. This test is not standardised; consequently, its reliability or validity is not established. Its popularity and use are related to the way it promotes discussion, focusses the patient's attention and aids clinical reasoning.

Health assessment questionnaire and the modified health assessment questionnaire (HAQ/MHAQ)

The Stanford health assessment (Fries *et al*, 1980;1982; Fries, 1983), known as the HAQ, was developed as a simple, self-report method to assess functional ability in rheumatoid arthritis and is well validated. Kirwan and Reeback (1986) found that the American phraseology was difficult for British patients to understand; having modified the questionnaire, they found that patients were able to interpret all questions correctly. The questionnaire has 20 questions relating to activities of daily living on dressing and grooming, rising, eating walking, hygiene, reach, grip, and activities. The patient is asked to comment on the difficulty of carrying out prescribed tasks during the last week and chooses from the following categories:

- without any difficulty
- with some difficulty
- with much difficulty
- unable.

The questionnaire also takes account of aids used; however, this can lower the score (Hammond, 1996).

The MHAQ (Pincus *et al* 1983) poses eight questions relating to the eight activities on the HAQ. Patients are asked to evaluate the eight activities in four ways (degree of difficulty, satisfaction with function, change in function, and the possible need for help). The MHAQ has the advantage that scores are not lowered when devices are used (Hammond, 1996). The scores between the HAQ and MHAQ have been shown to be highly correlated, but the MHAQ indicated a restricted range with an increased number of low scores (Blalock *et al*, 1990).

These questionnaires were shown to be used relatively infrequently by therapists. In a survey of occupational therapists (n=61), 48% used the HAQ, the majority only occasionally, and 16% used the MHAQ (Hammond, 1996). Although the tasks are not specific to the hand and of limited use in treatment planning, the questionnaire can be a useful, sensitive tool, highlighting the patient's concerns (Hammond, 1996). Some therapists send out the questionnaire with an appointment letter and use the results to guide the assessment interview. This has the advantage that the patient has thought about his/her difficulties in a logical and guided way prior to attending.

Arthritis impact measure scales (AIMS and AIMS 2)

The arthritis impact measurement scales (AIMS), another self-report questionnaire, was developed to profile health status in arthritis (Meenan *et al*, 1980). The arthritis impact measurement scale 2 (AIMS 2) was revised and expanded to give a more accurate, comprehensive and sensitive version (Meenan *et al*, 1992). This gives a potential score of ten in each of the following areas:

- mobility level, walking, and bending
- hand and finger function
- arm function
- self care
- household tasks
- social activities
- support from family and friends
- arthritis pain
- work
- level of tension and mood.

The questionnaire takes an average of 23 minutes to complete (Meenan *et al*, 1992). The advantage of this scale is that it covers a broader range than the HAQ and includes satisfaction with function, attribution of problems to arthritis, and self-identification of priority areas. It has been found to be little used by therapists working in the field of rheumatology. In a survey of occupational therapists working in rheumatology (n=61), only four used this scale occasionally (Hammond, 1996). A comparison of the hand and arm function section with the Jebsen indicates that AIMS 2 can be used as a quick, alternative outcome measure to the Jebsen. However, it does not evaluate certain aspects of hand function, e.g. pronation and supination (Hammond and Freeman, 1996). The disadvantage of the scale is that it is not suitable for use in other conditions. Also, the timescale considered is longer than for MHAQ—one month. This period of time seems to give patients problems with recall, and there is no reference to the use of gadgets that enable a patient to complete a task easily.

Michigan hand outcomes questionnaire

The Michigan hand outcomes questionnaire (Chung *et al*, 1998) has six questions relating to overall hand function, activities of daily living, pain, work performance, and patient satisfaction with hand function. There is also a final section relating to hand dominance, gender, ethnic background, and education. A mixture of time scales is used—one week and four weeks. The self-administered questionnaire takes about ten minutes to complete; reliability and validity have been established in a one-centre trial in the United States.

The DASH outcome measure

This measure was developed and sponsored by the Institute for Work and Health, The American Academy of Orthopaedic Surgeons, the American Association for Hand Surgery, the American Society for Surgery of the Hand, the American Orthopaedic Society for Sports Medicine, the American Shoulder and Elbow Surgeons, Arthroscopy Association of North America, and the American Society of Plastic and Reconstructive Surgeons. It measures disability and symptoms related to single or multiple upper limb musculo-skeletal disorders. It is a 30 item self-completed questionnaire, including 21 functional items, six symptom items and three social/role function items. There are also two optional modules, one for athletes and performing artists and the other for working populations. Use of the questionnaire is closely monitored to ensure that all results are co-ordinated and that the questionnaire is not amended in any way. The questionnaire can be obtained via the Internet address given below upon agreement of the conditions of use. There is a detailed user's manual that gives comprehensive information on the background, use, and evidence of reliability and validity (Institute for Work and Health, 2000). The form is easier to complete than the Michigan questionnaire and understandable for British people to complete, American phrases being limited, for example, 'yard work'. It has been shown to have test-retest reliability, validity and responsiveness on an American population (Beaton *et al*, 2001; 2001a).

Recording

All test results and completed questionnaires should be retained with the patient record.

The next step

Having tested function and identified and prioritised the patient's problems, it is necessary to analyse the cause of any loss or problem. The next step will be to consider how best to intervene. It may be necessary to act to restore function, for example, by increasing strength where weakness is causing the problem, or if sensation is deficient, by undertaking sensory re-education. Alternatively, it may be necessary to decide how to adapt the environment to enable the patient to function. Retesting will indicate the success of any intervention.

To summarise

- select a test suitable for the patient, condition, purpose, and place where it is to be tested
- use standardised tests whenever possible—resist the urge to amend them
- refer to original articles and study these carefully to ensure tests are carried out consistently and correctly—small changes make big differences

References

Apfel ER, Carranza J (1992) Dexterity. In: Casanova JS, ed. *Clinical Assessment Recommendations*, 2nd edn. American Society of Hand Therapists, Chicago: 85–94

Beaton D, Katz J, Fossel A, Wright J, Tarasuk V, Bombardier C (2001) Measuring the whole or the parts? Validity, reliability, and responsiveness of the disabilities of the arm, shoulder and hand outcome measure in different regions of the upper extremity. *J Hand Ther* **14**(2): 128–46

Beaton DE, Davis AM, Hudak P, McConnell S (2001a) The DASH (Disabilities of Arm, Shoulder and Hand) Outcome Measure: What do we know about it now? *Br J Hand Therapy* **6**(4): 104–18

Bexon C, Salter M (2000) Assessment. In: Salter M, Cheshire L, eds. *Hand Therapy Principles and Practice*. Butterworth-Heinemann, Oxford: 51–53

Blalock SJ, Sauter VH, DeVellis RF (1990) The modified health assessment questionnaire difficulty scale. A health status measure reviewed. *Arthritis Care Res* **3**(4): 182–88

Chung KC, Pillsbury MS, Walters MR, Hayward RA, Arbor A (1998) Reliability and validity testing of the Michigan hand outcomes questionnaire. *J Hand Surg* **23A**: 575–87

Dellhag B, Wollersjö I, Bjelle A (1992) Effect of active hand exercise and wax treatment in rheumatoid arthritis patients. *Arthritis Care Res* **5**(2): 87–91

Dellhag B, Bjelle A (1995) A grip ability test for use in rheumatology practice. *J Rheumatol* **22**(8): 1559–65

Fisher AG (1992) Functional measures, part 1: What is function, what should we measure, and how should we measure it? *Am J Occup Ther* **46**(2): 183–84

Fries JF (1983) Assessment of disability: From first to future principles. *Br J Rheumatol* **22**(Suppl): 48–58

Fries JF, Spitz P, Kraines RG, Holman HR (1980) Measurement of patient outcome in arthritis. *Arthritis Rheum* **23**(2): 137–45

Fries JF, Spitz PW, Young DY (1982) The Dimensions of health outcomes: The health assessment questionnaire disability and pain scales. *J Rheumatol* **9**(5): 789–93

Hammond A (2000) *Assessing Hand Function*. British Association of Hand Therapists Annual Conference, October 2000. University of Derby

Hammond A (1996) Functional and health assessments used in rheumatology occupational therapy: A review and United Kingdom survey. *Br J Occup Ther* **59**(6): 254–59

Hammond A, Freeman K (1996) Relationship between the Jebsen hand function test and AIMS2 scores in rheumatoid arthritis. *Arthritis Res* ARHP National Meeting Suppl S8 Item14

Institute for Work and Health (2000) DASH. Institute for Work and Health, 250 Bloor Street East, Suite 702, Toronto, Ontario M4W 1E6. http://www.iwh.on.ca

Jebsen RH, Taylor N, Trieschmann RB, Trotter MJ, Howard LA (1969) An objective and standardised test of hand function. *Arch Physic Med Rehab* June: 311–19

Jeffreson P, Hammond A (1997) Upper limb/hand function assessments in current use with rheumatology patients. *J Natl Ass Rheumatol Occupat Therapists* **11**(1): 33–37

Kirwan JR, Reeback JS (1986) Stanford health assessment questionnaire modified to assess disability in British patients with rheumatoid arthritis. *Br J Rheumatol* **25**: 206–9

McPhee SD (1987) Functional hand evaluations: A review. *Am J Occup Ther* **41**(3): 158–63

Mathiowetz V, Rogers SL, Dowe-Keval M, Donahoe L, Rennells C (1986) The Purdue pegboard: norms for 14 to 19 year olds. *Am J Occup Ther* **40**(3): 174–79

Meenan R, Gertman PM, Mason JH (1980) Measuring health status in arthritis. *Arthritis Rheum* **23**(2): 146–52

Meenan RF, Mason JH, Anderson JJ, Guccione AA, Kazis LE (1992) AIMS2. The content and properties of a revised and expanded arthritis impact measurement scales health status questionnaire. *Arthritis Rheum* **35**(1): 1–10

Murray K, Topping M, Simpson C (2000) Investigation of the hand assessment techniques used within the United Kingdom. *Br J Hand Ther* **5**(4): 125

National Literacy Trust (2000) *Literacy Issues and Database*. Swire House, 59 Buckingham Gate, London, SW1E 8AJ

O'Connor DO, Kortman B, Smith A, Ahern M, Smith M, Krishnan J (1999) Correlation between objective and subjective measures of hand function in patients with rheumatoid arthritis. *J Hand Ther* **12**: 323–29

Pincus T, Summey JA, Soraci SA, Wallston KA, Hummon NP (1983) Assessment of patient satisfaction in activities of daily living using a modified Stanford health assessment questionnaire. *Arthritis Rheum* **26**(11): 1346–53

Roberts C (1989) The Odstock hand assessment. *Br J Occup Ther* **52**(7): 256–61

Rosén B, Dahlin LB, Lundborg G (2000) Assessment of functional outcome after nerve repair in a longitudinal cohort. *Scan J Plastic Recon Surg* **34**: 71–78

Sharma SH, Schumacher R, McLellan AT (1994) Evaluation of the Jebson hand function test for use in patients with rheumatoid arthritis. *Arthritis Care Res* **7**(1): 16–19 (Corrections in 7: 109)

SODA (1995) *SODA Manual*. St. Maartensklinieck, Department Research/Development, Hengs Stdal 3, 6522 vv Nijmegen

Sollerman C, Sperling L (1978) Evaluation of ADL-function—especially hand function. *Scan J Plastic Recon Surg* **6**: 139–43

Sollerman C, Ejeskär A (1995) Sollerman hand function test. *Scan J Plastic Recon Surg* **29**: 167–76

Tiffin J, Asher EJ (1948) The Purdue pegboard: norms and studies of reliability and validity. *J Appl Psychol* **32**: 234–47

van Lankveld W, Graff MJL, van't Pad Bosch P (1999) The short version of the sequential occupational dexterity assessment based on individual task's sensitivity to change. *Arthritis Care Res* **12**(6): 417–23

van Lankveld W, van't Pad Bosch P, Bakker J, Terwindt S, Franssen M, van Riel P (1996) Sequential occupational dexterity assessment (SODA) A new test to measure hand disability. *J Hand Ther* **9**: 27–32

World Health Organisation (1980) *International Classifications of Impairments, Disabilities, and Handicaps*. WHO, Geneva

Chapter 13
Weight bearing

Weight bearing through the hand is the most primitive of hand functions. Early hominoids used their hands for locomotion, either weight bearing through the primitive extended wrist or through the knuckles (Almquist, 1992). Weight bearing through the hand, to assist with mobility, is a part of normal development, starting in the first year of life (Smelt, 1989), and continues to be important throughout life for activities of daily living, leisure and rehabilitation; it should, therefore, be included in a full hand assessment (Simpson, 1997). This ability is dependent on the strength and stability of the entire upper limb. The forces involved are greater than those used for gripping, making this a useful test of upper limb health. Two tests exist to test this ability, the dystrophile and the dynamometer, and these are described here. The work simulator, when available, is particularly suitable for testing this aspect of function (see *Chapter 15*).

When to test

These tests can be used following a fracture of the lower third of the forearm or wrist injury to identify triangular fibrocartilage complex tears and wrist instability (Kasch, 1993). They can also be used to establish if a patient, who is returning to a job involving weight bearing, such as electrical work and carpet laying, can function. If unable to function, it can be used to quantify the problem and recovery. It may highlight instability where patients complain of vague wrist pain.

Do not test

Do not perform these tests when:

- where there is a restriction on weight bearing on the wrist (Kasch, 1993)
- in the presence of unhealed fractures of the upper limb. (Kasch, 1993)
- where there are tendon repairs performed less than 12 weeks earlier in the upper limb
- if the patient cannot assume the starting position
- the test causes pain or distress.

The dystrophile

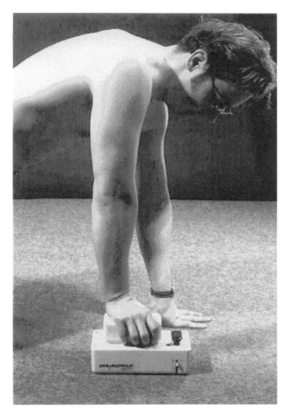

Plate 13.1 The dystrophile used to assess static stress-loading

This test, described by Kasch (1993), measures endurance; comparing static and dynamic stress-loading levels with the unaffected side. Consequently, this method is particularly suitable for fit manual workers (Simpson, 1999). The dystrophile works by displaying a light when a preset resistance is reached and a timer activates only when the resistance is reached.

How to test

- collect equipment needed—dystrophile, paper, chart and pen
- explain the purpose of the test to the patient and what he/she can expect
- test the unaffected arm first for static stress-loading
- always test on the same floor surface, as this may affect the resistance to dynamic stress-loading (Simpson, 1999)
- ask the patient to prone kneel, directly over the dystrophile and to press the top of it until the red light comes on, for ten seconds
- repeat this on the progressively harder resistances available. A normal arm will easily maintain the static stress-loading of the maximum six kilograms. Record the maximum resistance in the patient's notes
- repeat the sequence with the affected limb and record the maximum resistance. Also record the patient's reactions for each resistance, on the affected side, as 'comfortable/tolerable' or 'maximum'
- establish the dynamic stress loading by selecting the maximum resistance obtained statically on each hand. Start with the unaffected arm. The patient is asked to scrub with the dystrophile, moving it backwards and forwards, while maintaining the resistance (i.e. the light stays on). The patient is asked to scrub to the point of fatigue or mild discomfort, but not to go longer than five minutes. Record the time taken
- repeat for the affected arm, setting the resistance for the maximum described as comfortable/tolerable
- compare the raw data of pressure and timing by expressing the affected hand as a percentage of the unaffected arm.

Interpretation

There are no norms so progressive results can be compared if the test is being carried out to monitor progress. Kasch (1993) states that the test can be used to make predictions for function and suggests implications for treatment planning. If the static scores are similar, but the dynamic endurance is only 50%, then work tolerance activities could be added to the programme prior to return to work.

If static loading is considerably reduced, or the dynamic time is less than

Table 13.1: To show reduced endurance on dynamic testing

Date	Left	Right	% of unaffected
Static score	10	10	100
Dynamic loading	10	10	100
Time achieved	2.5 mins	5 mins	50

50%, then this is probably a sign of triangular fibrocartilage complex damage. Reliability testing results are not available.

The dynamometer

Static weight bearing can be tested using a dynamometer (Jamar or Baseline). This can be useful to chart progress after injury, especially where there has been a fracture of the lower third of the forearm and the flexor-radio carpal ligament and palmar ligaments are involved. Conservative treatment for wrist instability (Prosser, 1995) can be evaluated using this method.

How to test

- collect equipment needed—dynamometer, paper/chart and pen
- explain to the patient the purpose of the test and what will happen
- test the unaffected arm first
- choose a starting position that reflects the patient's functional abilities and requirements or matches the equipment available (Simpson, 2000). Three positions can be chosen:
  1 ask the patient to stand as close as possible to a hydraulic/electrically-operated table, but with his/her leg not touching it. Raise the table until it is at the level of the patient's greater trochanter. Place the dynamometer at the edge of the table, with the meter pointing in the direction the patient is facing. Instruct the patient to lean forward and place his/her hand on the handle of the dynamometer and push down as hard as possible for ten seconds

2   seat the patient on a table with the feet unsupported. Place the metered top of the dynamometer at the edge of the table, parallel to the patient's side. Ask the patient to place his/her hand on the handle of the dynamometer and to attempt to lift his/her body weight. This manoeuvre must be carefully supervised to ensure the patient does not overbalance

3   ask the patient to prone kneel. Place the dynamometer under his/her hand and ask him/her to push down as hard as possible on the handle of the dynamometer for ten seconds

- record the maximum score taken from the red indicator needle

- the procedure is repeated on the affected arm

- if a dynamometer is not available, a set of bathroom scales can be substituted for the dynamometer in the prone kneeling position. This has the advantage of being cheaper and readily available in almost all clinical situations. Patients also find scales more comfortable than either the dystrophile or the dynamometer (Simpson, 1999).

Interpretation

No norms are available, so it is necessary to compare with the opposite arm and previous readings. One patient tested on ten consecutive days by one tester showed 7.7% error in standing, 23.5% in sitting, and 46.8% in prone kneeling (Simpson, 2000). Inevitably after a fractured forearm, the ability to weight bear through the hand will be decreased; however, this should increase slowly, but is unlikely to return fully by three months (Simpson, 1997).

When this part of the assessment is complete, the therapist should be able to quantify static stress-loading of the wrist and, if tested, dynamic stress-loading. If results indicate wrist instability, a referral to a surgeon may be required. Other musculo-skeletal tests may be carried out to confirm suspicions (see *Chapter 14*). If generalised lack of strength or endurance is present, strengthening regimes may be useful.

To summarise

- choose a testing method reflecting the patient's particular needs and the equipment available.

References

Almquist EE (1982) Evolution of the distal radioulnar joint. *Clin Orthop* **275**: 5–13

Kasch MC (1993) Stress testing of the wrist using the dystrophile. *J Hand Ther* **Jan–Mar**: 48–49

Prosser R (1995) Conservative management of ulnar carpal instability. *Aus Physiother* **41**(1): 41–46

Simpson C (2000) *Weight Bearing Through the Hand: Postural Considerations for Measurement.* Poster Book VII, Congress of the Federation of the European Societies for Surgery of the Hand and VI Congress of the European Federation of Societies for Hand Therapy: 135

Simpson C. (1999) *Weight Bearing Through the Hand: Clinical Assessment.* Poster presented at Fifth Congress, The European Federation Of Societies for Hand Therapy, Athens. Freepapers and Poster Abstracts: 23–24

Simpson C (1997) Measurement of Functional Recovery Following Fracture of the Lower One Third of the Forearm. Research Project for Postgraduate Diploma in Biomechanics. Strathclyde University

Smelt HR (1989) Effect of an inhibitive weight-bearing mitt on tone reduction and functional performance in a child with cerebral palsy. *Phys Occup Ther Paediatr* **9**(2): 53–80

Chapter 14
Special tests

The tests in this chapter are useful adjuncts to the clinical assessment process, but do not easily fit in with the topics elsewhere. They are in alphabetical order for convenience.

Allen test

Originally described by Allen (1929) and subsequently modified, this reliable test quickly demonstrates arterial patency in the hands and digits. It is useful where the hand or fingers are pink, but the patient complains of pain and a cold feeling in the fingers (Ashbell *et al*, 1967). If circulation is deficient, this will have implications if any form of compression, elevation, electrotherapy or exercise are contemplated.

How to test

In his original paper, Allen suggests the compression of one artery at a time. However, it is recommended that the test be performed using bilateral compression (ASSH, 1990; de Herder, 1992).

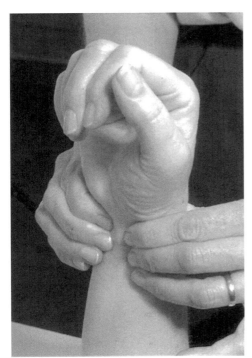

Plate 14.1: Performing the Allen test

- seat the patient at a table. Stand facing the patient
- ask the patient to put his/her elbow on the table, with the hand elevated. Compress the radial and ulnar arteries at the wrist (in the radial groove and Guyon's canal). Ask the patient to open and close the fist a few times, to exsanguinate the hand. Alternatively, Allen (1929) recommended maintaining a clenched fist for a few minutes, which is thought preferable by many practitioners
- ask the patient to open the hand in a relaxed position (i.e. partially extended). It should remain blanched
- release the radial artery; if the arteries are intact the hand should flush and then gradually fade to its normal colour (Allen, 1929)
- note the time taken for normal colour to return to the whole hand. This is usually five seconds in a healthy hand (ASSH,1990; de Herder, 1992). Record this as 'Allen test radial artery five seconds'
- repeat the test and release only the ulnar artery
- the test is negative if, on both occasions, the whole hand flushes, indicating arterial patency. If one side takes con-

siderably longer, this suggests that the artery is less dominant than the other

- the test can be performed on individual digits (Ashbell *et al*, 1967).

Finkelstein's test

The name of the Swiss surgeon, Fritz de Quervain, has been associated with a stenosing tendovaginitis, affecting the tendon sheath of abductor pollicis longus and extensor pollicis brevis, since 1895. De Quervain (1997) credits his former chief, Professor Kocher, with the first written description and treatment of this condition. Patients generally present with pain around the radial styloid, which has a gradual onset and is worse on grasping, abduction of the thumb, and ulnar deviation. Wrist pain is increased if resistance is applied to abductor pollicis longus and extensor pollicis brevis (Moore, 1997). Finkelstein's test (Finkelstein, 1930) continues to be the most pathognomonic physical sign of de Quervain's tenosynovitis (Moore, 1997) and involves a maximal stretch to the entire tendon sheath.

How to test

- ask the patient to hold up the hand and make a tight fist with the thumb against the palm
- take the fist into extreme ulnar deviation. The test is positive if this position causes intense pain, which is relieved when the thumb is extended. This confirms the presence of the tenosynovitis.

Plate 14.2: The painful position in a positive Finkelstein's test

Froment's sign

Froment first described this test in 1915 and his work was helpfully translated and reprinted by Kaplan (1972). It is used to establish if adductor pollicis, which is innervated by the ulnar nerve, is working.

How to test

- offer the patient a piece of paper. Froment used a folded newspaper
- the patient takes it in both hands; he/she will almost certainly take it between the thumb of each hand and the radial border of the index finger

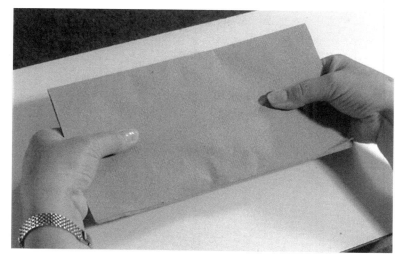

- ask the patient to pull forcibly on the paper
- the test is positive, showing that there is an ulnar nerve paralysis, if the thumb flexes at the interphalangeal joint and the volar surface of the thumb is not in complete contact with the paper. Establish this by comparing with the opposite hand.

Plate 14.3: Testing for Froment's sign

Gilliatt's test

Carpal tunnel syndrome, first identified by Sir James Paget in 1854, is a compression neuropathy of the median nerve at the wrist (Simovic and Weinberg, 2000). Typically, such a patient will complain of paraesthesia or hypesthesia in the distribution of the median nerve. Symptoms can be aggravated by strenuous use of the hand and patients often describe night pain, which may be relieved by hanging the hands out of bed. Pain may be referred to the forearm, elbow or shoulder. Thenar atrophy may be present (see also *Phalen's test*). Gilliatt's test can be used to confirm the presence of carpal tunnel syndrome (Gilliatt and Wilson, 1953). The test was based on the chance discovery that the application of a pneumatic cuff to arrest circulation worsened symptoms of acroparaesthesiae (Gilliatt and Wilson, 1953). Acroparaesthesiae has been defined as extreme sensitivity at the tips of the extremities of the body caused by the compression of the nerves in the affected area or by polyneuritis (Glanze, 1986). Phalen (1966) argued that the application of a tourniquet might produce numbness and tingling in a normal hand. Gilliatt and Wilson (1953) showed that a pneumatic cuff, applied to an arm without any neurological disorder, produced a faint fluttering or vibrating sensation in the hand, which became a diffuse tingle over a period of two minutes. This occurred predominantly in the little and ring fingers. This contrasts with the application of a cuff to an arm with carpal tunnel syndrome, where tingling is experienced within 30–60 seconds in the thumb, index, and middle finger, occasionally in the ring finger, but never in the little finger (Gilliatt and Wilson, 1953).

A controlled comparison of Gilliatt's test with nerve conduction tests in 32 hands showed Gilliatt's test was helpful in establishing the presence of carpal tunnel syndrome and its severity (Docquier *et al*, 1987).

How to test

- equipment required is a sphygmomanometer, stopwatch paper, and pen
- explain the purpose of the test to the patient
- ask the patient to tell you when his/her symptoms are reproduced
- place the cuff of the sphygmomanometer above the patient's elbow and inflate it to 220mm Hg (Gilliatt and Wilson, 1953). Set the stopwatch
- note the time symptoms appear. The test is negative if this takes longer than 60 seconds (Docquier *et al*, 1987).

Intrinsic and extrinsic tightness

This test, to identify intrinsic tightness, was described by Bunnell *et al* (1948).

Intrinsic tightness—how to test

- hold the MCP joints in 0° extension
- maintain this position and try to passively flex the IP joints
- passively flex the MCP joints and then attempt to flex the IP joints
- the test is positive, i.e. there is intrinsic muscle tightness, if the IP joints can only be flexed when the MCP joints are flexed.

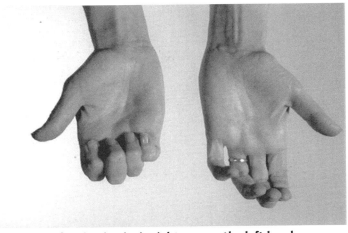

Plate 14.4: Showing intrinsic tightness on the left hand

It is important to distinguish between intrinsic and extrinsic tightness in order to make effective treatment plans.

Extrinsic tightness test

How to test—finger flexors

- passively fully extend the finger joints and try to maintain this while extending the wrist
- the test is positive, i.e. there is extrinsic tightness, if the fingers flex when the wrist is extended (ASSH, 1990).

How to test—finger extensors

- passively fully flex the finger joints and try to maintain this while flexing the wrist
- the test is positive, i.e. there is tightness of the finger extensors, if the fingers extend when the wrist is flexed (ASSH, 1990).

Kapandji method of testing thumb opposition

Thumb opposition is a complex movement, vital to function. It can be measured with a goniometer, measuring abduction and flexion, or radiologically, using two specific views of the CMC joint. These methods do not take into account the longitudinal rotation in pronation, which occurs when opposing the thumb fully; therefore, the simplest and most precise method is to use the Kapandji method, which gives a score for each component throughout the whole course of opposition (Kapandji, 1992).

How to test

- seat the patient at a table with the forearm pronated, the wrist extended naturally and the thumb on the lateral aspect of the proximal phalanx of the index finger. This position scores 0
- ask the patient to touch the lateral aspect of the middle phalanx of the index finger with the thumb. When achieved this position scores 1
- ask the patient to touch the lateral aspect of the terminal phalanx of the index finger. When achieved this position scores 2
- ask the patient to touch the tip of the index finger with the thumb. When achieved this position scores 3
- ask the patient to touch the tip of the middle finger with the thumb. When achieved this position scores 4
- ask the patient to touch the tip of the ring finger with the thumb. When achieved this position scores 5
- ask the patient to touch the tip of the little finger with the thumb. When achieved this position scores 6
- ask the patient to run the tip of the thumb down the little finger beyond the distal interphalangeal crease. This position scores 7
- ask the patient to run the tip of the thumb down the little finger beyond the interphalangeal crease of the little finger. This position scores 8
- ask the patient to run the tip of the thumb down the little finger beyond the proximal crease of the little finger,

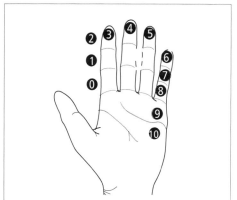

Figure 14.1: The Kapandji method scoring points

which corresponds with the base of the first phalanx. This position scores 9

- ask the patient to run the tip of the thumb down to the distal palmar crease below the little finger; this position scores 10, provided it is possible to slide a pencil through the arch made by the thumb (Bexon and Salter, 2000).

Recording

The score can be easily recorded, as thumb opposition, Kapandji and the score. It is possible to be even more precise (Collings, 1997).

Phalen's test or wrist flexion test

Another test to confirm the presence of carpal tunnel syndrome was devised by Phalen (1966). Quicker to perform than Gilliatt's test, it is preferred by many practitioners. This test cannot be used where there is an advanced degree of sensory loss in the hand.

How to test

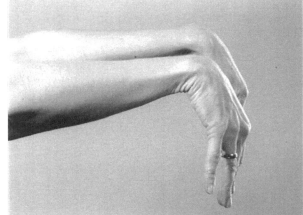

- ask the patient to hold the forearms vertically and allow both the hands to drop into complete flexion at the wrist for a minute. This position increases the pressure on the median nerve
- the patient is asked to say when pain is felt
- time the test and record when symptoms appear. If longer than a minute, this is regarded as irrelevant
- the test is positive if the symptoms are experienced.

Plate 14.5: A provocative position for Phalen's test

Reliability

Phalen (1966) found that, of 515 cases of carpal tunnel syndrome, the test was positive in 74% (380) and negative in the remaining 135.

Tinel's sign

This sign is often attributed to Tinel (1915) and refers to the tingling sensation or formication sign produced by slight percussion after injury to a peripheral nerve. The nomenclature of this sign is an interesting legacy of the Great War, which sadly created incalculable numbers of severe nerve injuries. In 1907, Trotter and Davidson described the stroking method of eliciting cutaneous anaesthesia. They discussed an area of altered sensibility surrounding the area of anaesthesia; this area extended over a period of time and correlated to recovery of sensation. In March 1915, Paul Hoffmann, a German neurophysiologist and military doctor, published work on a method of evaluating the success of nerve repair, demonstrating that stimulation of the nerve distal to the site of the injury produces sensation. 'Moderate finger pressure—-produced a tingling sensation' (Hoffman, 1915, translated by Buck-Gramcko and Lubahn, 1993). In October 1915, on the opposite side of the trenches, Jules Tinel, a French neurosurgeon, published his work on the formicating sign; formicating meaning a sensation like the crawling of an ant or barely perceived electrical shock in response to stroking distally following a nerve repair. In German speaking countries, the sign is known as the Hoffmann-Tinel sign, while the Anglo-American literature prefers Tinel's sign (Buck-Gramcko and Lubahn, 1993).

Tinel (1915; 1917) stated that this sign indicates the presence of regenerating nerve fibres and the absence or presence of migration to follow the progression of regeneration. The sign appears 4–6 weeks after injury. It is regarded as a favourable sign if the point at which it is experienced moves distally, in line with the distribution of the nerve, as it gives evidence of axonal regeneration (Tinel, 1917; Tubiana, 1996). The test should never cause pain; if pain is elicited by tapping, it should be regarded as evidence of a neuroma (Tinel, 1917; Moldaver, 1978).

How to test

- ensure that the patient is comfortable and the arm supported
- explain the purpose of the test to the patient and ask him/her to report if he/she experiences any mild tingling
- start distally, and gently and slowly stroke (Moldaver, 1978) or tap using the tip of the finger or felt-tipped pen the patient's skin over the route that would have been taken by the injured nerve (Tubiana *et al*, 1996)
- record the point at which the tingling ceases. This is known as a positive advancing Tinel sign (Bexon and Salter, 2000)
- mark the point and measure from a convenient bony landmark. If the point of the lesion is known, calculate the difference (Stone, 1992). If not known, repeat the process starting proximally until the sensation is expe-

rienced or a static positive Tinel sign is obtained (Bexon and Salter, 2000). Measure the distance between the two positive signs

- repeat the process every 4–6 weeks either until the positive distal point reaches the fingertips or there is no further recovery.

Reliability

The sign will be difficult to elicit if the nerve underlies a large muscle mass, and cannot be demonstrated if the lesion is proximal to the posterior root ganglion. However, sometimes it is absent even if the nerve is regenerating. Consequently, the sign should be interpreted in conjunction with other clinical findings (Tubiana *et al*, 1996). Standardisation of this test is poor; recent work has attempted to standardise and grade the tingling response using a vibrostimulator (Spicher *et al*, 1999).

Watson manoeuvre

This test, described by Kirk Watson *et al* (1988), can be useful in diagnosing scapho-lunate instability. Typically, the patient will present with wrist pain, weakness of grip, and clicks or clunks may be reported. This is often accompanied by a history of trauma (if presenting unilaterally) or rheumatoid arthritis. If a static instability is present, it will be visible on X-ray; however, if it is a dynamic instability, it will not be visible unless the wrist is placed in the position in which displacement occurs (Leslie, 1994). Sometimes this test is known as the scaphoid shift test (Tubiana *et al*, 1996), although it is provocative manoeuvre rather than a test (Watson *et al*, 1988).

How to test

- face the patient across a table with diagonally opposed hands (right to right), and elbows on the table, as if about to arm wrestle
- slightly pronate the patient's forearm. Grasp the wrist from the radial side, placing your thumb on the palmar prominence of the scaphoid and wrapping fingers round the distal radius
- using your other hand, grasp the patient's hand at the level of the metacarpals to control wrist position. Take wrist into ulnar deviation
- exert pressure with the thumb on the palmar aspect of the scaphoid and simultaneously press with the fingers on the distal radius
- move from ulnar deviation to radial deviation maintaining the pressure
- note any clunks, pain reproduction and the feel of the movement.

Plate 14.6: The Watson manoeuvre

Interpretation

The usual rotation of the scaphoid as the wrist moves from ulnar to radial deviation lies behind the scaphoid shift. If the scaphoid:

- quickly pushes the examiner's hand out of the way, it suggests rigid periligamentous support
- pushes onto the radius and when thumb pressure is withdrawn a loud 'thunk' is heard, it suggests ligament laxity
- moves with a gritty sensation, it suggests loss of smooth articular cartilage
- moves with a click, it suggests bony change producing impingement.

If dorsal pain is produced as the scaphoid shifts, this indicates rotary subluxation of the scaphoid. Patients with scaphoid fractures or non-union will experience pain similar to that which they experience on loading.

To summarise

- select a clinical test to:
  - confirm diagnosis
  - monitor recovery
  - measure activity.

References

Allen EV (1929) Thromboangiitis obliterans: Methods of diagnosis of chronic occlusive arterial lesions distal to the wrist with illustrative cases. *Am J Med Sci* **178**: 237–44

American Society for Surgery of the Hand (1990) *The Hand Examination and Diagnosis*. Churchill Livingstone, New York: 45–47

Ashbell TS, Kutz JE, Kleinert E (1967) The digital Allen test. *Plastic Recon Surg* **39**(3): 311–12

Bexon C, Salter M (2000) Assessment. In: Salter M, Cheshire L, eds. *Hand Therapy: Principles and Practice*. Butterworth-Heinemann, Oxford: 24–25

Buck-Gramcko D, Lubahn JD (1993) The Hoffmann-Tinel sign. *J Hand Surg* **18B**: 800–5

Bunnell S, Doherty EW, Curtis RM (1948) Ischaemic contracture, local, in the hand. *Plastic Recon Surg* **3**: 424–33

Collings J (1997) A handy tip. Kapandji's thumb opposition evaluation. *Br J Hand Ther* **2**(6): 16

de Herder E (1992) *Vascular Assessment in Clinical Assessment Recommendations*, 2nd edn. American Society of Hand Therapists, Chicago: 29–39

de Quervain F (1997) On a form of chronic tendovaginitis. Trans: Illgen R, Shortkroff S. *Am J Orthop* **Sept**: 641–43; Original published in: *Korrespondenzblatt für Schweizer Ärzte 1895*; **25**:389–94

Docquier J, Soete P, Forthomme JP, Twahirwa J, Godfraind P (1987) Le test de Gilliatt: Une alternative a l'EMG dans le diagnostic du syndrome du canal carpien. *Acta Orthop Belg* **53**(4): 495-97

Finkelstein H (1930) Stenosing tenovaginitis at the radial styloid process. *J Bone Joint Surg Am* **12**: 504–9

Froment J (1972) Prehension and the sign of the thumb in paralysis of the ulnar nerve. Trans: Kaplan EB. From article in: *Presse Medicale*. October 21st 1915, **23**: 409 ff

Gilliatt RW, Wilson TG (1953) A pneumatic tourniquet test in the carpal tunnel syndrome. *Lancet* **2**: 595–97

Glanze WD, ed (1986) *Mosby's Dictionary of Medicine and Nursing*. CV Mosby, St. Louis

Kapandji AI (1992) Clinical evaluation of the thumb's opposition *J Hand Ther* **Apr–Jun**: 102–6

Leslie IJ (1994) Carpal instability. Mini symposium: The wrist. *Curr Orthop* **8**: 14–22

Moldaver J (1978) Brief note: Tinel's sign. *J Bone Joint Surg* **60A**(3): 412–14

Moore JS (1997) De Quervain's tenosynovitis. *J Occup Env Med* **39**(10): 990–1002

Phalen GS (1966) The carpal tunnel syndrome. *J Bone Joint Surg* **48A**(2): 211–27

Simovic D, Weinberg DH (2000) Carpal tunnel syndrome. *Arch Neurol* **57**: 754–55

Spicher C, Kohut G, Miauton J (1999) At which stage of sensory recovery can a tingling sign be expected? A review and proposal for standardization and grading. *J Hand Ther* **12**(4): 298–308

Stone JH (1992) *Sensibility in Clinical Assessment*, 2nd edn. American Society of Hand Therapists, Chicago: 71–83

Tinel J (1917) *Nerve Wounds*. Auth Trans Rothwell F, revised and edited Joll CA. Ballière and Co, London

Tinel J (1915) Le signe du fourmillement. *La Presse Medicale* **47**: 388–89

Trotter W, Davies HM (1907) The exact determination of areas of altered sensibility. *Rev Neurol Psychiatry* **5**(10): 761–72

Tubiana R, Thomine J-M, Mackin E (1996) *Examination of the Hand and Wrist*. Martin Dunitz, London: 188; 355–56

Watson HK, Ashmead D, Makhlouf MV (1988) Examination of the scaphoid. *J Hand Surg* **192**: 481–84

Chapter 15
The future

The roots of hand assessment, the tools and techniques, described in this book, lie firmly in the past. The volumeter is based on the Archimedes principle, believed to have been described between 387–212 BC. The bulk of work has been undertaken in the nineteenth and early twentieth century by pioneers, such as Regnier (1807), Webber (1835), Von Frey (1896), Trotter and Davidson (1907), Wright (1912), and Fox (1917). It is hard to identify a genuinely recent development; the relative newcomer, the hydraulic five-grip dynamometer, was developed by Bechtol in 1954. The prime catalysts for change have been war and epidemic. Inevitably, the huge numbers of casualties in the First and Second World Wars led to increased knowledge. The poliomyelitis epidemic in the United States, in the early part of the twentieth century, provided a similar impetus. Sadly, war and epidemic continue throughout the world, but the catalysts for change will now, I believe, be technology and government intervention. This chapter gives a personal view of what the future might hold.

The technological developments in the last fifty years have been immense. Early computers filled whole rooms and performed limited functions; today palm tops have a much greater capacity and, as they enter mass production, become less costly. The Internet, or the information super highway, give huge opportunities in all areas of life, but so far there has been limited impact on hand assessment and hand therapy. In Britain, this has been slower than in the United States of America, where Fess (1995; 1998) has urged caution on the use of computerised tools. Currently, two types of system are available for clinical hand assessment in Britain, but are not widely used, largely due to cost pressures on individual departments. The first is the work simulator, the best known being the BTE (Baltimore Therapeutic Equipment), and, secondly, there are computerised systems that use the physical tests currently in use. These systems are described below. The chapter will then consider the potential for change through technology and government intervention.

Work simulators

Possibly the most expensive of the modern systems, these are located at a few major centres in the United Kingdom and can be used for assessment and/or treatment of patients. The idea for the work simulator came from Raymond Curtis, a Baltimore hand surgeon, who envisaged one clinical device to simulate all motions of the 'real world' and of work activities. The aim of the simulator was to rehabilitate injured workers, using the activities to which they were to return and possibly were performing when injured, using a single piece of apparatus. Curtis and a retired engineer, John Engalitcheff, developed the first device in 1979. Many users are very enthusiastic about the benefits of the systems (van Iderstine, 1996; Williams and Wolfe, 1997; Woodbridge, 1993).

There are three major components: the electrically controlled variable resistance device, multiple tools, which can be attached to the device, and the computerised controls consisting of the console, visual display screen, and keyboard (Curtis and Engalitcheff, 1981). All results are shown on a visual display unit and recorded by the computer for print out. By selecting the appropriate tool, the forces involved in a wide selection of tasks, from pinch grip to pulling a trolley, can be assessed. The system enables maximum static and dynamic strength to be tested, repeated and compared with the opposite hand or previous records. It is possible to restrict range and to perform repeated measurements, over a specified period, to assess endurance and the effects of repetition on pain. The coefficient of variation is calculated on repeated efforts and a graphical display is possible (BTE, 2001). Normative values have been calculated for some of the functions (Bhambhani *et al*, 1994; Esmail *et al*, 1995) and good correlation on grip testing with the Jamar dynamometer has been demonstrated (Beaton *et al*, 1995). Patients appear to enjoy the high tech appearance and are, themselves, quickly able to set it up for treatment.

Role of assessment with the work simulator

- all age groups and conditions can be tested on the work simulator, but clinical judgement is needed to ensure that no inappropriate or harmful tests are selected for the individual patient
- the options for positioning enable it to be adapted to assess or treat any individual irrespective of size
- the range of devices and versatility of the simulator enable it to be used to assess almost any work position and task. It can be used to define the position, tool, repetitions, pace, and forces involved in a particular work task. The patient can use his/her own tool or adaptations to tools can be made and assessed. These factors are helpful when assessing fitness to return to work, or the type of job or tool to be avoided, and can be useful when preparing medico-legal assessments. Caution has been advocated on using BTE results alone (Kennedy and Bhambhani, 1991)
- through the reproduction of presenting pain, it can be used to assist in the diagnosis of physical problems, such as an impaction disorder of the carpal bones. The use of controlled repetitions and quantification of forces involved facilitates this; however, it does not give an instant diagnosis—the therapist's knowledge and clinical judgment are required to select the tests and interpret results
- specific manual handling procedures can be assessed, to establish if correct technique is used
- changes over a period of time can be monitored, for example in neurological conditions that follow a fluctuating or unknown course

- cognitive problems could be highlighted when following instructions. It is always helpful to be aware of these

- assessment of endurance to isotonic activity providing numerical data (Woodbridge, 1993)

- consistency of effort can be assessed when used in conjunction with other findings (Woodbridge, 1993).

Disadvantages of work simulators

- concerns have been raised over the calibration of the BTE Systems by several authors (Fess, 1986, 1993; 1995; 1998; Cetinok *et al*, 1995; Coleman *et al*, 1996). It has been recommended that the W10 model of the BTE should not be used in the dynamic mode for evaluations requiring constant torque (Cetinok *et al*, 1995). It should be noted that the new models (Simulator 11 and Primus) have tried to address these criticisms

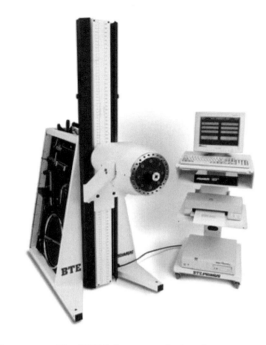

Plate 15.1: The BTE Primus work simulator. Reproduced by kind permission of Baltimore Therapeutic Company

- the units displayed are not always meaningful to the therapist or patient (e.g. newtons and watts)

- in view of the cost of any work simulator, it is necessary to invest some considerable time developing familiarity with its operation, in order to use it to best advantage. If not used fully, it represents a poor investment.

Computerised systems

In America, the computerised process is further developed; for example, there is a system that incorporates video, X-ray, and note-keeping facilities, as well as the conventional hand assessment methods used (Dexter System). This system is in use at one centre in the United Kingdom (Pratt and Burr, 2000).

Two systems available in Britain are computerised versions of the conventional methods described in this book. These are the HATS (hand assessment and treatment system) and the E-LINK System. Other systems are currently under development.

HATS

The HATS system was developed and evaluated between January 1997 and May 1999, and funded by the European Telematics Commission for the Elderly and the Disabled DG XIII. The development team included therapists, surgeons and engineers from Britain, Germany and Sweden. The acronym HATS stands for 'hand assessment and treatment system'. There is no treatment component; this is a historical part of the development phase. The concept grew out of discussions to find a further application for the Handy 1 Robot (Rehab Robotics Ltd, Staffordshire) (Topping and Smith, 1999). The system uses the traditional methods of assessment with which therapists are familiar.

HATS (Rehab Robotics Ltd, Staffordshire) comprises push button tools to measure range of movement, grip strength, pinch strength, circumference, and

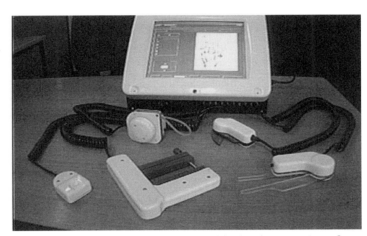

span. A computer with touch screen and Windows™ software records all relevant patient data at each visit. There are several screens for storing data achieved by other methods (sensibility, other tests, and information related to the whole patient). These results can be printed out quickly if attached to a printer, or electronically transmitted to others in the team. Automated report writing facilities are incorporated that can represent information graphically, as well as in written form (Heck *et al*, 1997; Perlick *et al* 1997; Topping, 1997; Topping *et al*, 1999).

Plate 15.2: HATS system (Reproduced by kind permission of Rehab Robotics Ltd)

The clinical evaluation of prototype systems was carried out over an eight-month period and compared HATS with conventional tools; 438 assessments were carried out on a wide range of subjects (assessments included healthy subjects and patients). The evaluation showed that HATS maintained its calibration in the clinical setting better than the conventional tools concurrently in use. Limits of agreement (Bland and Altman, 1986) for intra-rater and inter-rater reliability were calculated for all tools and were broadly similar or superior to the conventional tools; this superiority was particularly noticeable for the span gauge. Comparison of speed of assessment showed that HATS was significantly faster than the conventional tools, saving 29.2% on measurement times alone. Further considerable timesavings can be made by the reporting facility. Questionnaires showed that HATS was perceived as being quicker, more accurate, and more comfortable by patients and normal subjects than conventional tools. Furthermore, therapists preferred the system. HATS proved to withstand daily cleaning and department use well. Several areas for improvement were fed back to the developers for action. Report writing was not included in the evaluation (Heck *et al*, 1999; Murray *et al*, 2000; Murray *et al*, 1999; Simpson *et al*, 2000; Simpson *et al*, 1999).

The system is not in widespread use in Britain. In large or busy hand departments multiple systems may be necessary.

E-LINK

E-LINK (Biometrics Ltd, Gwent) is a development of the computerised upper limb exerciser to incorporate hand assessment. It has a range of accessory kits, with a large and small goniometer, a dynamometer, and a pinchmeter. These enable measurements to be taken and stored. Like the HATS system, these are more sensitive at low values than the conventional dynamometers and pinch gauges. The E-LINK registers forces as small as 0.1 (kilograms or pounds). It is possible to carry out a rapid exchange test (see *Chapter 8*), calculate the coefficient of variation, and measure sustained grip over time. There are also a variety of screens for incorporating data and tests from other sources. There are more screens than for the HATS system relating directly to the hand, such as manual muscle testing, dexterity, and provocative diagnostic tests. The system has the advantage of being relatively portable when used with a lap top computer.

The makers of E-LINK purchase Jamar dynamometers, unpainted and unassembled, directly from the manufacturer. The handles are coated in the company's trademark purple colour prior to assembly by the engineering and production team in South Wales. It is claimed that, through the assembly process and the use of a precision sensor, the end result is a dynamometer that is accurate to 1% full scale. (This is ±1kg at 100 kg). Furthermore, calibration is maintained over time. The manufacturer states that, as the exterior of the Jamar is not modified, the Jamar normative values do apply. The analysis portion of the E-LINK software compares results against norm values in both graphic and table form. The norm values are based on the patient's age, sex and dominant hand, so this information must be documented in the patient information for the comparison to be made (Miller, 2001). Results are printed out in a clear and easily understood form.

In departments where the upper limb exerciser is in constant use, it may be necessary to purchase an additional computer for assessment, and multiple systems may be needed.

Choosing a system

The cost of any work simulator or computerised system will be high and, for most departments, this would probably involve the production of a business case to obtain capital or charitable funds. As part of this process, it would be necessary to appraise the options available. This usually involves seeking assistance from the supplies department, engineering department, and information technology experts. It should involve the following:

- explore all relevant literature to make an informed decision on calibration and reliability. Take independent engineering advice whenever possible
- assess the suitability of methods for local use. This will depend on the profile of cases seen in a department and sociological factors of the catchment area. Consider the conditions that it would be used for and the frequency of use
- consider the potential advantages to the department and weigh against any problems, such as space constraints
- consider how each system would fit into plans for the electronic patient record (EPR), which involves the computerisation of medical records. It will be necessary to contact the Trust's information technology experts about this
- whenever possible, trials are beneficial to experience ease of operation. The results of these should be included in the business case. Prior to embarking on a trial, ensure that indemnity and insurance are arranged
- investigate the training provided in the use of any system following purchase
- investigate any hidden costs or consumables. Investigate rental and purchase options
- investigate the maintenance and repair of the systems for ease and cost.

The way forward

Technology, economic and social factors have wrought great changes in working and social life. Consequently, it would be unreasonable to assume hand therapy assessment will continue as before. Working life in Britain has changed radically over the last 25 years, with fewer people employed in heavy industry, such as coal mining and steel production, and there is an increased emphasis on safety in the work place. Leisure time in Britain has also developed markedly in importance, and the opportunities available are greater. The resultant injuries, and the demands of the workplace and leisure, will change treatment needs. Furthermore, surgical techniques have become more sophisticated and complex—replantation and transplantation of the hand are now possible. These factors will, in turn, affect the type of therapeutic assessment required and this will be facilitated by new technology and government intervention.

Technology developed in unrelated areas, with greater resources, present wonderful opportunities for therapists, combining accuracy and portability of measurement with the understanding of the normal. Load cells, developed through Formula 1 motor racing, are the size of a shirt button, yet they can sensitively measure less than 1 kilogram or up to 100 kilograms. This technology has great potential for the measurement of grip, pressure, and torque (Novatech, 2001). Fibre optic strips, developed to design and produce precision tools, can be used to measure movement in single or multiple joints. This has resulted in a portable device (Shape Tape) that will measure and create a 3-D computer image and data set of its shape in real time (Measurand Inc, 2001). This could give an exact range of motion measurement, in addition to information on patterns of movement in function. Developments such as these could make it possible to calculate the forces exerted by each muscle, and the cumulative forces needed for function can be quantified and norm values established. The clinician could then test the patient and calculate exactly the amount of improvement needed and achieved. The measurement of tremor could be carried out simply in the clinic, by measuring the frequency. This has the potential to evaluate the effects of medical and therapeutic intervention and possibly confirm diagnosis in tremor (for example, Parkinsonian tremor tends to have a frequency of 3–6Hz while alcohol-induced tremor is 8.5Hz). Our understanding of sensibility could be clarified by the work being carried out on active touch and the sensory landscape; this could greatly improve our ability to test sensibility accurately. Perhaps new devices would safely and non-invasively unlock the mystery of carpal bone movement in the normal wrist, permitting diagnosis of abnormalities when there is pain and/or loss of function. Technological developments such as these could enable us to measure the exact size and shape of the limb quickly. The biomechanical laboratory could be portable and available to all in the clinical setting.

Government intervention in public healthcare in Britain has markedly increased in response to the technology available, public dissatisfaction, and the effects of infinite demand on finite resources. Two major developments are the Information for Health Care Strategy (Department of Health, 1998) and the Plan for the NHS (Department of Health, 2000). These will have a far-reaching impact on all aspects of assessment and treatment.

The Information for Health Care Strategy requires that, by 2003, 35% of all acute hospitals must have an integrated communication system, and 100% by the year 2005. This will create the electronic patient record and the electronic health record, where all interventions are recorded in one electronic record that could be transferred to a patient-held swipe card. Consequently, patients' history will be with them wherever they go in the country, perhaps even the world. The multidisciplinary team makes every effort to communicate and avoid duplication, but integrated documentation offers the opportunity for increased communication between all involved in the patient's care. Communication will become faster—no waiting to have letters typed or records photocopied—the results of tests will appear as soon as they are carried out. A further benefit is the eradication of any duplication—each professional will no longer record the same information in a variety of records. Currently, it is possible that the doctor, physiotherapist, and occupational therapist may each record the same data (e.g. grip strength) on the same day—with the integrated electronic record available, this need only be done once. Some health professionals are concerned by the potential reduction of interaction with the patient, to the detriment of the relationship. An example often given is that of the detailed history-taking that establishes rapport between therapist and patient. It is suggested that, by merely accepting the history already taken by another professional, this opportunity is lost. This need not be so; the therapist has the opportunity to check the history with the patient, thus eliminating any errors. It also gives the chance to elaborate on the history, which may give more detailed, revealing information and the opportunity to explore other areas, such as how the patient feels about his/her injury. When evaluating the HATS system in the clinical setting, it became clear that the device facilitated discussion and permitted increased eye contact between therapist and patient (Heck *et al*, 1999). It is the therapist's communication and social skills that build a rapport with patients, not the questions asked.

The greatest potential advantage of the electronic health record, and the technology of the digital camera, is to permit assessment to be carried out from a distance. Already, a dermatologist is able to screen patients from one practice, presenting with skin lesions, and ascertain who needs further investigation (MSGH, 2001). This can easily be extended for hand problems, with the patient assessed at a distance using electronic questionnaires, interviews, and televised functional activities. This would enable a patient, in a surgery in a remote corner of Britain, speedy access to a highly specialised team based elsewhere, perhaps even in another country. This has advantages for everyone in the team, as well as the patient. A therapist with limited experience could consult a specialist therapist in the field about a problem case. This provides an opportunity for on-the-job learning, as well as ensuring that the patient has the best possible treatment. The European Telematics Commission for the Elderly and Disabled actively encourages such programmes throughout the European Union. Continuing improvements in technology will improve the safety of remote assessment; clarity of the picture will almost certainly improve. Furthermore, haptic—kineasthetic—tactile technology already exists to feel through the computer control what is seen on a computer screen. This could permit palpation from a distance.

The digital camera is another device that could be used to provide a record of function and treatment, giving recall of a whole session. This might be helpful where there is a complaint or litigation against the therapist.

The Beveridge Report (1942) laid the foundation for the National Health Service. A basic assumption of the report was the effects of prevention of illness and restoration of capacity for work. The report states that 'Diminishing and controlling sickness—may affect the finances of the Social Insurance Fund' (Beveridge Report, 1942). Consequently, in 1948 when this part of the report was implemented, it was generally believed that, once tuberculosis was conquered, the costs of the National Health Service would decrease. This has not been the case. Demand and costs have continued to grow, as new conditions are discovered and previously terminal conditions become treatable. In consequence, clinicians realised the importance of treatment being effective, as well as efficient. It is useless to treat two patients, if there is no change, it is preferable to treat one effectively. It is imperative that scarce resources, in this context the therapists' skills and time, are correctly targeted. The concept of outcome measures to evaluate the efficacy of treatments, both individually and comparatively, has been developed and the purchaser/provider split in the NHS gave further impetus to the concept (Macey and Burke, 1995). There has also been intense activity in the United States of America on outcome measures. Outcome measures will almost certainly continue to grow in significance in Britain, and their further development increases the importance of accurate, objective, meaningful baseline and subsequent measurements. Currently, there is copious data held on individual records throughout the country. Extracting evidence from this data is a virtually impossible task. The electronic patient record and telemetry make this a real possibility, and multicentre research and audit projects could become the norm, advancing practice considerably. To do this, the use of non-standard measures must be eradicated.

The last 15 years have seen periods of radical change in the way the British health service operates, as successive governments tried to reconcile demand for services with the resources available. The resulting, frequent changes and restructuring of services has led to many NHS staff being stressed as they struggled to adjust. Many have become disillusioned and ceased practice. Furthermore, the annual winter pressures on services, as beds and accident and emergency departments fill up, have given rise to great public debate. These factors resulted in a massive consultation exercise of both staff and public, and the formulation of the new plan for the NHS (Department of Health, 2000). This plan increases funding, and staff are to work more flexibly and keep the patient, rather than the process, at the centre of activities.

Joint training at the start of courses for health professionals will be introduced. Consequently, professionals will share skills, and therapists, doctors, and nurses will undertake work that they previously did not do. Interdisciplinary and multidisciplinary working will increase and roles will change, giving opportunities for sharing of information. An illustration of the need for this is the work done on hand dominance by psychologists, which may have huge implications for the results of therapeutic assessments on grip and function; but has generally gone unnoticed by therapists. Likewise, therapists must share their knowledge and skills with other professionals; the challenge of this must not be underestimated, for the potential benefits are real. Nursing colleagues can provide useful information on the level of function of ward patients to aid assessment and reinforce treatment techniques. An important aspect of the plan for the NHS is prevention. This could give the opportunity for multidisciplinary workplace assessments and action to ensure hand health of the general population.

Perhaps the most exciting aspect of the NHS plan for therapists is that of the consultant therapist. Already, there are advanced practitioners in hand therapy who give injections, select patients for surgery and admit and discharge inpatients—formerly the sole preserve of our medical colleagues. The thorny issue of prescribing rights will inevitably be reconciled as part of the reform process. Coupled with the changes of the electronic patient record and measurement technology, this must surely mean the need for more and more sophisticated assessment methods. As assessments will be available for others, challenges on the content and conclusions from other professions can be anticipated, and this can only be met with a sound knowledge base.

Future possibilities are endless and very exciting. Measurement and communication technology are advancing constantly; the ruler, tape measure, volumeter, pocket goniometer, manual muscle test, and Moberg's collection of hardware to test sensibility could be gone for good. To achieve this Utopia, three objectives must be met:

- a huge increase in funding is required, as this area of research has been significantly underfunded
- a frank interchange of knowledge between engineers (communication, biomedical, and mechanical) and clinicians. As therapists, our knowledge of measurement technique is often comparatively poor, yet our knowledge of the feel of tissues needs to be quantified
- therapists must develop the qualities needed to facilitate the process—vision, imagination, determination, and courage to change the way we practise. The proposals for the Health Professionals Council (Department of Health, 2001) will facilitate this by ensuring that practitioners are competent to practise, and practise in a reflective manner.

To summarise

- h.and assessment has changed little during the last 50–75 years
- work simulators and computerised systems must be selected carefully
- technology and government action have opened up huge potential for change in hand assessment.

The path is not easy, but the potential benefits are huge. Therapists must use every opportunity to advance the assessment process, as it is through this that treatment techniques will be evaluated and developed.

References

Baltimore Therapeutic Equipment Company (2001) Company Profile. http:/www.bteco.com/Company.html

Beaton DE, O'Driscoll SW, Richards PR (1995) Grip strength testing using the BTE work simulator and the Jamar dynamometer: A comparative study. *J Hand Surg Am* **20**(2): 293–8

Beveridge WH (1942) *Social Insurance and Allied Services Report*. HMSO, London: 120; 159

Bhambhani Y, Esmail S, Brintnell S (1994) The Baltimore therapeutic equipment work simulator: biomechanical and physiologic norms for three attachments in healthy men. *Am J Occup Ther* **48**(1): 19–25

Bland MJ, Altman DG (1986) Statistical methods for assessing agreement between two methods of clinical measurement. *Lancet* **i**: 307–10

Cetinok EM, Renfro RR, Coleman EF (1995) A Pilot study of the reliability of the dynamic mode of one BTE work simulator. *J Hand Ther* **8**: 199–205

Coleman EF, Renfro RP, Cetinok EM, Fess EE, Shaar CJ, Dunipace KR (1996) Reliability of the manual dynamic mode of the Baltimore therapeutic equipment work simulator. *J Hand Ther* **9**(3): 223–37

Curtis RM, Engalitcheff J (1981) A work simulator for rehabilitating the upper extremity—preliminary report. *J Hand Surg* **6**: 499–501

Department of Health (2001) *Establishing the New Professions Council*. Department of Health, London, SE1 6XH. Overview. http://www.doh.gov.uk/hpcconsult1pdf

Department of Health (2000) *The NHS Plan: A Plan for Investment, A Plan for Reform: A Summary*. Department of Health, London, SE1 6XH: http:/www.doh.gov.uk/

Department of Health (1998) *Information for Health: Executive Summary*. Department of Health, London, SE1 6XH: http:/www.doh.gov.uk/nhsexipu/strategy/summary/1.htm

Esmail S, Bhambhani Y, Brintnell S (1995) Gender differences in work performance on the Baltimore therapeutic equipment work simulator. *Am J Occup Ther* **49**(5): 405–11

Fess EE (1998) Making a difference: The importance of good assessment tools (Guest Editorial). *Br J Hand Ther* **3**(2): 11

Fess EE (1995) Guidelines for evaluating assessment instruments. *J Hand Ther* **8**: 144–48

Fess EE (1993) Instrument reliability of the BTE work simulator: A preliminary study. *J Hand Ther* **6**: 59–60

Fess EE (1986) The need for reliability and validity hand assessment instruments. *J Hand Surg* **11A**(5): 621–23

Heck H, Bühler Ch, Suppelna G, et al (1997) *The Development of a System for Hand Assessment—An Overview of the HATS Project*. Proceedings of the Conference for the Advancement of Assistive Technology: 179–83

Heck H, Simpson C, Murray K, Smith J, Alcock S, Fathmann M (1999) *HATS Evaluation Study Workpackage 13*. Telematics Project DE3208 (DE). Staffordshire University

Kennedy LE, Bhambhani YN (1991) The Baltimore therapeutic equipment work simulator: Reliability and validity at three work intensities. *Arch Phys Med Rehab* **72**(7): 511–16

Macey AC, Burke FD (1995) Outcomes of hand surgery. *J Hand Surg* **20B**(6): 841–55

Measurand Inc (2001) *Miniature Joint Angle Shape Sensor. Shape Tape*. Product Information, Measurand Inc. Fredericton. Canada: http://www.measurand.com

Miller L (2001) Personal E-Mail Communication 5/3/01

MSGH (2001) *Booked Admissions Newsletter* March 2001. Mid Staffordshire General Hospitals NHS Trust: p4

Murray K, Simpson C, Topping M, *et al* (1999) Clinical evaluation of a computerised hand assessment system: An overview of results. British Society of Surgery to the Hand. *Br J Hand Ther* **4**(4): 151

Murray K, Simpson C, Topping M, Jones P, Loynes RD (2000) Hand assessment and treatment system. *J Integr Health Care* **4**(1): 32–3

Novatech (2001) *Company Profile and Product Information*. Novatech Measurements Ltd, St. Leonards-on-Sea, Sussex

Perlick O, Heck H, Fathmann M, Simpson C, Topping M, Blomsjo G, (1999) HATS: Development and Clinical Evaluation of a Computerised Hand Assessment System. *Proceedings of the Conference for the Advancement of Assistive Technology*, Dusseldorf, November 2nd 1999

Pratt A, Burr N (2000) Evaluation of the Dexter computerised assessment tool. *Br J Hand Ther* **5**(4): 123

Simpson C, Murray K, Topping M, Jones P, Loynes RD (2000) HATS: A computerised hand assessment system—An overview of clinical evaluation results. *J Hand Surg Br Eur* **25B**(Suppl): 85

Simpson C, Murray K, Topping M, *et al* (1999) The development of a clinical evaluation protocol for use with a computerised hand assessment system: Preliminary findings. *Br J Hand Ther* **4**(2): 68–73

Topping M (1997) Healthcare telematics—hand movement assessment. *Ethos Newsletter*. September 1997: 2

Topping MJ, Smith JK (1999) *The Development of Handy 1, A Robot to Assist the Severely Disabled. Research and Development in Europe*, Part 11. IOS Press, Netherlands: 96–105

Topping M, Heck H, Blomsjo G, Wickramasinghe Y (1999) *HATS Final Report*, DE 3208 (DE) HATS. Report lodged with European Telematics Commission for the Elderly and Disabled.

van Iderstine C (1996) BTE Primus: Technology meets demands. Products at work. *Adv Rehab* **Oct**: 60

Williams R, Wolfe J (1997) Technology that helps client and therapist. *Occ Ther* **11**: 4

Woodbridge S (1993) BTE work simulator—The Derby experience. *Br J Hand Ther* **1**(6): 13

Abbreviations

The following abbreviations appear in the text:

ASHS	American Society of Hand Therapists
ASSH	American Society for Surgery to the Hand
CMC	Carpometacarpal joint
BAHT	British Association of Hand Therapists
DIP	Distal Interphalangeal joints
IP	Interphalangeal joint
MCP	Metacarpophalangeal joints
NRS	Numerical Rating Scale
PIP	Proximal Interphalangeal joints
TAM	Total Active Movement
TPM	Total Passive Movement
TROM	Torque Range of Movement
VAS	Visual Analogue Scale

Index

Hand assessment:
A clinical guide for therapists
Second edition